HIGHER EDUCATION FOR EVERYONE

Higher Education for Everyone

E.G. Edwards

with a foreword by Caroline Benn

Spokesman

First published in Great Britain in 1982 by Spokesman
Bertrand Russell House, Gamble Street, Nottingham NG7 4ET

British Library Cataloguing in Publication Data

Edwards, E.G.
Higher Education for Everyone
1. Education, Higher — Great Britain — History — 20th Century
I. Title
378.41   LA36.8

ISBN 0 85124 335 5
ISBN 0 85124 345 2 Pbk

Printed by the Russell Press Ltd., Nottingham

Contents

List of Figures

6

List of Tables

Acknowledgements

The author expresses his grateful appreciation to the Leverhulme Trust for the award of an Emeritus Fellowship and to the University of Bradford for the provision of additional research assistance, both of which contributed considerably to the research underlying the present book. Most of the statistical data presented in the first four chapters was collated by my research assistant Mr I.J. Roberts, who also contributed very significantly to the theoretical analysis and to several papers which have appeared in research journals. Claudette Wild typed and checked most of the manuscript with patience and precision.

The errors and infelicities which remain are the sole responsibility of the author.

Foreword

The positive educational forces which produced the revolution against a divided secondary system in post-war Britain are still well at work. The comprehensive reform which resulted from that earlier revolution is nothing like complete, for selection and privilege still hang on. But the extended common educational experience has gone far enough to have added considerable fuel to the demand for continuing education in life as a new universal right. Demand is being passed up the line. The 16 to 19 age group is experiencing dramatic changes of which most people, even in education, are as yet unaware. Even fewer are aware of the demands which lie beyond, including the right to higher education for all.

Ted Edwards is particularly suited to articulate the higher education demand, for he alone of all the United Kingdom's university vice-chancellors was willing to stand up and be counted among the growing band of reformers arguing for comprehensive education in the 1960s. At a time when so many of his colleagues were denouncing this now popular change as a threat to educational civilisation, he saw how clearly necessary it was in order to raise society's standards.

In this book he looks ahead again, and sees that for the sake of those same standards, higher education, like secondary education before it, cannot remain the privilege of a largely middle class minority. It must be transformed into an experience all can share.

Higher education's nature, methods, content and structures will have to change dramatically before they can meet the majority's needs or match their lives, particularly in the case of women. But once the process really begins, the experience of making continuing education a reality in all parts of the post-education, will itself produce the new ways and means, and a withering away of unacceptable divisions. For this is what is happening at secondary level now, if only slowly.

First, however, myths have to be demolished about adults as they once had to be about children. The main one is that most adults do not have the capacity for rigorous, extended education. As one who had worked in extra mural university teaching and Open University preparation during the last fifteen years, I have n o doubt that what is missing is not people's ambition, interests or capacity, but society's agreement to encourage that ambition, cater for that interest, and provide for that capacity to be realised through a new radical development of our education service.

Before this, however, there must be a new consensus on universal educational rights. As this book documents so well, the extension of higher education which the Robbins era produced was impressive. But higher education was only available still to those who could 'qualify' or who were thought 'able to benefit'. Decisions about both these crucial matters were delegated to the same small elite who had already qualified and already benefited. Not until there is a new agreement that these decisions be taken by society as a whole — by people themselves — will the gates be open and the resources found.

This book argues the case for opening the gates and finding the resources, not merely to extend social justice to individuals, but, equally important, to meet society's own real needs. If post-industrial Britain is to 'grow on' harmoniously and productively, the struggle for social change, including a higher education revolution, becomes a practical necessity.

What must begin now is the long slow process that has characterised the struggle for all the educational advances of the past, starting with the extension of simple literacy to all. The very same argument that started it must be brought into higher education: that which was once a privilege for the few shall in future be agreed as a right for everyone who wants it.

Caroline Benn

Preface

This book is intended to demonstrate the feasibility, indeed the ultimate social necessity, of extending to virtually the whole population the same expectation of enjoying higher education that they now take for granted in the case of primary and secondary education. It is therefore not primarily concerned with the detail of the future curriculum of higher education nor of the precise forms of future institutional organisation, except insofar as these matters bear on its main theme. They are, of course, important matters and the author has written on them elsewhere and would hope to deal with them at a greater length in a future book. They bear on the associated theme of the relevance of higher education to those who engage in it, to society and to its cultures, its economy and its social development. However, although some treatment of them cannot be omitted from a book such as this which is mainly concerned with the franchise of higher education, a precise blueprint for their elaboration is neither necessary nor desirable to the demonstration of its thesis.

The content and forms of higher education have changed more or less proundly during the century or so of continuous exponential expansion which is reviewed in the earlier chapters of this book. But these changes have been mainly as a result of the social and economic thrust which motivated that expansion rather than its driving force. So the nature of future higher education will be largly determined by those who participate in it and refashion it to serve the purposes for which they pursue knowledge.

In spite of all these changes, higher education has served continuously as the preparation for responsibility at the top. It may be defined as the level of education associated with policy making, with managing, with setting the goals and overseeing the standard of economic, social and cultural development.

It will become obvious to the reader that the author is not an impartial observer of these functions of higher education. He is prejudiced enough to consider that these social functions which it serves, which have always been the prerogative of the ruling class and their professional servants should be taken over by the ordinary people.

To realise this aim they will need universal higher education. This book is intended to help to persuade them to demand it.

Some 40 years' experience at all levels and in all sectors of higher education have convinced the author of the credibilty and indeed urgent necessity of this goal, not only for future social stability, but for the survival of the best of the inheritance of culture and science, albeit in the context of new social purposes and with a greatly diversified content and much wider institutional forms.

After the first chapter, the succeeding three or four are inevitably concerned witha fairly detailed analysis of the expansion of higher education in the past century and particularly in the post-Second War period. This exploration is necessary in order to identify the main driving forces which have caused higher education to break out of the comparative stasis of the preceding centuries and to multiply over a hundred times during the latest period of a mere one eighth of its nearly thousand-year-old life in Europe. The following chapters are concerned to discover whether there is any reason why this relative explosion in the search for knowledge and those who participate in it have to rest at the present level or whether, on the contrary, new waves can carry the surge forward to the full cultural emancipation of the vast majority. The quantitative treatment of these trends is inevitably a compromise between rigid academic formality and readability but is aimed at being comprehensible to an intelligent reader who will take the trouble to study it carefully. At the same time a sufficient indication of sources of data and a reference to the authors own research in this field should enable those who wish to check the methodology of the analysis to do so.

Those who would like to obtain an overall appreciation of the nature of the argument more quickly may turn in the first place to Chapter 10 where the thesis built up in the earlier chapters is summarised and drawn to a conclusion. This will enable them to return to the beginning or even to the sections which most immediately interest them.

An academic referee, of one of the author's research papers, once described him as prejudiced, insufficiently concerned to discover how to "disclose the innate educational conservatism of discover how to "dislodge the innate educational conservatism of cause of their children's poor educational performance.

This book is dedicated to those same children who will certainly prove such patronising arrogance as unfounded as it is irrelevant.

E.G.E.

CHAPTER ONE

The Importance of Being Educated

The modern world, at least in its material, social and economic aspects is changing more rapidly than ever before. Our work is largely dominated by machines and technologies which were unknown in the childhood of most of us. The most evident sign of this is the computer, which has not only transformed the nature of a vast number of manufacturing processes, but has even more invaded the clerical world. Our means of travel have been invented largely in our own lifetimes. Our recreation is dominated by television, which was largely unimagined a few decades ago. And we coexist under the shadow of means of destruction of such ultimate power as would have been unthinkable to previous generations.

A word that has been coined to express this rapidly changing world we find ourselves in is the "immediacy" of our everyday environment, our ways of work and recreation and of the threats to their stability and survival.

These changes are most evident in what are called the advanced or developed countries, which are nearly, but not quite, the same group as the rich countries, though their effects are equally if not more unsettling on the vastly larger populations who constitute the desperately poor majority of the human race. We shall be concerned directly only with the advanced countries and with Britain in particular, but must bear in mind that trends of change which seem dominant and self-propelling in these may be liable to sudden and overwhelming disruption and transformation from social political and economic upheaval in the world of underdevelopment which surrounds them and increasingly presses its claims on their privileges. Indeed, this claim is most significant in the theme of our book, the privilege of higher education; and we shall not be able to avoid discussing the significance of this demand which is sometimes (we believe falsely) held to conflict with the needs of our own population.

Nevertheless, the "immediacy" of the dominating factors in the lives of most of us is characteristic above all, of the rich countries and in them it has affected both rich and poor. But it has affected them in different ways and the different relation in which rich and poor stand towards the effects of science, technology and the level of education which generates them and controls them will demand

13

treatment in this book. Some positive changes, such as the control and elimination of many infectious diseases, have benefited all classes of society. Others, such as the rapid rise in the diseases of affluence and rich living have struck at the middle and upper classes. Changes in the environment are largely shared by most of us, though the privileged can more easily escape to temporary sanctuary in the yet unspoilt areas. But the changes which have had the most diverging effects on the lives of different levels of society have been the changes in the nature of work. The higher levels of average material wealth have only been achieved at the cost of introducing the continual spectre of obsolescence and redundancy into the working lives of the majority of the manual working population. Of course, this is not a new threat; the whole development of industrialisation was preceded by the uprooting of the majority of the population from their previous form of life on the land and proceeded in a series of transformations which periodically caused the wholesale redundancy of large numbers of workers and their skills. But the new feature, or rather the feature which has now become dominant, is the possible permanence of obsolescence, the endemic instability of employment, the continual recurrence of redundancy. We shall return to this question in Chapter 6, but here we shall note that this threat of semi-permanent, so-called "structural unemployment or unemployability", has quite different effects on the different sectors of the workforce, and in general on different social levels of society. The same technological changes which throw the semi-skilled operative on the scrap-heap can be an exciting new challenge to the manager or professional worker. Survival is relatively easy at the top. Once there, one can usually find plenty of room. Professional expertise is widely transferable and is usually associated with levels of income and property ownership which makes possible periodic shifts to different parts of the country, or even the world. Management skills at the higher levels are usually even more continuously sought after and may even be at a premium in times of sharp technological change.

It is a different story for the more routine levels of junior non-manual administration and clerical work which are the newest section of vulnerable skills. Manual workers with the most generally adaptable skills, essentially the polyskilled workers whose training has included a wide range of techniques in shaping basic materials can adapt reasonably, provided they can overcome the difficulties of home mobility. But this is only a small section of the manual working class. Skills which are tied to specific industries, like textiles, metal foundries or basic heavy industries are vulnerable either to technological restructuring or, even more, to absolute decline, as whole industries are downgraded in the advanced countries and are

14

taken over by previously under-developed countries. Even more vulnerable are the semi-skilled and operatives in the mass production industries and their counterparts in routine non-manual work in the public services. The majority of manual workers and particularly the unskilled, are also vulnerable in another way. Unlike those from the professional, technical and managerial sections, they lack the financial reserves to be readily mobile. A much smaller proportion, particularly of the younger workers, have the basis of home ownership, nowadays, essential to changing the place of one's home, they depend more on several incomes per family, which makes simultaneous moves from one region to another very difficult. Above all, they lack the basic know-how of retraining; they cannot initiate their own retraining. They depend largely on public retraining organisations, whereas it is the hallmark of the professional that he has already acquired the method of renewing his own skills. He can, if necessary, initiate a new career for himself and has the basic techniques of getting the new knowledge, or at any rate, is familar with the routes through which he can gain it. Indeed, the world of changing techniques is largely his world because he is largely the initiator of these changes. The methods of adapting his position, his work and lifestyle to a new world are much of the same kind as those demanded by his normal work role. This role of the so-called technocracy; the core of managers, technologists and technicians, senior administrators, scientists, communications experts of all kinds and the upper levels of public service is one in which continual change of function is a part of everyday existence. They are used to the speed of change because they start it, regulate it and manage it. As we shall see later, the immediacy of so much of the modern world is reflected in the immediacy of the existence of most professionals. They are the section of society which is expanding in numbers at a pace which matches its speed of transformation. The number of jobs in these sections is increasing much faster than the total work force — at any rate in the advanced countries. As we shall see in Chapter 6, this rate of expansion of employment of the so-called highly qualified is itself an index of the material prosperity of a country or region. In recent decades, which have seen such an hectic expansion of the education of graduates, graduate unemployment has, nevertheless, always been less, usually only a fraction of the rate of general unemployment.

Unemployment, on the other hand, strikes first at the unskilled, the semi-skilled and generally at the least established, for example in Britain, among the West Indian arrivals and in the USA amongst the most unskilled and deprived of the minority groups. In the early stages of the American recession in 1979 a satirist cartoonist put into the mouth of a leading economist the definition of what affluence would be "Affluence is when only 3% of the white middle class is unemployed . . . and minority unemployment has levelled off at 25%".

The professional, technical and managerial sectors of society have another advantage over the majority of their fellow citizens which is related to all their other privileges and, indeed, is now becoming more and more a condition of retaining them. They have ready access to higher education. This may seem a strange statement in these days of supposed equality of opportunity when no-one is prevented from going to university or college because of lack of means to pay the fees and, indeed, when all have the opportunity to obtain maintenance grants which at least cover the bare cost of subsistence. The so-called Robbins principle that higher education should be available for all those qualified and willing to benefit from it apparently still governs Governmental policy, or at least did until recently.

We shall have occasion to examine the consequences of that policy later. Meanwhile, the real gulf in participation in higher education is shown by the following comparison: the son of a professional man has an 80% probability of taking (and completing) a full-time course of higher education in a university or college. For the daughter of an unskilled labourer the corresponding chance is less than 1%. This measured the range of inequality of participation in higher education in 1976. And in the intervening few years the gap has been widening rather than lessening.

The significance of this divergence is that higher education is closely related to the capacity to cope with the rapid changes of the modern world, to be able to control them rather than be controlled by them. Indeed, as we shall see later, it is precisely this latter quality which distinguishes higher education from normal education and which enables us to strip it of the mystery with which intellectuals who are professionally engaged in it like to surround it. Underlying the structural and technical changes which are more and more rapidly transforming the nature of work and production are the continual advances in scientific knowledge and its translation into technical applications.

Underlying the continual developments of new methods of organisation and management in both private and public sectors of industry, as well as in the public services, are the rapidly expanding social and economic sciences and their applications in management, systems theory and what is coming to be called social engineering. Finally, the thoughtful upper middle class father will encourage his son (and even, though to a lesser extent, his daughter) if they show any interest in literature, the arts or history or politics, understanding well their close relation to ease and power of communication which are the essential personal instruments of advancement on the one hand, and to political channels of control on the other. It is a mistake to think of some subjects such as science and engineering as being almost the sole keys to control of the modern technological world. While they underly its material and physical structure and are inseparable from changes in the mechanical and material aspects of production, the economic social and cultural changes which continually accompany them are even more complex and generate problems which are usually much more difficult to solve than those of the so-called hard sciences.

In all these fields the modern organisation, both for pursuing the new knowledge which is both the initiator and key to control of change, and for the training of those who are to apply it and advance it, is the institution of higher education. There sometimes appears to be a conflict between the teachers and researchers in universities (and even other colleges of higher education) and those in authority in industry or Government about the role of higher education. It sometimes appears that there is a battle between those who believe that knowledge should be pursued for some abstract ideal, for its own sake, and those who think that it should directly serve those who pay for it, by which they usually mean themselves (together with the other fortunate people who have the privilege of paying higher taxes than the majority). As we shall discover it is largely a mock battle about form rather than substance and without either side having a clear idea of their own goals. It is true that some academics retain a quite unworldly if somewhat inaccurate image of higher education, largely devoted to the ideal pursuit of knowledge for its own sake. Conversely even large scale employers have often only a dim notion of the ways in which advances in fundamental knowledge can rapidly change the economic viability of their enterprises. But the vast majority of students, predominantly from the upper and upper middle classes, who dominate higher education, undertake it because they think it more or less essential to preserving or advancing their status in the modern world. And even though it could be doubtless improved as an instrument for carrying out this purpose, they are right, they are on to as good a thing as one can get in an imperfect world.

Higher education tends, as we have hinted above, to surround itself with an aura of mystery. It cultivates the image of a rarified atmosphere where only the exceptionally gifted can survive. At the time when there were about 5000 university students in Britain, a leading professor forecast the catastrophic degeneration of standards if the numbers should increase. Today there are upwards of 500,000 in all degree level higher education.

At far as one can compare standards, a subject we shall explore and expose later, the examination papers in any particular subject seem more searching now than then, and the percipient teacher will usually admit that students are now more critical and independent in mind than in his time. Certainly, the syllabuses which tend to accrete knowledge mechanically rather than to prune themselves, are much more comprehensive than a few decades ago. Yet the myth of decline of standards persists. It is perhaps the perpetual plaint of the old men. A similar tradition tends to preserve the image of the limit of "graduate level" employment in spite of the plain fact, noted above, of its actual exponentially fast increase. One is reminded of the debate in 1870 when Forster introduced the first Education Act; everyone should have the opportunity to learn to read and write. But what a degeneration in standards of the quality of literacy would follow! One cynic said universal education increases the number of people who can read but decreases the number who are literate. And the opposition in Parliament were quick to point out that the majority of jobs in the country did not require the ability to read and write so that to teach ordinary people to do so was bound to foster discontent.

Let us therefore, devote a little time to what we may call the myth of the sanctity of academic standards, a subject to which we shall return in more detail later. This myth tends to still any disquiet one might feel for the enormous disparity of participation in higher education by assuming that it is at a level of intellectual excellence which is somehow absolutely governed and that those who do not participate are in the main those who are unfitted to participate. We may note immediately that it is difficult on this theory to account for the fact that the numbers of students have multiplied about 20 times in just over a century and actually rose by nearly three times in one recent period of about 12 years. During all this rapid change there was little sign of a change in the proportions of those in the various class of honours; indeed, these proportions stay so generally constant that one is tempted to believe that academic excellence in any field is decided by the laws of arithmetic. The top 10% or so are always first class! It is still more difficult to discover how the standards in, say, fine art are, compared with those in, say, computer science, or those in history with those in theoretical physics, in the same university. Finally, we shall see later that in the vast majority of European countries, with very different lengths of courses, conditions of entry and contents of curriculum and examination methods, the course of development of higher education has followed remarkably similar quantitative laws over the past 150 years.

We do not wish to dismiss the concept of academic standards

completely. In its proper place it has a necessary role. But there is simply no evidence that they have anything important to do with the numbers of students entering higher education, their reason for entering or their average rate of success. The plain fact is that if you come from a family that is determined that you should enter higher education in a class where it is regarded as normal, you have to be almost moronically stupid to avoid the fate, whereas if you come from a background where higher education is abnormal and strange, you have to be unusually devoted to learning, and possibly unusually gifted, to get in.

We shall purpose to develop the theme throughout this book that the supposed conflict between quality and quantity in higher education is largely irrelevant to its most general functions and, indeed, not necessarily inhibiting to its more specialised pursuits.

Of course, there can be a degeneration of quality, but it has little to do with expansion. The great periods in particular regions or countries, or universities or colleges have often been precisely when a kind of liberation of the minds of previously untouched sections of the people caused a rapid expansion of higher education. Such a period occurred in Scotland, for example, at the turn of the 18th and 19th centuries. The enormously faster growth of American higher education in the past 100 years has coincided with the steady but remorseless overtaking of Europe by the USA in most of the accepted standards of intellectual achievement. On the other hand, old and traditionally famous universities have sometimes fallen so badly behind as to have demanded investigation by official commissions. And such periods of recession have often coincided with that stagnation which accompanies the fear of extending the scope and social breadth of their growth.

We are approaching the point when we should make a preliminary definition of the theme of this book "higher education".

We shall do so by considering for a moment the processes of getting, conserving and transmitting knowledge. They are, of course, not confined to schools and colleges. They start with the infant learning from its mother both the meaning and method of growth and survival. They continue throughout childhood and in every activity of work and leisure of adult life. Knowledge is, after all, simply the remembered lessons of practice, the mental tools we build up to enable us to both achieve our purposes and enlarge our vision of them. Institutionalised education arises because of the increasing stores of organised knowledge necessary to life cannot any longer be entirely assimilated directly from the limited experience of practical application available to us in a reasonable time. After all, it is reasonably important to have some idea of where Europe and America are before one has the opportunity of actually travelling over them.

Nevertheless, education never escapes from the ultimate necessity to justify itself in practice in its relevance to all the things we live for and live by and work for and enjoy as a result of our work. We can now see in terms of the different relations of different sections of the population to higher education how to define it in terms of its relevance to life and work and practice and purpose.

Higher education is that level of education which belongs to being able to cope with the rapid changes in work and life, especially those changes arising from the continual impact of new knowledge and new techniques.

Higher education is associated with taking decisions in the modern world, with giving orders, with managing, or with being able to be independent and run your own professional function.

By contrast, compulsory education is the level of education necessary to understand how to carry out the decisions made by others to obey orders, to be managed, to be dependent, to serve adequately the independent professionals. The professional engineers or managers are people who formulate decisions, the operative carries them out. The consultant or professional diagnoses and prescribes. The unqualified assistants undertake the routine work. The senior civil servant prepares administrative policy, the routine civil service worker operates it. Broadly speaking, higher education is associated with management in its various forms, and the various jobs which demand higher education all, to some extent, participate actively in shaping the goals; developing the methods and giving the orders involved in management. While it is not yet true, at any rate in Britain, that all those who achieve this level have qualifications in higher education, it is correct to say that this is the normal level at which it finds its place and ultimately demands that it be regarded as normally essential.

And higher education is, in any case, a normal feature of the social, cultural and economic life at the management level of society. The children in the professional and managerial social sectors are, therefore, as used to the notion of higher education and the presence of the highly educated in their normal surroundings as they are to using a cloth table napkin at meals.

This concept of higher education as the level normally associated in the country concerned at the time concerned with making rather than obeying decisions, with independence rather than dependence, with managing rather than being managed, enables us to remove a great deal of magical aura from it and at the same time give a less arbitrary place to the idea of standards of academic or intellectual attainment. The standards of knowledge and ability of higher education will tend to be just those that are necessary in the field concerned in the country concerned at the time concerned to cope with the existing role of the highly educated.

Hence its standards will not be absolute, but will properly tend to depend on the actual complexity of management and decision taking, or the actual scope and needs of professional practice in the country or region concerned and in the field concerned. These standards are continually changing, generally becoming more complex, although they can also be simplified as a result of breakthroughs in general scientific principles. In a group of similarly economically and culturally placed countries such as Western Europe, professional and managerial levels may tend to settle at rather similar levels and hence an appearance may develop of some standard level of attainment necessary in a more absolute sense to the concept of higher education. On the other hand in the USA, where the managerial function and the professional status are much more widespread than in Europe, and where a host of various new professions have established their independent status, higher education includes courses and qualifications which seem bizarre to the conservative European academic, but they are as proper to its function of preparing for independent decision taking, as even the oldest of the recognised fields of higher education in Europe. And in the developing countries it may be said that the main error in higher education has been to ape the so-called sanctity of academic standards of Europe rather than develop forms and content suitable to the problems of their own policy making and management.

There is, of course, one field which higher education prepares for which appears to have less arbitrary standards of academic content, and that is for the academic profession itself. Yet it is precisely here that as much divergence is shown as anywhere in the actual length of training, examination requirements and record of intellectual achievement in the different advanced countries. However, this field does have this in common, that nearly everywhere it requires actual experience in research, though it would be impossible to compare the standards of originality normal in different fields, let alone different countries. On the one hand this has the apparent disadvantage that academics who tend to class students according to the degree in which they resemble themselves and indeed, set themselves before their students as the goal of higher education, tend to think that the primary function of higher education is to train academic research workers. Of course, the large majority of students have no such future before them. Even those who become school teachers, which was until recently, one of the major outlets for graduates, rarely had the opportunity to continue research after leaving university or college. On the other hand, it is, of course, this other research function of higher educational institutions which nowadays creates a very large part of the fundamental new scientific knowledge which we have seen is a major factor in ultimately changing the nature of industry and public service and hence the nature of the professional and managerial functions in them. Hence the association of even those students of the large majority who will never undertake academic research with teachers who are mainly so preoccupied, has its advantages, though we need not conclude at this juncture that the way these two functions are brought into relationship in higher education is necessarily the optimum solution.

It follows from all the above that the standards, the content of the curriculum, the mix of subjects, the examination practices in higher education do not arise as some immutable intellectual certainty. They are inevitably and properly conventional. In other words they are not a product of the intellectual genius of an inevitably scarce gifted few. They are a social product. They are controlled by the content of decision making in the actual field concerned at the time and in the profession concerned in the place where the role is carried out. They are the entry ticket to a social group of decision makers. Even so, the new entrants, because of their association with the advancing front of knowledge relevant to the professional role concerned will be the main agents in changing entry conditions, the carriers of the advancement of practice and the appliers of the new techniques.

In the above definitions we may have appeared to neglect the whole range of "non-professional" studies, particularly those in the "pure" sciences, arts and humanities which many academics would consider to be the essence of the university curriculum and to justify their claim to pursue knowledge for its own sake. But originally almost all university disciplines were openly devoted to professional social functions: law, medicine and theology. The modern abstract studies of the sciencies, natural and human, and of the arts, have developed as the knowledge to pursue the main professional functions in the State and community became more complex. The division of labour which ensued has given rise to a series of scientific professions and analogous formal or informal associations who determine standards of taste in the Arts.

These are the cultural professions who claim the same prerogative of decision making and management in the different fields of culture as do their counterparts in the field of medicine, law and in the technological, management and economic areas of industry and the State.

Indeed, the cultural professions perform the vital and central stabilising role of legitimising the autonomy of all the other professions, since they assert effective control of the ultimate standards of truth, rationality, taste and communicability.

Of course, these more "abstract" studies appear at every level of education as "tool" subjects. Indeed, they predominate most at the secondary level where they establish that base of communication, that minimal acceptance of the ruling culture which is necessary in all citizens.

But at the level of higher education they are associated closely with the decision making, managing, professional function in society, either because that is the level required for their use as tools by the other professions in the world of practical affairs or because it is needed for their own professional role in the fields of culture and communication.

Of course these definitions of higher education, and by contrast, of normal education, are not intended to convey a complete educational apartheid in the entrances or exits to or from the upper circle of those who give orders to the rest of us. Nor in modern society are the orders completely unquestioned or unopposed. But even a successful strike does not yet change the self-image of the management nor indeed does it give the strikers any illusion of their own relation to policy making.

Again, many, indeed far too many, managers (though not many professionals nowadays) do not have a full higher education, and some of those with higher education never achieve much in the way of professional, independent or managerial status. And, of course, there are a great many people in intermediate sections with some further education, and a great many occupying semi-professional or junior management positions. These intermediate layers of educational attainment or levels of participation in decision making emphasise the contrast between the two levels which we have used to define the essential difference between higher and normal education and their associated social functions.

As we shall see later, we may treat these middle sections as a group which share some of the characteristics of the two upper and lower main socio-cultural strata of society. It has always proved difficult in practice to obtain agreement about any special intermediate level of education for these middle strata, compared with the general consensus of what is appropriate for the two extremes of the working class and the managerial or professional class.

Some of these intermediate professions eventually move up into their own independent status and the education associated with them becomes properly speaking higher education. Many of the engineering professions once occupied a half-way stage in status (and associated education) between that of the skilled craftsman

23

and the manager or member of the older professions. Britain was particularly late in recognising the need to promote the status of engineering and this tardiness played a large part in the relegation of British industry to a technical level uncompetitive with relative newcomers such as Germany and the USA. As recently as the 1960s a majority of British qualified mechanical engineers had been trained by traditional apprenticeship supplemented by night school or part-time courses, whereas the vast majority of German engineers had followed full courses in Technological Universities for the greater part of the century. The delay in recognising engineering as a full profession coincided with the delay in insisting on its place in higher education. Even now the social status of a professional engineer in Britain does not compare with a doctor or lawyer. It may be noted that these older professions have been part of university life for hundreds of years; they virtually constituted the first universities in Europe in Italy of the 11th Century.

A similar move from semi-professional to full professional status has taken place since the war in the so-called para-medical professions ranging from pharmacy, where the higher education required has risen from one year to four within a generation, to nursing, which is just moving up to this status, with the simultaneous provision of degree courses. A large number of new professions are being created by the natural evolution of what used to be regarded as junior levels of management, and as they move up in status they move in the field of higher education.

This tendency has become particularly widespread in the United States. In contrast to Britain, which has only very recently introduced degree courses in management, the American college and university enrols more management students than in any other subject.

Many fields which were until recently considered fully served by technicians with an intermediate level of training now require so-called technologists, i.e. with full higher educational qualifications.

Thus there is now a range of materials technologists with degree level qualifications evolved out of semi-professionals such as welders who were previously largely trained on the job.

On the other hand the reverse process of the disappearance of certain intermediate roles and the forms of training associated with them is also taking place. This is particularly evident in that previously strong group of complex techniques that sustained the older industries, textiles, heavy metals, foundry work and, of course, industries that have either disappeared, such as coal gas manufacture, or are rapidly disappearing, like ship building. The levels of education associated with these roles were the highly specialised aristocracy of craft training supplemented with the

24

elements of the basic sciences of the materials concerned and the basic mechanics of the machinery involved. Like the highly specialised craftsmen in the same industries these intermediate level technicians are equally vulnerable to change and obsolescence and the education previously associated with their training does not normally reach a sufficiently independent level to protect them. As we have already noted, the intermediate levels of non-manual work, when they do not evolve into professional status and acquire a place in higher education, are liable to suffer a similar fate.

Of course, the constant movement of modernisation also produces the need for new kinds of intermediate trained personnel. An obvious example is the rapid expansion of work at this level associated with the computer. And as the number of professions increases they tend to spawn the demand for their own separate semi-professionals. So it may appear that this intermediate layer halfway between the highly educated professionals and managers and the main body of workers with only basic education, remains fairly constant in size.

Nevertheless, although new intermediate roles may be created as old ones disappear, they do not have that continuity and individual stability that belongs to the upper managerial and professional levels. This is inevitable because professional level stability and continuity of career arises from that command of the levers of change which comes from an adequate knowledge of the sciences and arts which are basically causing the changes. Hence, it is characteristic of the semi-professions that they strive to move to full professional status, that is, independent status, precisely the status of autonomy in decision taking. And they simultaneously strive to raise the education and qualifications necessary to practice their role to higher education level. This desire to move upwards in the educational world is sometimes deplored by those who think that it is vital to have this intermediate layer as a buffer between the upper levels who decide policy and the organisation and the workers who are supposed to do what they are told. From the point of view from above, the social ambitions of the semi-professions disturb the existing pattern only slightly less than the more primitive dissidence of the workers at the bottom. But from the point of view of the members of the intermediate work strata the strategy of moving educational requirements upwards is a sound one. Only by doing so can they aim to secure the relative security of the professional. And incidentally those countries in the modern world who are encouraging such upward mobility of educational requirements and the extension of professional status are precisely those who are rapidly overtaking or already leaving behind the others, at least in terms of economic prosperity.

25

To sum up, we may say that the intermediate levels of education, like the semi-professional and junior technical roles they are associated with, are less stable in their purpose and less defined in their form and content than either basic normal education on the one hand or higher education on the other. These latter are the poles between which the currents of knowledge pass into social and economic life. At one pole there is education for independence for the policy makers and decision takers, for those who give the orders or solve the problems. This is higher education.

At the other pole is compulsory general education, which is the level and scope of learning necessary to understand orders, to carry out decisions, to perform the obligatory duties of citizenship in the country concerned. This general level of education is not designed to equip for participation in policymaking or to share in management. It is for the modern equivalents of the hewers of wood and drawers of water. Its limits are so drawn as to leave most of its participants incapable of grasping the nature of the forces in modern society which are increasingly changing and controlling their lives. It leaves them largely dependent on and at the mercy of decisions and policies created and controlled by the highly educated.

We shall return to examine in detail the social stratification of higher education in Chapter 4 and to investigate the effects of the knowledge explosion on production, employment and economic growth in Chapter 6. To close this review of the impact of the knowledge revolution and the expansion of higher education on the nature of our working lives we may express them both in terms of what Derek Price has called the coefficient of immediacy. Most of the enormous store of factual (largely scientific) knowledge and the collated schemes for its practical application is of such recent discovery that it was simply unknown in the childhood of today's old men. Of all the people in every country who have been through higher education in the history of the world, about 80% are alive today.

To understand the cause of this immediacy of higher education and to grasp the nature of the forces which propelled it forward and those which press it towards the future we shall have to examine, in the next chapter, the history of its expansion since its growth started accelerating. We shall find that this take-off was not so recent as many think. Indeed it dates from that same period when the basic pattern of modern industrial life was cast, the latter half of the 19th Century.

CHAPTER TWO

The Century of International Expansion

At the beginning of the century there were about 29,500 full time students in higher education in Britain. Of these most, about 24,000, were in universities, the rest were mainly in Teacher Training Colleges, with only a small proportion in all other forms of higher education, for example, technical colleges. However, these proportions will not greatly concern us in what immediately follows, since we shall find that the expansion of higher education has probably not depended much on the nature of the Institutions provided to meet it, but rather on the rise of the demand for it by would-be students.

By 1960 the numbers had risen to about 180,000 — a multiplication of about six times, and by 1970, after a decade of hectic acceleration to fifteen times the enrolment of 1900 at about 446,000. It may be noted that the total British population in 1900 of 37 million rose to about 49 million by 1960 and to 53 million in 1970, so that its rate of increase played little part in the very much faster growth in the number of students. Indeed, we shall see differential population growth in different countries of Europe has borne almost no relation to their comparative expansion rates of higher education. Whatever caused the ever-increasing flow of students, it was certainly not merely because there were more young people of student age about.

At this point it is useful to make a quick comparison with the total growth in the group of major countries in Europe for which comparable statistics are available. We shall call this group "Little Europe". It is the total of Britain, France, Germany, Italy, Belgium and the Netherlands. In 1900 all the universities and institutions of higher education in this group of countries had a total of 163,000 full-time students. By 1960 it had become 1,021,000 again a ration of six times and by 1970 had reached 2,445,000 which happens to be almost exactly fifteen times the figure for the beginning of the century.

We will suggest later that this remarkable identity of the ratios of growth between Britain and Europe is not accidental. On the other hand we shall have to consider evidence that this parallelism is no longer in evidence and that during the last ten years Britain has commenced to fall very far behind the other countries of Europe.

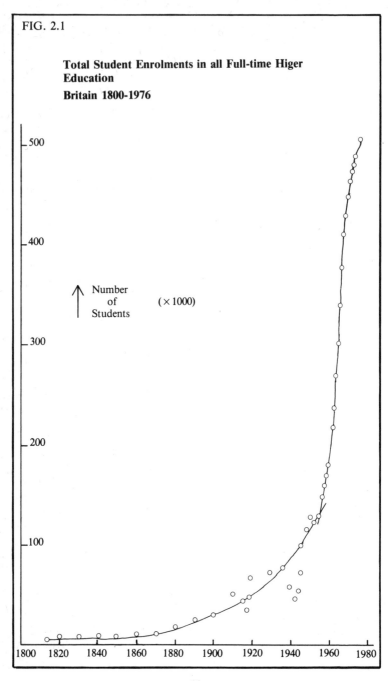

FIG. 2.1

Total Student Enrolments in all Full-time Higer Education
Britain 1800-1976

Number of Students (× 1000)

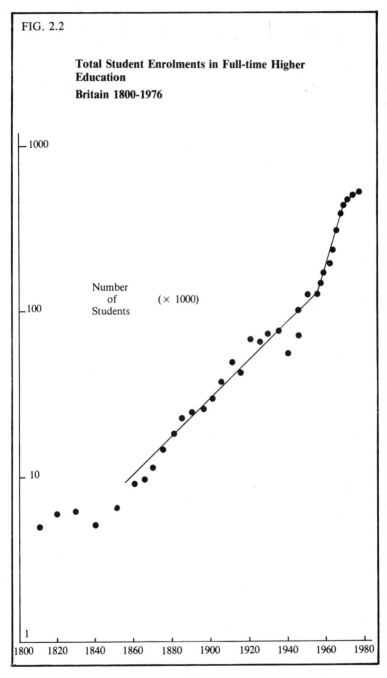

FIG. 2.2

Total Student Enrolments in Full-time Higher Education
Britain 1800-1976

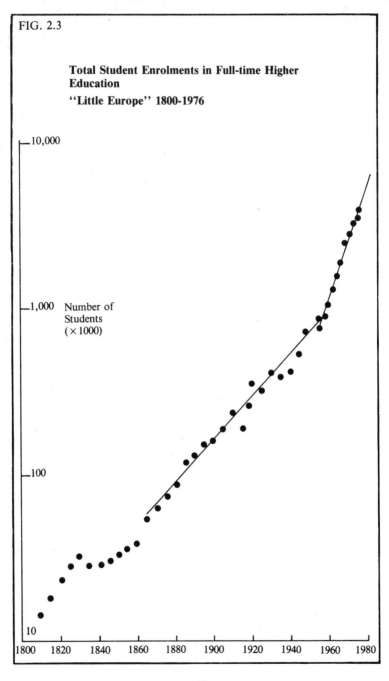

FIG. 2.3

Total Student Enrolments in Full-time Higher Education
"Little Europe" 1800-1976

Number of Students (×1000)

However, this expansion over the century has not proceeded at a constant speed. Rather, it is broadly true to say that from about 1860 to 1960 the rate of growth was continually accelerating and that in the decade from 1960 to 1970 the process of acceleration itself escalated to an higher level. In Fig. 2.1 we show graphically the growth of student numbers in all higher education from 1800 to 1976.

At first glance this graph would seem to show that almost all the expansion during this century has occurred very recently and in the simple numerical sense this is true and, indeed, sustains the notion of the "immediacy" of higher education that we mentioned in Chapter 1. On the other hand, those familiar with the growth curves of many natural processes will recognise it as an exponential curve, or rather, as we shall see, as the union of two exponential curves. This form of expansion is essentially the same as that of the accumulation of capital invested at compound interest. We shall see that between 1860 and 1960 student numbers accumulated at an average rate of compound interest of nearly three per cent per annum, whereas between about 1955 and 1970 the rate rose sharply to a very steady value of nearly ten per cent per annum.

Nevertheless, between about 1860 and 1960 the rate of compound interest at which student numbers expanded was remarkably even.

We can show this if we draw the graph of expansion as shown in Fig. 2.2. Now the rise in student numbers, the vertical scale, is shown, not arithmetically, but logarithmically. This means that the base line represents 1,000 students, the next main division 10,000; and the third 100,000; and similarly for the intermediate divisions. The exponential curve of Fig. 2.1 now appears to have become a fairly straight line from the middle of the 19th Century until about the mid-1950s. Then there was a sharp change of slope which lasted for about fifteen years. Before examining this course of expansion of higher education in Britain in greater detail, it is interesting to compare it with the growth graph for the total students in the group of countries we have called "Little Europe". This is shown in Fig. 2.3, though, because the number of students in "Little Europe" is about ten times that in Britain, we have multiplied the vertical scale ten times. It is immediately apparent that the similar ratios of growth over the century in Britain and Europe is simply a result of the process of expansion following the same course.

In Figs. 2.2 and 2.3 a straight line means a steady constant rate of annual compound interest of expansion and, indeed, the slope of the straight line is proportional to this annual rate. It follows that in both Europe and Britain the percentage increase in students each year remained pretty constant from about 1860 to 1960 and then, as mentioned previously, made a sharp change to a rate of about three times as high which was then maintained till the early 70s.

The ideas introduced above are important for analysing the nature of development of higher education. We have seen that not only has the number of students grown more or less continuously for over a century, but the rate of growth has been accelerating the whole time. The actual form of the accelerated expansion has been exponential. Steady exponential growth is characterised by a constant annual rate of percentage increase and this shows up as a straight line if we plot student numbers on a logarithmic scale against time. Finally, we may speak of an explosion or escalation of growth when the rate of annual percentage increase multiplies suddenly. If steady exponential growth is a sign of some underlying continuity of development, such a sharp change is a sign of some fundamental change in an important factor of growth.

Higher education in the form of universities has existed in Europe since the 11th Century. For most of the period since, although they played a vital part in providing the chief servants of the State and the corpus of so-called learned professions, their numbers of students fluctuated around a level of between one and two per cent of their numbers today. Indeed, there were periods of long slow decline, as for example, in England between 1600 and 1750, when entering students (predominantly in Oxford and Cambridge) were reduced from about 1000 per year to less than 300. The beginnings of the modern acceleration began in the 19th Century. In a number of countries of Northern Europe there was an early peak about the 1820s, though in Britain this was particularly pronounced in Scotland and, indeed, the great leap forward in that period was probably caused by forces of popular thirst for knowledge that kept Scotland well ahead of England right up to the present day. We shall have occasion to comment briefly on that when we come to consider the social aspects of higher education in Chapter 4.

For the moment we will concentrate on the period dating from about the middle of the 19th Century, and taking Europe as a whole as being more "typical" than any of its individual countries, we shall fix the beginning of the great acceleration of higher education at about 1860. This is, of course, only a provisional date since information about the early part of the 19th Century is not yet precise enough to fix the time when the long stasis of the previous centuries gave way to the modern upward trend. Indeed, there is evidence that the first half of the 19th Century was a period of considerable fluctuations in several of the principal countries of Europe. But by 1860 they began to move forward together, and soon came into a reasonably close degree of equilibrium. By 1870 the numbers of full-time students per 100,000 of the total population in the different European countries was as shown in Table 2.1. The comparable figure for the USA at that time is only given at this stage to indicate that the state of affairs there was very different from Europe.

TABLE 2.1

Ratios of Full-time Students to Total Population

Average of Years 1870-1875

Country	Number of Students per 100,000 Population
Great Britain	50
Germany	54
France	40
Italy	64
Belgium	57
Netherlands	38
"Little Europe"	49
USA	166

From 1860 to 1970 the similar trends of growth in the different European countries are shown in Fig. 2.4. It can be seen that the number ratios of students in the different countries are scattered fairly evenly and remarkably closely to the line for "Little Europe" as a whole. In this diagram as in Fig. 2.3 the vertical scale is logarithmic so that the straightness of the line is an indication of the evenness of the rate of compound interest of expansion and the slopes of the lines for the different countries are proportional to the different rates.

Table 2.2 shows the comparison between the different countries from 1860-1960 in numerical form. It will be seen that the percentage rate at which the number of students in each country was expanding each year (the rate of compound interest of expansion) was remarkably similar to that in the others and to that for "Little Europe" as a whole. This similarity in the rates for the different countries will be seen to be even more striking when we come to compare the more or less equal rates during that century from 1860 to 1960 with those of the vastly escalated explosion in student numbers in the period from 1955 to 1970.

Also in Table 2.2 we give for each country a coefficient r^2 which

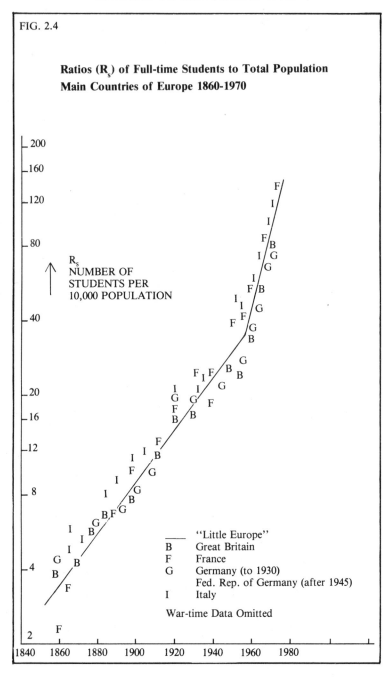

FIG. 2.4

Ratios (R$_s$) of Full-time Students to Total Population
Main Countries of Europe 1860-1970

R$_s$
NUMBER OF
STUDENTS PER
10,000 POPULATION

_____ "Little Europe"
B   Great Britain
F   France
G   Germany (to 1930)
     Fed. Rep. of Germany (after 1945)
I   Italy

War-time Data Omitted

measures the regularity of exponential growth, or in other words, the regularity of the rate of compound interest of growth. This factor, r^2, is conventionally called the coefficient of determination. If the actual number of students in any one year was exactly that predicted by the straight line which has been drawn as nearly as possible evenly between them in the above diagrams, Fig 2.2, Fig. 2.3 and Fig. 2.4, then the value of the coefficient r^2 would be 1.

TABLE 2.2

Annual Percentage increase in Number of
Full-time Students in Higher Education 1860-1960

Country	Percentage Annual Increase	Coefficient of Determination (r^2)
Great Britain	2.7	.93
*Germany (1860-1933)	2.9	.97
France	3.2	.92
Italy	3.4	.96
Belgium	2.3	.92
Netherlands	3.7	.98
"Little Europe"	2.9	.98

*Germany was divided after the war of 1939-45 and its Universities had been decimated in the Hitler period. Hence, we have included the data for the period 1860-1933 only.

If, on the other hand, the line has no predictive value at all, and the figures for individual years were scattered randomly over the diagram the value of r^2 would be zero. Actually it will be seen that the individual figures for individual years do not lie exactly on the straight line, but, though fairly near to it, some lie slightly above and some below. The significance of the coefficient r^2 is that it expresses exactly the extent to which the average rise in student numbers in any particular year is explained by the general overall expansion expressed by the straight line. Thus a figure of .95 for r^2 means that, on average, 95% of the actual rise in the number of students at any particular date is a consequence of the regular exponential expansion in numbers since the beginning of the period, 1860, while the remaining 5% must be attributed to random, accidental, unpredictable variations.

Such dislocations of the regular trend of exponential growth are easily detectable at the dates of the two world wars and there is also clear evidence of the slow down which occurred at the time of the great depression of the late twenties and early thirties. However, it is quite striking how, in spite of the enormous social upheavals of these great catastrophies, the trend of expansion jumped, as soon as they were over, quite rapidly to the figure which would have been expected if they had never occurred. It is as though the force of student demand, pent up during the war, was immediately released and even tended to overshoot the mark as soon as the crisis was over. And indeed those of us that remember the hectic clamour for higher education in those immediate post-war days know that was exactly what happened. To put it another way, suppose someone from a far country knew only the growth in student numbers in Europe between 1860 and 1910 and arrived on the scene in 1960, knowing nothing of the period in between nor of the great wars and depressions that had taken place in the intervening half century. He would have found the further growth in student numbers, which actually multiplied about four times, almost exactly what he would have expected had the regular growth of the earlier period gone on without any interruption.

It is useful at this point, at the cost of a little repetition, to draw together the main conclusions from a study of simply the course of development of student numbers in the different European countries over the century from 1860 to 1960. In every case the growth is exponential; i.e. the speed of growth is continuously accelerating. Nevertheless, the average percentage growth per year is remarkably constant. In spite of the great disturbance of wars, depressions and near revolutions, we can account for an average of over 95% of the expansion that actually took place on the assumption that it was governed by a perfectly regular accumulation by a fixed rate of compound interest. Moreover, in spite of all the differences which might be supposed to exist between the different countries, this rate was remarkably similar in each. Indeed, the range of variation was only from 90% of the average European rate to about 115% of it.

Now in all the above we have purposely neglected all the detail of differences in systems of higher education in the different European countries. As yet we have not taken into account the fact, for example, that in a number of the countries we have been concerned with, there is no selection for higher education, everyone who passes the final secondary school examinations has a legally guaranteed right to a place in a university. On the other hand in others, such as Britain, there is no such guarantee. Neither have we taken into account the different educational laws in the different countries or the quite different extents to which they have charged fees or subsidised students by maintenance grants. These factors have considerable effects on the individual students in the different countries and on the pressure on the resources of higher educational institutions and it will be proper to deal with these matters when we come to consider the future of educational policy in a later chapter. Nor have we attempted to differentiate between the academic standards in different countries; to see from that point of view whether higher education in, say, Britain would be recognised as such in Germany. As we pointed out in Chapter 1, we know of no way of fixing standards for such a comparison in general, and it is fairly clear as we shall see in more detail later, that a great deal of what passes for wisdom in this field is either misinformed or based on prejudice. Although all such differences between the different countries and between the different periods in any one country will deserve attention in their own place, for the purpose of detailed analysis of particular educational fashions and applications, and for the detailed design of planning and policy, they appear to have little bearing on understanding the main forces which propelled higher education forward at an ever increasing speed for the century we are studying. If they did, it would be difficult to understand the overall remarkable regularity of the exponential growth, its persistence in re-establishing itself after major social upheavals and the almost exactly parallel behaviour in each of the major European countries. We shall have to look for explanation in some deeper social roots which were continuously feeding the growth of higher education throughout the whole period and in behavioural forces which were largely common to the main European countries in spite of their difference in legal, financial and institutional provision.

We might expect the growth in higher education to reflect the increase in the total population. Over long periods the population of a large region also tends to grow by compound interest. This is true for the population of Europe as a whole. Between 1860 and 1960 it grew fairly steadily at the rate of about 0.7% per annum. It will be seen however that this is only about one quarter of the annual percent increase of student numbers. If we look at the populations of the separate countries of Europe the regularity of the population expansion is somewhat similar in the individual nations, but their comparative rates of growth bears no relation to the comparative rates of student expansion. This is shown if we compare Table 2.2 and Table 2.3. It will be seen that France, for example, which had one of the fastest rates of student expansion had by far the slowest population growth. The number of entrants to higher education in a particular country seems to have borne even less relationship to the number of young people of student age. Fig. 2.5 illustrates this for Britain between 1900 and 1960.

We may conclude that the simple expansion of the total number of young people can have played only a small part in the increase in

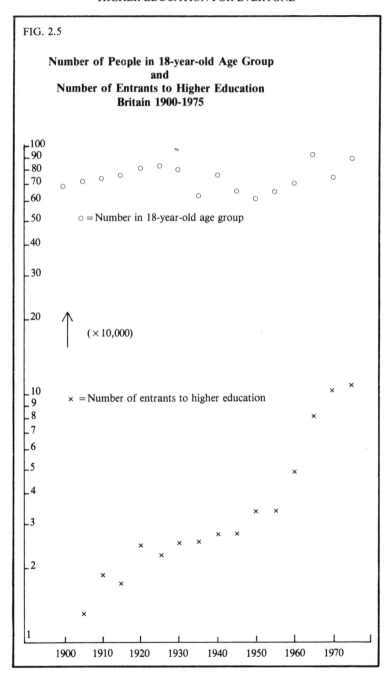

FIG. 2.5

**Number of People in 18-year-old Age Group
and
Number of Entrants to Higher Education
Britain 1900-1975**

o = Number in 18-year-old age group

(× 10,000)

× = Number of entrants to higher education

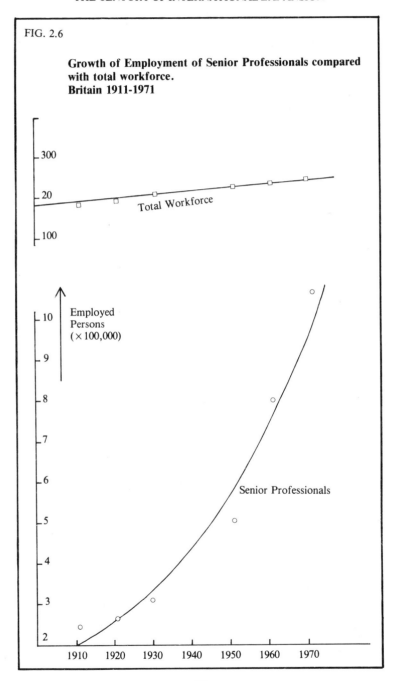

FIG. 2.6

**Growth of Employment of Senior Professionals compared
with total workforce.
Britain 1911-1971**

the demand for higher education in a period of sixty years when this demand grew by six times. We shall return to this particular comparison in Chapter 5 in relation to the recent official projections which base estimates of future demand for higher education on calculations of the rise and fall of overall birth rates. We may at least consider that if this had been the basis of similar estimates of student growth at the beginning of the century we are reviewing, they would have borne little relation to the actual reality as it developed.

TABLE 2.3

Average Percentage Annual Increase in Population 1860-1960

Country	Percentage Annual Increase	Coefficient of Determination (r^2)
Great Britain	.8	.95
Germany	.9	.95
France	.2	.85
Italy	.7	.95
Belgium	.7	.95
Netherlands	1.2	.95
"Little Europe"	.7	.85

On the other hand, if we look not at the total population, but at the growth of the numbers of senior professional workers in the population there is evidence of a possible connection with the expansion of student numbers. Here again we have the same kind of continually accelerating, exponential, expansion. Fig. 2.6 shows how the numbers of those in this sector of the employed population have multiplied in the period from 1911 to 1971 compared with the much slower rate of growth of the total work force. The regularity of exponential growth in the former case is again striking and is expressed by a coefficient of determination of .95 i.e. 95% of the accelerated growth conforms to that which would be predicted from exactly regular compound interest rate of 2.4% per annum. This value is very close to that found in British student expansion in Table 2.2. The connection is not now accidental since this section of the population supplies a much greater part of the total demand for higher education than the average as we have already noted in Chapter 1, and as we shall see in greater detail in Chapter 4. Additionally, graduating students are one of the most important sources of recruitment to the managerial and professional classes, indeed, as we shall see later they probably are becoming the dominant source in the last quarter of the 20th Century. The above relationship gives us a clue to an important cyclical feature of the development of higher education which lies at the core of its continual acceleration. The sections of society which provide the largest proportions of students are the continually expanding ones, and one of the reasons for their expansion is that all graduating students, including those that filter up from lower sections of society are potential recruits to them. Finally their own work of changing the technical and organisational nature of production and public service provides the very impetus for increased demand for their services.

We shall examine the evidence for various aspects of this thesis in several later sections of this book. To begin with we shall touch on one feature which is frequently found to be characteristic of natural processes which show exponentially increasing growth. As we have seen, these include a number of developments which are transforming the modern world like the growth of scientific and technical knowledge, the expansion of the professional and managerial personnel, the speed of transportation, the use of electricity, the sale of computers. This feature is their high degree of self-momentum. Within a large enough region such as Europe or America, or even in one of the larger individual countries, they seem to grow steadily in spite of fairly large variations in economic, social and legislative background. One may contrast this apparent autonomy of growth with the slow decline of the older industries, the ebb and flow of sales of specific consumer goods or commodities in general, the fluctuating employment of the lower grades of technical and clerical manpower and the slow decline of manual labour, all of which seem much more vulnerable to the short term variations in the overall economic and social environment. Of course some of the older industries and forms of employment and the older sources of energy or transport had their own period of exponential expansion before they passed into a steady state or even a decline. During the period we are presently considering, higher education has clearly been in such a rapidly expanding phase. The analogy of an epidemic is sometimes used to picture the spread outwards into society of movements which grow in this way. The very process of expansion appears to be caused by the agent which is expanding. The speed of growth at any point of time is proportional to the amount of growth which has already occurred, indeed, it is precisely this proportionality which must result in the continually increasing speed which is mathematically expressed by an exponential growth curve. A grimmer analogy is the growth of a cancer in a living being and a happier one is the growth of an unborn child in the womb. In each case it is easy to grasp why the speed of growth is

41

continuously increasing. It is because each living cell automatically divides into two daughter cells at fixed intervals of time. Within wide limits the speed and the acceleration of this growth process is unaffected by what is happening to the body in which it grows. We shall suggest that higher education has had an analogous self-propelled mechanism of expansion. In brief, we may say that the speed of growth of student numbers depends on the number of people who have already been highly educated, or perhaps more accurately, on the number of people in the social classes where the graduates find their place. As we shall demonstrate in detail later, this gives rise to the kind of spiral development at the heart of higher education which we have suggested above. It also enables us to understand in a preliminary way why the growth of higher education does not seem to be correlated very strongly with the overall rate of growth of the population nor is simply proportional to the number of young people of university age. These are, as it were, the body within which it grows but whose fluctuations do not much affect it within wide limits. We may also begin to appreciate how it can be that the apparently autonomous multiplication of student demand persists through considerable variations in social and economic conditions. It is, as it were, protected from short term ups and downs in the general climate of prosperity or depression by the overriding social and cultural stability of the social strata from which it is either initiated or finds its place. We may also suppose that like other natural, apparently self-propelling processes of this kind, its acceleration of expansion must ultimately come to an end, if only when the whole population participates in it, when at last its growth curve would slow down to that of the population itself. Alternatively it could be limited long before that point either because the number of potential students could no longer increase, exhausted by lack of motivation or because of some barrier in the social environment, or by sufficiently stringent limits imposed by the political restriction on the necessary resources for its continued development.

These questions are important, at least as much to those who do not and possibly would never participate in higher education as to those who do or will. They may indeed underlie, not merely the future of the universities and colleges, but possibly the future nature of society. They concern particularly the future of the division in society between those who decide on its goals and its organisations and those who in the main will be subject to its forms of organisation and carry out objectives decided by others.

To put the questions in this way is to suggest already that they are not merely objective matters to be decided by some arbitrary selection rules but, even more basically, moral and political. In the rest of this book we will survey a further range of evidence and principles which bear on whether there should be any limitation to universal access to higher education.

To conclude this chapter on the century of the epidemic growth of students we may examine briefly how it started and the most characteristic of the symptoms that it developed.

The start of exponential growth must often be found outside the thing which is growing. Before the foetus becomes self-developing there must be the conception. Epidemics start because of particularly favourable external environment. New industries arise because of changes in possible technology usually initiated outside of industry. After centuries of a fluctuating stability in the size of university populations the modern period of accelerated expansion took off in the 19th Century and thereafter became apparently self-fuelling. But the start is probably to be found in massive changes erupting in 19th Century society and particularly in industry. These changes had been fermenting in the first part of the century. From about 1850 to 1870 they transformed the nature of industry and industrial society. During this period the momentum of the older craft-based industries of the industrial revolution, coal and steam, textiles, pig iron, railroads, began to sag and the initiative passed to a new and different group that were to require a different level of scientific and technological expertise and a more complex and sophisticated management. Typical of this new group were steel, electricity, chemicals and their numerous offshoots, the internal combustion engine and its many embodiments. The industrial world became critically dependent on materials such as oil and on metals such as nickel, chromium and aluminium, which had been laboratory curiosities a generation before. As the century which followed gathered momentum the age of synthetics began; substances which did not exist as such in nature, but which were a product of scientific laboratories. The innovations were also to transform the nature of those basic industries which were age-old but could never become obsolete since human survival depended on them, like the production of food and shelter. Artificial fertilisers, which were virtually unknown before this period, became essential for continued human survival as the world population was no longer decimated to the same extent by infectious diseases, succumbing one after the other to medical science.

At the same time many sciences were taking their modern shape and their pursuit was passing from the amateur to the professional, usually the holder of a position in a university.

Indeed, the typical science of the 20th Century, which expanded so rapidly as to equal in growth all the other branches of organised factual knowledge put together, organic chemistry, was given its shape in the twenty years between 1850 and 1870. Thereafter, for almost a century, most of the enormous accumulation of new organic chemical compounds which were to transform the shape, colour and texture of our man-made environment were logical developments of the pattern worked out in those decades. At this time also was invented the idea of the modern specialist. The actual word "specialist" did not exist in the English language before 1856.

In the century which was to follow, it was to dominate the intellectual life of the entire civilised world, so that to be a specialist became the only respectable intellectual role, replacing almost entirely the older, wider concept of culture. It was to dictate the goals of much of university teaching and scholarship above all, in Britain.

It is not our purpose to trace all these climactic changes in the closing decades of the lst century to a single cause. However, they pervaded the cultural climate of the advanced world, which is to say that of the most prosperous classes of Europe and America. These classes which ranged from the small group of the traditional upper class to the mill managers of the industrial towns and the different sectors of independent or statutorily established professions and even the aristocracy of the highest skilled workers already knew about higher education. Previously it had been merely one of minor alternative ways of establishing and conserving one's social poisition. Generally more important was to have gone to a good school and to have thereafter entered as quickly as possible into a protected position in the social hierarchy of employment.

It may be assumed that during the latter part of the 19th Century the changes in the mental and cultural climate that we have briefly outlined above, associated above all with the changing requirements for knowledge in the more rapidly rising and influential areas of employment began to create a new level of demand for higher education.

In Britain this demand spread into the industrial areas of the North and expressed itself in the successive founding of a series of new civic universities in the closing decades of the 19th Century. Some of these evolved from the larger technical institutes which were themselves often an extension and development of the Mechanics Institutes which had reached their heyday in the first half of the 19th Century. These newer universities followed the tradition of their founding institutes by concentrating much more immediately on the sciences and applied sciences and even began to convert engineering into a subject of serious systematic scientific study — a process whch was to proceed much more speedily and thoroughly in the even more committed Technischen Hochschulen which had been initiated in Germany in the previous decades.

At the same time the older craft traditions of the Mechanics Institutes were continued and supplemented by the development of a
new wave of technician-level training, usually in after work evening
classes, in the Technical Colleges which were founded by many
municipalities in the industrial areas. These also had their own,
usually small, portion of full-time higher technological and scientific education, though it lacked the autonomy of growth of the
Universities and came to depend more and more on external subor-
dination to London University as the following century unfolded.

At this point we may note in passing a pattern of recurring
transformation in the development of further and higher education
in Britain. Training associated with the needs of industry has been
frequently conceived of in the first place as merely "vocational"
and hardly worthy of attention by the upper and middle classes, except insofar as the more far sighted members of the latter class were
concerned in the needs (and incidentally with the productive efficiency) of their skilled workforce. Thus, the Mechanics Institutes
were founded largely by philanthropic manufacturers for the
education (after a 12-hour working day) of the most energetic and
able members of the industrial working class. In the early days the
workers were even drawn into initiating some of the schemes of
study and into the management of the Institutes. But as they
developed, and as the applied arts and technical subjects they
fostered began to attract the interest of scientists and intellectuals
and as their usefulness as socio-cultural centres in the rapidly growing industrial towns became known, they were gradually infiltrated
and eventually to a large extent taken over by the more ambitious
and energetic members of non-manual clerical and supervisory
workers. The Technical Colleges which followed them became
rapidly dominated by the needs of these levels of "technician"
training and the original clientele of skilled and semi-skilled
workers, though still catered for, became a subordinate section of
the enterprise. In an analogous process of upward drift the civic
universities, which grew largely from some of the Technical Colleges, soon discarded the lower levels and concentrated on "degree
level" courses. At the same time they became fairly quickly filled
with students drawn mainly from middle and upper class
backgrounds. This pattern of takeover by universities of areas of
study previously considered beneath their interest, and often
pioneered in institutions of lower level intellectual prestige and
lower level class initiative, was to recur throughout the next hundred years and indeed, is still happening today. Even the ancient
centres of learning, so class-dominated that at the beginning of our
period attendance at an expensive public school was infinitely more
important for admission than any test of intellectual merit, even-

tually embraced the education of engineers and technologists, though very late in the day and to the disgust of those more traditional of their members who could not get used to the idea of these "plumbers" being admitted. And, of course, such is the attractiveness and financial superiority of the life they offer that they have inevitably attracted to themselves some of the brightest of technological talent.

In drawing attention to the fact that the impetus for an accelerated growth in higher education in the closing decades of the last century coincided with a new phase in industrial development in the advanced countries, we are not suggesting that it was a simple process of demand by the latter and supply by the former. Although the new industries were to become much more dependent on the inputs of higher education, particularly its scientific and technological products than the older industries could ever have been, the demand was not necessarily immediately apparent. It is characteristic of employing enterprises, both industrial and service, that their consciousness of their demands for a higher level of professional and managerial expertise always lags behind their real needs; not surprisingly because demands are expressed by the old management which is based in the past, whereas new needs develop precisely as the new expertise enters and creates the future.

It was rather that the momentum of the new industrial revolution, coming as it did after decades of unprecedented economic growth which made it both possible and necessary, was at the centre of a broader wave of buoyant expectation of continued material progress. The scientific revolution of the 19th Century gave an intellectual basis for this optimism, and the new universities and colleges were expressions of faith in the contribution of higher education to it, just as the General Education Act of 1870 was aimed at giving a very modest part in it to the industrial working class.

The force behind the expansion of universities (and to a lesser extent the other forms of further and higher education), which took off then, was more the push from would-be students than the direct pull from the careers into which they were to enter. The expansion took the same course throughout a series of European countries independently of whether they created new universities or continued with the old.

We shall note the same fact in more detail in the much more hectic acceleration of almost a century later. Although both increasing industrial and civil employment needs and university provision doubtless played their part in sustaining the ever-increasing demand for higher education as it got under way, they did not actually create it. It arose essentially from a new consciousness of its potential value among the growing managerial and professional sections of the middle class and among the industrial employers and entrepreneurs, which was a response, not to any particular pull from employment or any particular provision by universities, it was rather a product of the whole new climate of social, cultural, scientific, economic and industrial winds of change. This climate was not confined to any one of the advanced countries. In Europe, in particular, such a change in the socio-cultural atmosphere was bound to diffuse more or less rapidly throughout the individual countries. As we shall see later, some of the European countries were nevertheless able to adapt their institutions, particularly their industries, more successfully than others; to take advantage of the outputs, both of research and education, developing in the universities. Such a differentiation indeed, has persisted to this day, even through periods when the actual course of expansion of higher education has followed parallel paths. The application of knowledge does not always keep even pace with its potential. The evenness of the growth of higher education in Europe throughout the century from 1860 was a reflection of the growth of a common consciousness of its importance among the classes who commonly dominated it throughout Europe, rather than a common path of economic and industrial application in the individual countries.

To conclude this survey of the century of continuous acceleration, we may remark that it was during this period that all the modern features and institutional forms of higher education were established and consolidated. Indeed, it may be said that the self-image of most present day academics still reflects the ideas of university studies and research as they developed in the heyday of this century. We have already remarked on the all pervasive rule of the specialist which became established in this century, epitomised and satirised by Shaw in *The Doctor's Dilemma*. In the newest countries to joint the race for scientific hegemony, those of the Soviet bloc, the word specialist has become synonymous with intellectual, or indeed with anyone who has received higher education. The universal form of greeting in academic circles became "What is your subject?" It became decidedly suspect to voice opinions in a university except within the narrow confines of one's "discipline". The older concept of a "Universitas" where the common advance of common knowledge was the concern of all, decayed into a narrow departmentalism. The centre of intellectual concern became the accumulation of more and more factual knowledge. The value of a university teacher became measured by the number of research papers he had published, without concern about their human significance. The intellectual creed of the period, the dominant philosophy of knowledge, was positivism; with its enthronement of facts as the only repository of meaning.

As Wittgenstein, the outstanding theoretician of the century remarked at almost precisely its mid-point in 1918 "The world is the totality of facts".

The accepted academic dogma became "the pursuit of knowledge for its own sake", without reference to practical application or moral or ethical significance. Indeed, it became universally regarded as unethical to ask whether a goal of research or education was ethically justified. As for practice, although higher education was required of course, to continue to provide for the education of the older professions and, indeed, for an increasing number of new ones, its centre of gravity moved to the area of fundamental pure research in the specialised disciplines and in the single h onours degrees which were seen by the academics as the only possible feeders to them. We shall have occasion to deal further with the consequences of the overall cast of moral neutrality which came over the face of the universities in the next chapter. A word of comment is necessary here on the apparent dichotomy between the purism of university studies as they expanded and the new momentum in industrial production and its associated public services which we have associated above with the take-off of higher education at the beginning of the modern era. We must note that this separation of the internal goals of higher education from the goals for the application of knowledge and for the careers of graduates differed in different countries. Above all the courses of higher education began to follow quite a different path in the United States, where its more rapid development coincided with much closer integration with application.

As far as Britain and, to some extent, other countries of Europe are concerned, the divergence was rather a consequence of the indirect path through which the growing tide of new knowledge, especially scientific knowledge penetrated the barriers of tradition and vested interest to its applications in practice. Research, higher education and industry and new forms of social administration were to develop side by side, parallel to each other, impelled together by their common transformation in the last decades of the 19th Century. Though they were to become more and more closely dependent on each other, feeding each other's development, the dependence remained implicit rather than explicit. The course of development of each of these social institutions whose changes and interactions marked a sharp break with the past, nevertheless appeared to be largely self-powered, autonomous. They each showed separately the feature of ever-accelerating exponential growth which, as we have seen above, is the hallmark of processes whose momentum of change apparently comes from within. It is not indeed, until we come to our own day that the close, but previously largely hidden connection between the growth of knowledge and its application comes out into the open. It is not unexpected that this latest transformation coincides with the beginnings of another revolution in the nature of industry and industrial, or perhaps post-industrial, society. Again, this appears to be heralded by an escalation in the growth of higher education. We shall deal with the evidence for this in the next chapter.

CHAPTER THREE

The Student Explosion of the 1960s

Almost as soon as the Second World War ended, higher education started to revive. Student numbers commenced to grow in the latter years of the war and by 1946 had already reached the level which would have been predicted if the regular trend of acceleration of the previous 80 years had not been interrupted by conscription to the fighting forces. Indeed, the backlog of returning ex-servicemen anxious to make up for lost time caused a surge of enrolments which temporarily flooded the Universities and brought an unusual boom in full-time students into the Technical Colleges and Colleges of Education. This temporary pressure reached its peak by about 1950 and then began to recede until, by 1954, it was back on trend. The detailed course of this immediate post-war tide is shown in Table 3.1, where the number of annual entrants into the three main streams of full-time higher education are given for each year from 1943 to 1955.

It will be noticed in passing that the biggest proportional ebb and flow took place in the further education system essentially the Technical Colleges. In the period from 1943 to 1950 their numbers of entering full-time students rose by 140 per cent (and in addition their numbers of advanced part-time students rose even more rapidly) compared with the corresponding peak rise of about 45 per cent in University enrolments. In the subsequent recession from 1950 to 1954 the Technical Colleges suffered a drop to 52 per cent in full-time students, whereas the Universities only fell to 90 per cent of their highest total. This indicates a general feature of the way the flow of students tends to divide itself between the different streams of higher education in Britain which persists to this day. The main thrust of the advance has been towards the Universities. Teacher training numbers have been much more definitely controlled by the State to meet the calculated requirements of the schools. The Technical Colleges however, have frequently acted as the reserve provision, catering for the excess which could not temporarily get into the Universities. This is not unrelated to the fact that the Technical Colleges, catering predominantly for evening, and latterly, part-time students from industry have been much more predominantly representative of working class sections of the population. Their incursion into full-time higher education, largely the preserve of the professional and managerial strata has only been sporadic at times of overflow. At such times they have stretched their facilities to an extent that would have been unthinkable to University academics and would have occasioned a revolt among University students.

TABLE 3.1

New Entrants to Higher Education 1943-1955

Year	University Entrants	Teacher Training Entrants	Further Education Entrants
1943	12911	4450	2250
1944	14057	5600	2500
1945	14380	9250	3500
1946	17650	12450	4250
1947	18400	14250	4800
1948	19450	13550	4950
1949	19050	12006	5150
1950	17400	11250	5350
1951	17750	11650	4800
1952	16720	11700	4150
1953	16560	12050	3450
1954	17593	11943	2786
1955	18767	11914	3025

Sources: University Grants Committee Annual Reports.
Report of Committee on Higher Education, Lord Robbins. HMSO 1961-1965.
Annual Abstracts of British Statistics.
Higher Education into the 1990s, DES London 1978.

Comparison of Figs 2.2 and 2.3 of Chapter 2 will show that a similar post-war surge was characteristic of Europe. Indeed, after the drop in student numbers in the early war years, Europe was back on course by 1945 and reached a temporary comparative peak by about 1948. Thereafter, the speed of advance slackened, as in Britain, and was back on trend by about 1953-4. The individual countries of Europe showed broadly similar behaviour. Those who were effectively out of the war soonest, such as France and then Italy, recovered the momentum of University enrolments before the end of the war and peaked earliest, but by the early fifties all (except Germany, which had suffered the additional trauma of a split down the middle) were about back where the trend from the pre-war half century would have predicted.

In the mid-1950s occurred a sudden break in the continuity of the long-term trend. From then, for the next fifteen years, there was an extraordinary unpredicted and unpredictable explosion in University and higher education expansion, common to all the countries of the advanced world.

There is still a belief in Britain that this great escalation was a product of projections and government policies of the post-war years, especially the adoption of the recommendations of the Robbins' Report of 1963. It is therefore necessary to review briefly the scene of the reports and projections of this period. It is true that the closing years of the war saw a considerable concentration of attention on the problems of post-war education. A series of reports on secondary education from 1943 on was eventually disposed of in the Education Act of 1944. From our point of view, that of recruitment to higher education, the relevance was the possible liberation of undeveloped talent, particularly among the lower socio-economic levels, by the raising of the school leaving age to 15 and the universalisation of secondary education. (The next twenty years were necessary to show what little difference these changes in themselves were to make). Then followed a series of official papers on higher education or its product, the supply of qualified man-power.

In 1945 the special committee on High Technological Education under the chairmanship of Lord Percy (the first of a series placed by the government in the hand of its most noble Lords) recommended that a number of Technical Colleges should be developed to sponsor technological courses at degree level to be validated by a "National Council of Technology". It is interesting to note, in parenthesis, that the reservation by the chairman, Lord Percy, that this device of nominating another third party to take the place of the University of London as academic nursemaid to the Technical Colleges in their newly proposed role, would only delay their acceptance as a university equivalent, has proved, unhappily, well founded. Given a choice between autonomous institutions which award their own degrees and those still under tutelage, would-be students nearly always choose the former if they can. The same problem dogs the Polytechnics of our day. In British Higher Education, given a choice between status, especially social status and relevance, for example, industrial and economic relevance, status wins every time.

In 1946 a committee on "scientific manpower" chaired by Sir Alan Barlow, recommended that the Universities should be expanded so as to double the output of scientists. Nevertheless, it considered that this increase should not be at the expense of students studying humanities. The report stated that "we attach the greatest importance to the atmosphere of an association of men and women which takes all knowledge as its province . . . such as atmosphere has a great part to play in completing any student's education and prevent him from becoming a narrow and cloistered specialist". These sentiments tended to get eroded in the following decades as the panacea of manpower planning became fashionable. The report also concluded that "only about one in five of the boys and girls, who have intelligence equal to that of the best half of the University students, actually reach the Universities"!

In the 1950s, because of the continued preoccupation with the supposed shortage of scientists and technologists, a group of committees started the business of surveying the future needs for scientifically qualified manpower. The broad method of the surveys was by questionnaires to all sorts and conditions of employers inquiring about their needs for such personnel in the following decade or so. As the subsequent decade unfolded the results of the surveys proved extraordinarily wide of the reality. It was fortunate if the error in particular fields proved to be less than 50 per cent. We shall return to a critical examination of the subject of the planning of future needs of graduates in Chapter 7. Here we may just note that in spite of the emphasis of policy on the production of scientists, it was in the key subject of mathematics that the underestimation of future needs proved most disastrous.

In 1956 another White Paper on technical education appeared which attempted once and for all to divide the two levels of applied studies which, as we have seen, had been uneasy bedfellows for a century. At the lower level was that development upward from craftsmanship on which much of the original industrial revolution had been based. This was now to be fixed as the sphere of the technician, and to be the preoccupation as before, of the majority of Technical Colleges. At the higher level were those applications drawn from academic science by the newer industries emerging in the 20th century. These were the functions of the technologist. It was this second concept that the White Paper really made claim to have discovered and to offer to the larger Technical Colleges, which were to become Colleges of Advanced Technology. Thus Britain was re-discovering the invention of the German Technischen Hochschulen, the best part of a century later. Within a decade the old cultural habit had asserted itself and the Colleges of Advanced Technology had become Universities. This, however, was a consequence of a report to end reports on higher education, the Robbins Report of 1963.

In the hagiology of British Higher Education since the war there is no name more revered on the one hand or regretted on the other than that of the chairman of the Committee on Higher Education appointed by the Prime Minister in 1960, Lord Robbins. According to established legend, both the headlong expansion which multiplied the number of students by three times in about twelve years and the supposedly new principle "that courses of higher education should be available for all those who are qualified by ability and attainment to pursue them and wish to do so", were the legacy of his Report. We shall examine the significance of the principle later in Chapter 4; here we are concerned with the allegations that, for better or worse, the escalation of the 60s was the responsibility of the Robbins Report issued in 1963.

The elaborate calculations of the Report were based on surveys and research on a scale unprecedented in British higher education. Eventually its recommendations arose from two main kinds of consideration. The first was that comparisons with abroad revealed that "If, as we believe, a highly educated population is essential to meet competitive pressures in the modern world, a much greater effort is necessary if we are to hold our own". The second arose from evidence which suggested the existence of "large reservoirs of untapped ability in the population, especially among the girls . . .".
On that basis, and on the assumption that a steady trend of demand reflecting these latent resources would continue to increase up to 1980, and asserting the "Robbins principle" mentioned above, the Report recommended targets of about 390,000 places for full-time students in higher education by 1973-4 and about 560,000 places by 1980. The main targets of the Report were adopted by the government and it has been assumed by disciples and critics ever since that Robbins was to blame, or praise, as the case may be, for the flood of students which followed.

TABLE 3.2

Annual Percentage Increase in Numbers of Full-time Students 1955-1970

	Percent Annual Increase 1955-1970	Coef. of Deter- mination r 2	Doubling period 1860-1960 Years	Doubling period 1955-1970 Years	Transition Date
Great Britain	9.3	.99	26.4	7.7	1956
West Germany	7.3	.95	23.9*	8.9	
France	9.4	.99	22.0	7.6	1957
Italy	7.6	.96	20.6	9.5	1958
Belgium	8.1	.99	30.4	8.8	1954
Netherlands	8.9	.99	19.0	8.0	1955
"Little Europe"	8.4	.99	23.5	8.7	1957

*All Germany 1860-1933

However, inspection of Fig 2.2 again shows that the sharp upturn in student expansion dates from much earlier than the Robbins Report and can be placed almost exactly at 1956. Fig. 2.3 shows that precisely the same change occurred in Europe at about the same date. Fig 2.4 demonstrates that the course of student expansion was extremely similar in each of the main European countries. At some point in the mid-1950s the slope of the graph changes more or less sharply to nearly three times its former value. In Table 3.2 we estimate a notional transition date for each country from the point of intersection of the regular trend line from 1860 to 1955, and the new trend line from 1955 to 1970. Also in this table are given the new annual percentage rates of expansion and the coefficients of determination as described in Chapter 2. The sharpness of the transition is seen from the fact that in each country the annual percentage increase had risen to about three times its former steady value. The estimated date of transition in each country only varies by two or three years from that for Europe as a whole. For ease of visualisation Table 3.2 also includes the calculated "doubling periods" for student growth in each country before and after the mid-50s.

The conclusion is inescapable that the explosion in the number of students in higher education which has so often in Britain been attributed to the Robbins Report of 1963, actually started about seven years prior to that date and was almost exactly duplicated throughout the individual countries of Europe. It may be noted, in passing, that the actual immediate course of expansion in Britain differed sharply from the target figure of the Robbins Report, since it reached 481,000 students by 1973, compared with the Report's figure of only 390,000 (but considerably below the figure of 600,000 which would have been achieved if the trend of regular escalation of the period from 1955 to 1970 had been maintained instead of entering the recession of the 70s as we shall describe later).

One must also conclude that the remarkable new impetus of expansion must have had its source in factors which were common throughout Europe; unless Monsieur Robbins, Herr Robbins, Signor Robbins were simultaneously conspiring together in each of the European Governments.

Although we have mainly limited our comparisons to Western Europe in order to avoid the more complex factors that will have to be taken into account in describing the wider world scene, the remarkable escalation of this time undoubtedly affected the whole advanced world. Even in the United States, where full-time student enrolments have always far surpassed the proportions in Europe, and had reached the staggering total of about three-and-a-half millions by 1960; they more than doubled in a decade. Such countries of East Europe where the statistics are in a form most comparable with the West, such as Yugoslavia, showed an even bigger proportionate jump. In Japan, which had started late in the field of

University growth and did not catch up with Europe till the early part of the 20th century, precisely the same thing happened, though in her case, as to a lesser extent that of the USA, the transition was not so sharp because of the already much higher growth rate in the pre-1955 period. Table 3.3 shows the comparison of growth rates for Europe, the USA and Japan for the two stages 1900-1960 and 1955-1970.

TABLE 3.3

Comparative Annual Rates of Expansion of Student Enrolments 1900-1960/1960-1970

| | 1900-1960 | | 1960-1970 | | |
	Percent Annual Increase	Coef. of Deter-mination	% Annual Increase	Coeff. of deterioration	Transition Date
"Little Europe"	2.9	.95	9.2	.99	1958
Japan	5.5	.99	9.7	.99	1962
USA	4.6	.97	8.7	.99	1960

The very simultaneity and closely parallel course of the post-1955 escalation in higher education in so many different parts of the world, and particularly in virtually every country of Europe, makes it difficult to connect with the policies of particular governents or with reforms in the educational system in particular countries, which by no means kept in step. Though in Germany and France, for example, there was some detailed broadening of the scope of secondary education after the war, in neither country was there legislation of such scope as the British Education Act of 1944.

Nor did the successive attempts to upgrade the Technical Colleges in Britain, which culminated in the creation of ten Colleges of Advanced Technology in 1956, have any simultaneous parallel in the other European countries. Although, in Britain these colleges contributed to the accommodation of the rapidly increasing number of students, there is no evidence that they attracted a basically new source of student supply. Indeed, in that formative period they suffered, as the Technical Colleges had before them, and the Polytechnics were to do later, the role of taking the overflow from the Universities. There is little doubt that had they never been brought into existence the existing Universities and Colleges would have taken the whole expansion, provided of course, they have been fed the necessary extra resources.

The main source of the simultaneous world-wide explosion of higher education could hardly have been an equally internationally simultaneous set of measures to increase the supply of the number of higher education places. It must rather have come in the first place from a new level of urgency in student demand. There is no evidence that the universal cause of this was a sudden rise in the numbers of young people of University age, a consequence of a post-war bulge in the birth rate. In Fig 3.1 are shown the steady exponential rise of first year entrants to higher education in Britain from 1954 to 1971 and also the ebbs and flows of the number of 18-year-olds in the population. During each of two periods when student numbers rose by about 30 per cent, there was in each case a net fall in the size of the age group, in the second case from 1965 to 1971 by as much as 17 per cent. A similar disparity was shown, for example, in France, where, between 1954 and 1964 the total size of 18-22-year-old age groups remained virtually constant, while the total number of students rose from 194,000 to over 400,000. We shall advance later, reasons which will support the view that there is no necessary relation between student enrolments and the total number of people of the age to become students, precisely because the majority of young people have no real possibility to do so. On the other hand, there may well be a close relation with the number of young people in the social classes from which higher education is predominantly recruited.

The new urgency of student demand probably represented a relatively sudden change in the evaluation of higher education (or the qualifications it led to) comparable with the change that had taken place a century or so before. We shall advance evidence in Chapter 4 that it did not, at any rate in the main countries of Europe, herald a sudden change in the scope of the franchise of higher education. At the end of the period, in the 1970s, there was still the extreme disparity of social participation in Britain which we briefly enumerated in Chapter 1. The vastly increased numbers of students were not new to the idea of a University, nor did it suddenly become easier for them to attend. It became more attractive. More than that, the consciousness grew rapidly that whereas before, higher education had been merely one of several ways of conserving (and for a minority of gaining) social and economic status, at this stage in the 20th century it was becoming a virtual necessity for many of the roles played by the upper and middle, professional and managerial classes.

In Britain, one of the signs of this change was the appearance of new academic barriers to entry to the Professions. During the decades after the war, successive branches of the many new technological professions began to demand completed higher education as a condition of entry. Engineering, where the lines of division between craftsmen, technician and technologist had been traditionally blurred, was now separated out into more or less distinct streams. The possibility of transition between them which

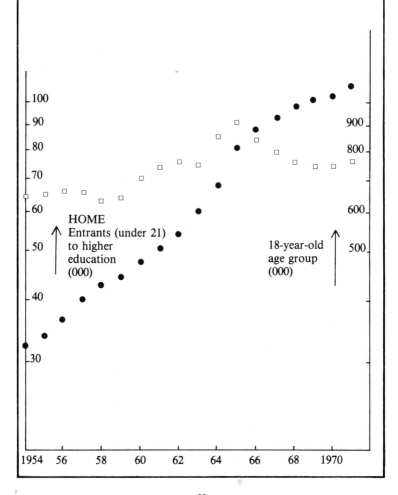

FIG 3.1   **Home entrants (under age 21) to Higher education and 18-year-old age group Britain 1954-71**

Age group   □

Entrants   ●

Sources: Statistics of Education. HMSO. Relevant Years' Higher Education into the 1990s. HMSO 1978.

had been a particular feature of the British system reflecting the growth of the Applied Sciences of Engineering from craft background in the industrial revolution, was drastically reduced. The same changes were becoming imminent in the non-technical professions, including those in the para-medical field like pharmacy, ophthalmic optics, physiotherapy and in the commercial and managerial areas such as accountancy, personnel management etc. At the same time the rapidly growing complexity of public administration created a clutch of new planning roles and functions requiring higher education as a necessary preliminary base.

These were merely some of the reflections in Britain of a new world-wide climate of opinion in the advanced countries; a new sense of significance of the post-war knowledge explosion, particularly in science and technology. By the early years of the 1950s there was a growing prescience of the imminence of what one British politician called the "White Heat of the new Technological Revolution". Just as the great technological changes of the period of about 1850-1870 had laid the basis for the second industrial revolution of the 20th century, so it now appeared that the basis was being laid for another great transformation of the methods of production and the systems of industrial and public organisation.

This latest discontinuity in social and economic development had begun to have the drastic effects on the nature of work and social life described in Chapter 1. We shall be assessing its possible course of development in Chapter 7. Here, we will merely mention some of the signs it cast before it, such as the epidemically rapid spread of the influence of the computer; the growth of new industries, based for the first time in history on the discoveries of the laboratory, such as nuclear power, electronics in its multitude of applications; and again dramatic changes in the methods of agriculture and food production.

The great changes in material life brought about in the rich countries during the hundred or so years from 1860 and the enormous comparative rise in higher education which accompanied them, nevertheless took place steadily throughout the period. We have noted the almost constant annual percentage increase in the number of students. There was a parallel steady overall development of gross material product, but more to the point, the basic technologies of production only changed gradually. As we have seen, although industry and public service continually found employment for the exponentially increasing numbers of graduates and professionals who were the principal agents in modernising and changing them, major changes rarely appeared to spring directly from the sources of new knowledge, the research laboratories or the Universities. To put another aspect, in most cases policy in the largest enterprises was more heavily weighted by considerations of capital sunk in existing processes than by the potentiality of the new.

The changes that appeared to be imminent in the new age which seemed to be developing in the second half of the 20th century, could be of quite a different kind. The 1950s were, perhaps, what an American economist called a time of discontinuity; analogous perhaps with the earlier discontinuities of the first industrial revolution and again with the climactic changes of the closing decades of the 19th century; but possibly more sudden and severe in its consequent social upheavals than either.

The escalation of higher education of the 1960s, concentrated as it was among the informed sections of the population, can be interpreted as a race for cover before the coming storm.

This sense of discontinuity pervaded the decade of the 1960s. All the traditions and sacred conventions of Universities throughout the world seemed to be in the melting pot. In 1968 student rebellions broke out simultaneously in several countries and spread rapidly to every major centre in the developed world. This period is so close that many members of the public have hardly noticed that it almost vanished as quickly as it came, and can still anxiously inquire about the problem of "student" unrest. Of course there are still eruptions of outraged protest from time to time and from college to college, as there have always been, and in some countries where the university is almost the only institution with any vestige of freedom, violent revolt can still suddenly erupt and be as suddenly ruthlessly suppressed. But it is a far cry from the days of May 1968, when President de Gaulle found it prudent to leave Paris to check the loyalty of his Generals in the face of a student-initiated revolutionary movement which appeared to threaten the stability of the Fourth Republic itself. Or the time, a little later, when the greatest military power on earth was pulled back from the battlefields it had dominated and the countryside it had devastated in Vietnam, as much by the anti-war campaign initiated in its own Universities and Colleges as by the resistance of the enemy.

Like the explosion in student numbers which preceded and accompanied it, the explosion of student revolution was more or less completely unexpected, particularly in the Universities and Colleges. Indeed, the immediately preceding post-war bulge in student numbers, which, as we have seen, peaked in about 1950 with resources, both of staff and material facilities, infinitely poorer than those attained by the late 60s, gave no warning of the later outburst of discontent. The 50s were indeed a honeymoon period for the traditionalist, and even a source of irritation to many, even senior academics who found it difficult to attain any informal conversation with so conservative a body of students. As one Master of Cambridge College put it at a European conference on University Staff/Student Relations in 1956: "It is so difficult to make any real contact when the junion common room is so much to the right of the senior".

A conference of the International Association of Universities in Tokyo in as late as 1965 solemnly concluded that it would not be possible to include students into any formal policy making or governing body in the University. Within a decade there was hardly a University or College in the Western world which had not conceded this very principle. Indeed, in some countries where centuries old systems of University organisation and government were transformed within a few years of 1968, this was one of the least of the changes that followed from the troubles.

Yet internal university reform was not at the heart of the great waves of protest emanating from the students crowding into the Colleges. Nor, as we have said above, was it the inadequacy of facilities for the extraordinary rapid growth of classes. Though the provision of buildings undoubtedly did lag behind demand in some countries, that was not the case in some of those where the rebellion was most severe. And in any case, in most countries the provision of money and other material resources more than kept pace with the expansion. The general evidence in Europe and America is that public expenditure per student steadily rose in real terms throughout the whole decade (see Table 5.2, Chap.5). Certainly, in Britain, staff/student ratios generally kept pace with expansion. Indeed, in the newer Universities and Colleges they reached higher levels than had been customary for many decades. Generous expenditure rates on new equipment and technicians ensured that the resources available for research were probably higher than ever before. As far as the academics were concerned it would not be far from the truth to say that "they never had it so good".

There were some of the expected moans of the traditionalists about the decline of quality, of the difficulty of dealing with students from backgrounds which did little to fit them for cultural heights of University study. This was a myth. There was no larger a proportion of students from the "uncultured" classes than before. They came in the main from the same privileged families as before. But more of them came. Although the climate of opinion which swept them into higher education was, as we believe, a product of the larger changes in the industrial, economic and social life of the advanced countries, occasioned by the knowledge explosion, many of the students were, paradoxically, less directly concerned with the mere career value of a University or College education than their immediate predecessors, the pragmatic post-war classes of the previous decade. Indeed, it was precisely their political and social "idealism" which appeared to motivate the main thrust of their demands which were only obliquely concerned with the reform of the Universities and more directly obsessed with the revolution of society.

Another apparent paradox is that, though the impact of new knowledge on society, which is the great motor of change, arises most directly from the advances in the "hard" sciences of physics, electronics, polymer chemistry and molecular biology, the most popular field of demand in higher education temporarily passes to the social sciences. In one sense this may arise from the prescience that although the knowledge revolution starts from the material sciences, the most difficult of the challenges that it poses lies in the field of human relations and the social and political problems that reflect them. It is broadly true of any major technological change that for the first five years or so it stimulates the demand for technologists and scientists in its laboratory and design stage, but as it passes into development, production or implementation, its organisation and control calls for much broader knowledge, and the skills in demand become those of managing people.

As we have noted earlier, the actual course of qualitative development in higher education and its associated research may be only indirectly related to the underlying changes in the industrial, social and economic environment which provide the impetus for its sudden expansion. The general sense of new concern to climb on the higher bandwagon among the children of the informed sectors of society divided itself among the possible subjects of study, not by some precise calculation of their economic relevance, indeed, such a prophesy is, in any case, as we have seen a highly hazardous business, even to the professional statisticians; but, according to the influence of persuasive teachers or the impulses of idealism. So at the very time when the Universities and Colleges were constrained to accent the expansion of material sciences and technology, the student demand for these subjects often fell below capacity, whereas the pressure on the so-called human sciences, and to a lesser extent, the arts, exceeded the supply of places.

Nevertheless, if one looks for a basic common motivation correlating the extraordinary uniform swing of the middle classes towards higher education in almost every country during this decade, it can hardly have been other than a common premonition that it was a necessity for survival. It was indeed a necessity to retain that capacity for freedom, for self-direction, for personal autonomy, above all, for defence against that reduction to robots of the industrial state machinery of production or routine service which appeared to be the destination of the majority of the under-educated.

For the more pragmatic of the youth, industrial or public leadership or the independence of an autonomous profession might be the goal. For the more rebellious of their companions, it might be leadership of the revolution. It is not entirely cynical to consider that in some cases the difference in motivation was not as great as it appeared. Indeed, that is more or less what the factory workers of Renault told the student revolutionaries of the Sorbonne when the latter came to lead them to the barricades. In other cases whatever had been the tide of social class consciousness which had drawn the youth into higher education, the ideals survived and found that knowledge of every kind can also illuminate human understanding and be made to serve the cause of human welfare. The rebellions of 68-70 did not achieve social revolution and their leaders sometimes became conservative management consultants, but they nevertheless challenged and even changed the complacent self image of the Universities, and they reminded the widest areas of society of the moral implications of the enormous social impact of new knowledge and of the vacuum in the heart of the shining technological age.

The student disillusion which erupted into the troubles of the end of the decade of escalation were not a product of the failure of the higher education system to deliver the goods as before. There was no such failure. They were rather because it succeeded merely in its old role. This explains why they came as such an inexplicable shock to the academics, who were almost the last people to grasp what was going on. The confrontation between student and academic was one about the goals of learning. The academic was in the main nurtured in the tradition of the pursuit of knowledge for its own sake. That, after all, was the justification for the main emphasis of his work, fundamental research. The majority of students were concerned with preparing for careers in which knowledge was not a direct goal but a tool for application. They were destined rather than their teachers, to be at the sharp end of the impact of knowledge on society.

The euphoria of the late 50s gave rise to the vision of a new world (whether of scientific management or of social revolution) which appeared to be almost within reach, and higher education was the main key. In the short term neither the structures of society nor those of its industrial or State enterprises could respond quickly enough to the tide of expectations released. As we shall suggest later, in most countries the social base of higher education was, in any case, far too narrow to develop any rapid response to the new perspectives arising from it. It was essentially this failure of overheated expectation among the young intelligentsia, rather than any dramatic change in the general human condition or any sudden surge of general social unrest that led to the rise of student revolutions of the period. And the same factors were, of course, bound to lead to its relatively rapid subsidence. The fifteen years from 1955 had witnessed a trebling of the student population in most of the advanced countries. It was widely but mistakenly thought to have been a major step towards mass higher education and, indeed, was already deplored as such in the more exclusive academic circles. Reaction to this supposedly regrettable dilution of the essential élitism of the University began to mount. One revered traditionalist of the old school entitled his account of the period "The degradation of the Academic dogma". In Britain a counter-attack was led by a nondescript collection of disgruntled dons, minor politicians of the right, and once-trendy writers who had finally attained their room at the social top. Their magazine was aptly entitled *The Black Papers.*

In the more euphoric circles of expansionist educational administrators, politicians and journalists, it was believed for a short period that the phase of mass higher education had already begun and would henceforth roll inevitably forward. Much attention was given to discussing the forms it might take and the concept of "permament education" was born. The vast potentialities of television began to be exploited in higher education throughout the world. In Britain, the most successful breakthrough to a new methodology of higher education was given form in the Open University, where all forms of modern mass communication were combined with a systematic development of the techniques of programmed learn ing. Its great success was unprecedented and unexpected. Both in its recruitment of students and in high graduation rate, it exceeded the hopes of its most optimistic friends. But its students came mainly from the same social sectors as before. It absorbed those middle class professionals or housewives who had missed their chance of full-time higher education. It hardly touched the masses. In Britain also, the Polytechnics began for the first time to take a sizeable proportion of the students entering full-time higher education though as we shall see later they played little part in extending the social franchise. Their social composition apparently did not differ greatly from that of the Universities.

It was characteristic of both the optimists and the pessimists of the closing years of the period of escalation that they were so engrossed in the problems of intellectual standards or pedagogical methods that relatively little attention was paid to the continuing social apartheid that had survived. Until this is removed, mass higher education in most advanced countries simply means the intellectual emancipation of the middle classes. The 1960s raised for the first time the question of mass higher education, but provided no answer. Though the question of costs and benefits was to dominate the next decade, the crisis of the period was not economic. Indeed, there was a comparative abundance of resources. The poverty was in the imagination. The wave of dissent which swelled into rebellion challenged both the system of higher education and the failure of advanced societies to harness its potential for human welfare. The challenge has not yet been adequately answered. The decade which followed was rather to be one of uncertainty of purpose, failure of confidence and an obsession with the techniques of cost reduction and institutional management.

CHAPTER FOUR

The Persistence of Social Apartheid

The dreams of mass higher education of the closing years of the 1960s have suffered a rude awakening in the years that have followed. As we suggested in Chapter 3, they were inspired by a false reading of the social facts and a premature optimism about the spread of higher education to the working class. Before returning to the more pessimistic projections and the more restrictive policies of the decade which has followed, it is necessary to examine in more detail the nature of the social class differences in education.

To put the matter this way is to presume an inequality in higher education, and to imply the need or moral obligation to set it right, to achieve an eventual equality. In advanced countries both the social need and moral obligation have long been formally recognised, first in so-called primary education and secondly in universal secondary education, though considerable differences have emerged in the interpretation of the character and compulsory period and leaving age of the latter. In the case of higher education the simple question of equal participation has been clouded by substitution of the question of equality of opportunity, which has proved elastic enough in its interpretation to justify the extremely wide social apartheid which exists. Opportunity has been taken to apply only to those able and willing to make use of it, indeed, it seems at first sight that such a restriction is inevitable. The assumption has been that there is a certain quota of such deserving young people at any moment and that educational policy determines what proportion of them are enrolled as students and that the proper aim of policy is to make this proportion as high as possible. Such a concept of policy, which culminated in the adoption of the so-called Robbins principle in Britain, has coincided with the development of the meritocratic self-image of higher education. As we have suggested in Chapter 2, this is a relatively recent development in the long history of Universities. It arises during a period of the dominance of specialised factual knowledge, the rapid social rise of the professional specialist, the degradation of the nature of work of a large proportion of the population and the growth of an amoral culture where efficiency (as interpreted economically) is the ultimate arbiter of values. The Robbins principle is, perhaps, not really so new, the tests of ability have been slightly modified over the century, but never to the extent of changing much the social mix of the entrants. However, to obtain a deeper grasp of the nature of both the necessary ability and the equally essential willingness to enter higher education, we have to develop an explanation of the actual expansion of higher education, both during the period from 1860-1955 when it multiplied some 12 times, and the subsequent 15 years of hectic escalation at nearly three times the previous rate of growth.

We summarise below the essential facts which have to be accounted for:

In each of the main countries of Europe the expansion followed basically the same course.

From about 1860 to about 1955 the percentage rate of annual growth was remarkably similar in the different countries and they each jumped to a similar, but much higher, rate of growth from 1955-1970.

The expansion in each case followed a steady exponential growth curve, interrupted in a similar way by the Wars and the great depression, but in each case rapidly returning to the expected trend.

Once the expansion was under way it showed little dependence on variation in population, or even on the size of the total age group of young people for normal entrance to higher education.

The preliminary evidence is that during the whole period, higher education has been largely dominated by the upper and middle social classes. We shall be examining this in more detail later in this chapter.

For almost a century the continual expansion of higher education appears to have a high degree of internal momentum, or, in other words, to be self-propelling. This follows both from its relative continuity of acceleration and from the international uniformity of its growth rates apparently independent of indifference in national policies, institutional forms and academic standards.

On the other hand the sharp internationally synchronous and uniform escalation, post-1955, indicates that a sufficiently powerful change in the international climate of economic and social thinking can trigger off a rapid change in the demand for higher education.

The explanation we shall develop accepts that something like the Robbins principle has, in fact, prevailed throughout most of the modern expansion that, in the main, the provision of places has corresponded to the effective demand, that numbers of students have risen in proportion to those both able and willing to enrol. Indeed, this is almost self-evident in those countries of Europe where there has been a legal entitlement to a University place for all those successful in the appropriate secondary school leaving examinations, whereas in Britain, although there has been the formal right of Universities to refuse students, a fairly constant high proportion of qualified applicants has been accepted for most of the period and for the latter part when we have reliable statistical evidence, there were places for the remainder in the other sections of the system.

It is possible that the provision of the necessary places has temporarily been interrupted in individual years or in periods of acute economic restriction as at the height of the depression of the interwar years, but it is more likely that the demand had also fallen correspondingly; in any case such interruptions had little effect on the eventual onward march of demand and the corresponding supply. On the other hand it may well be true that the effective demand has been affected by such factors as the financial cost of being a student or conversely the financial sacrifice entailed in abstaining from paid employment during the three or four years of higher education and hence militated against those from poorer families. This is to merely specify one of the reasons why some of those able to qualify for entrance might not be willing. Though this may have been important in the early decades of the century, it is much less likely since the Second World War, at any rate in Britain. In any case we shall suggest that it has never been the most important reason for a social division which has remained little changed over the whole century.

To understand this we shall change our approach to analysing the nature of the effective demand. Instead of the two factors of the Robbins principle: ability and willingness, we shall describe the growth of demand in terms more generally applicable to all individual decisions. The first necessity is the consciousness that higher education is a possibility at all, that it is, with any semblance of reality a part of the possible future. To make this factor precise we will call it the "perception of the probability of success in achieving entrance to higher education". We will note that this may be similar or equivalent to the perception of the chance of achieving the status goals to which higher education is an essential preliminary. For ease of formulation we will give this "perception" factor the symbol P and the quantitative significance of the visualised calculated chance of success.

The second factor is the value set on achieving entrance which we will call V (or more generally on achieving the status goals which higher education is expected to lead to). This may be given a quantitative meaning by considering it as measuring the degree to which the goal of higher education is preferred to other choices open to the individual concerned at the time. The chance that an individual will decide to attempt to enter higher education will be proportional to the product of the two factors of perception and value, P x V. The value factor in this scheme is clearly of the same kind as the willingness to enrol assumed in the Robbins scheme. But the other factor, the perception of the possibility of higher education as a personal future has dimensions which are wider than those of simple attainment or even ability.

Though at some stage some evidence of attainment, usually success in Secondary School examinations is necessary for entrance to higher education, this is only the last stage of the process of preparation. It is the culmination, not merely of all previous education, but of the cumulative influence of family and cultural environment from the individuals' earliest years. In some cases the experience of the individual will have been saturated with contact with learning throughout his childhood. A large proportion of the adults with whom he has come into contact will have been graduates or their professional equivalents. The kind of work done by his parents and their friends will be at the level for which higher education is at least an important method of entry. It will have been expected of him that at each stage of his childhood he should read the books and prepare for the interim tests which will eventually ensure his smooth passage from School to University if he wishes to go. The concept of higher education and the kind of career it leads to will have become a familiar prospect in his personal future. His perception factor, P, will be very high.

In other cases the early childhood of the individual will have been almost devoid of any contact with higher education with the exception of the socially remote figure of the class teacher. The graduate or professional worker will be a rare intruder in the adult scene in which she lives and perhaps as socially comprehensible to her as a visitor from another planet. The notion that she might aspire to any career associated with higher education hardly ever occurs to anyone in her family or social circle and indeed, virtually none of her friends or her elder siblings have ever given an example of its possibility. By the time she comes of age to make choices it is already far too late. Higher education is about as real as pie in the sky. The perception factor P will be very low. Indeed, in the case we have described above, it hardly exists in any real sense.

The percipient reader will realise that we have now sketched out imaginary scenarios for the son of the professional man on the one hand and the daughter of the unskilled worker on the other, for whom we showed the enormous disparity in chances of entering higher education in Chapter 1.

We shall consider later the supporting evidence from social

research for the above picture of the two extremes of what we may call the socialisation of consciousness of higher education. And, of course, we will take into account that there is a range of behavioural patterns in the social layers inbetween. Here we shall assume that is a broad picture which can be checked by commonsense observation and consider what consequences would be expected to follow and how it would be expected to affect the rate of expansion of higher education. While participation in higher education will clearly be strongly affected by social class, the above approach suggests that in the modern period this is an effect of the prior contact with the influence of higher education, the extent to which it is part of the normal social environment, above all the extent to which the products of the universities and colleges are constant members of the same social circles and that the work roles of adults in these social classes require previous higher education. In other words the class dichotomy we are speaking of, as some researchers have observed, is that of the educated versus the uneducated class, rather than simply the richer versus the poorer classes. Of course, the educated class overlaps significantly with the richer classes or the senior managerial classes, though not exactly as we shall see later. In any case the difference we are highlighting is their familiarity with, their know-how concerning, and their confidence in dealing with, higher education, even more than their capacity to buy their way into some of the avenues of access via private secondary education, if need be.

Thus, we may consider that the perception factor, P, is very large for precisely that section of the population which is already in close touch with higher education. Another way of seeing this is to visualise the existing graduates, the past products of higher education as stimulating the demand for entry to it. It is reasonable to suppose that the number of young people in the population with a high enough perception, P, to be significant, is proportional to this influence of past graduates and will be concentrated in the social circles in which they are considered normal members. As a reasonable simplification of the main features of the expansion we may suppose that the number of young people applying for enrolment each year will rise according to the rise of this influence, that is, it will be proportional to the number of graduates in the population. On the other hand the majority of young people will not be subject to this close and continual example of what it is to have undertaken higher education and their perception of it will lack reality and hence their P factor will, on the average, be much lower.

In quantitative terms the above may be expressed as follows:

$$N_e \text{ is proportional to } N_g \times P \times V$$

where N_e symbolises the number of enrolments in a given year, N_g is

the number of graduates in the population and P and V are the average perception and valuation by those young people whose contact with higher education has been sufficiently close for entry to have become a real object of choice. It follows from this that the rate of annual increase of enrolments will depend on the rate of annual increase of graduates which is itself proportional to the existing number of students preparing for graduation, as well, of course, to P and V as defined above. We can put this as a formula for the speed of expansion of student numbers as follows: Rate of increase R_s is proportional to $N_s \times P \times V$
Hence the percentage annual increase
$$R_s/1000N_s \text{ will be simply proportional to } P \times V$$
This is the mathematical formula for exponential expansion provided that the perception and valuation of higher education remain fairly constant among the young people who are its main clientele. To put it another way, the scheme we have outlined above predicts that the annual compound rate of interest of expansion should remain constant unless there is a significant change in the perception or value factors. As we have seen, this is what happened. From 1860-1955 the annual percentage interest remained remarkably constant and again, but at a higher rate from 1955-1970.

In the above we have outlined in non-technical terms the demonstration that the assumptions we have made about the main factors propelling higher education forward accounts for one of its main features, its apparently self-propelling, steadily accelerating, exponential character. The international uniformity of the exponential growth in a continent such as Europe, where its entrants would in the main have a uniformity high percentage of it, is also explicable. The remaining factor, the value of factor V, would, understandably, be subject to the same long-term trend of steady reinforcement and consolidation, since the economic, technological and social significance of the impact of new knowledge on the role of the professional and managerial classes would be common to the advanced industrial countries.

The rate of growth of student enrolments was not much influenced by variations in the total population of University age because working class children who constituted the majority of this population were not much involved in it. The professional classes from which most students came were expanding exponentially, mainly by processes of net upward social mobility because of the rapidly increasing demand for their services from the economy. Recruitment from new graduates (including that source of graduates which filtered up from below), was a major factor in this steady growth of the proportions of the educated class.

Finally, the explanation outlined above can account in a

straightforward way for the discontinuity of 1955 and the sharp escalation in higher education of the following period. As we shall confirm later this sharp upturn was not accompanied by any significant closing of the social gap in participation. The main factor was a further jump in the already high participation rates of the educated classes. For these sections the perception factor was already very high and as we have suggested in Chapter 3, the main reason for the sudden escalation was a further rise in the value attached to higher education in comparison with alternatives such as direct entry to the professions or to assured careers in business or commerce. Although we have no such direct evidence of the social division in higher education for the earlier discontinuity of the 1860s, we may reasonably presume that an analogous earlier revision of the values of the corresponding upper social layers accompanied the epochal changes that were erupting in the nature of industry, economic life and social organisation in the closing decades of the last century, and gave impetus to that general take-off in the growth of higher education which persisted for the long period from 1860-1955.

We will now return to the more detailed examination of the social stratification of higher education in the light of the broad features described above and the explanatory model which we have developed to account for them.

As we have seen, the chief social characteristic which is likely to influence the individual's consciousness of the value and possibility of higher education is contact with, and confidence about it, gained from the prior participation in it of family, friends, relatives and young people of the immediately older age group with whom he or she is still in contact. We will discuss school influence later, but may note here that it would be a matter of common observation that the kind of school atmosphere and influence experienced by most children tends to reinforce the social influences mentioned above. It would be interesting therefore to attempt to correlate participation in higher education with the "educational" social background or what one might call the "educational" class of the students.

However, this is not directly possible since census information and additional data available from research about the class divisions in society are mainly based on classifications of the occupations follows by the adults, or in the case of children, by the occupational class or status of their parents, most usually the father. The basis of the Registrar General's classification has been changed several times during the period of a hundred years that we are interested in, and various research workers have used variants of their own which cannot always be exactly fitted together. Nevertheless, there would be broad agreement that from an educational point of view the extremes are represented by the professional class, consisting essentially of the senior professions such as doctors, lawyers, accountants on the one hand and the class of unskilled workers on the other. In 1976 the former class were about 4 per cent of the population and the latter about 8 per cent. Table 4.1 shows the comparative participation in higher education for children from these two classes in 1976 in Britain. This illustrates the range of social and sex discrimination actually obtaining at the present day. Table 4.2 shows that the social split has not materially changed over the past twenty years. Indeed, in terms of the ratio of numbers of students at universities the gap between the two classes has widened. On the other hand, the gap between the men and women from the professional class, has become noticeably less. In the case of the daughters of unskilled workers the numbers are still too small for much significance to be attached to the increase in their very small participation.

TABLE 4.1

Participation in Higher Education
Children from Professional Class and from Unskilled Workers. 1976

(Note: The classification used in this table and table 4.2 is based on the Registrar General's classification of occupations 1970)

| | MALE | | FEMALE | |
| | Professional | Unskilled | Professional | Unskilled |
Social Class	(RG Class I)	(RG Class V)	(RG Class I)	(RG Class V)
Nos. of University Entrants by class	9639	482	6124	266
18-year-old age group by parental class composition	16769	33538	16111	32222
Class APR (Univs) %	57.5	1.4	38.0	0.8
(Estimated) Entrants to all Higher Education by class	14280	714	9085	395
Class APR (All Higher Education) %	85.2	2.1	56.4	1.2
Total University Entrants	48193		26625	
Total H.E. Entrants	71400		39500	
Total Age Group	419220		402780	
Total APR (i) University	11.4		6.6	
Total APR (ii) Higher Education	17.0		9.8	

APR = Age Participation Rate

TABLE 4.2

Participation of children of Professional Class and Unskilled Workers in Universities 1957-1976

Year	MALE Professional Number of Students	A.P.R. %	MALE Unskilled Number of Students	A.P.R. %	FEMALE Professional Number of Students	A.P.R. %	FEMALE Unskilled Number of Students	A.P.R. %
1957	2460	25.7	246	.6	974	9.9	—	—
1961	3252	29.1	181	.5	1571	14.4	75	.2
1976	9639	57.5	482	1.4	6124	38.0	266	.8

Sources: 1957. R.K. Kelsall. Applications for Admission to Universities. London 1957.
Sources: 1961. Report of Committee on Higher Education (Lord Robbins) HMSO 1961-3.
Sources: 1976. Universities Statistical Record.

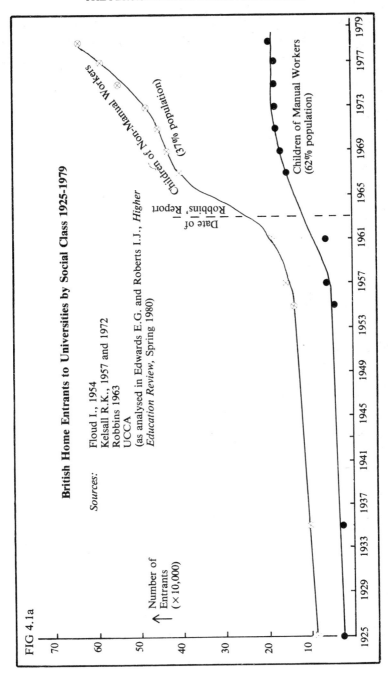

FIG 4.1a

British Home Entrants to Universities by Social Class 1925-1979

Sources: Floud I., 1954
Kelsall R.K., 1957 and 1972
Robbins 1963
UCCA
(as analysed in Edwards E.G. and Roberts I.J., *Higher Education Review*, Spring 1980)

Number of Entrants (× 10,000)

Children of Non-Manual Workers

Children of Non-Manual (37% population)

Date of Robbins' Report

Children of Manual Workers (62% population)

TABLE 4.3

Proportion of University Student Entrants by Social Class of Male Parent 1968-78 compared with proportions of employed males aged 45-59, Census 1971.

Note: The social classification of occupations used in this Table and table 4.4 are based on data from the University Central Council for Admissions using the occupation orders of the Office of Population Censuses and Surveys. The main difference between this and the classification used in Table 4.1 and 4.2 is that the Professional and Technical occupational class below is a somewhat broader group (of about twice the numerical strength) than the more senior Professional Class I of the R.G. 70 classification used in Tables 4.1 and 4.2.

Male Parental Occupational Class	Census 1971 Males 45-59	*Percentage of entering students*										
		1968	1969	1970	1971	1972	1973	1974	1975	1976	1977	1978
Professional Technical	9	28	31	30	30	32	34	34	35	35	36	37
Managers, Senior Administrators	7	14	15	14	14	14	15	15	16	16	16	17
Clerical, Junior Administrators	21	29	27	28	27	27	25	25	24	24	24	23
Manual Workers	62	29	27	28	29	27	26	26	25	24	24	23

Sources: Universities Central Council for Admissions. Statistical Supplements for relevant years. UCCA Cheltenham.

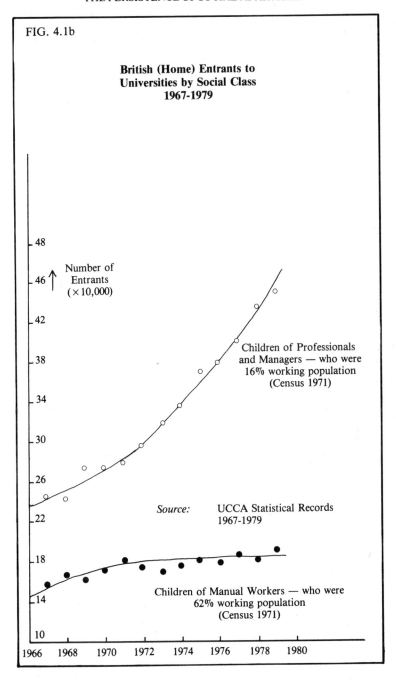

FIG. 4.1b

**British (Home) Entrants to
Universities by Social Class
1967-1979**

Number of
Entrants
($\times 10,000$)

Children of Professionals
and Managers — who were
16% working population
(Census 1971)

Source: UCCA Statistical Records
1967-1979

Children of Manual Workers — who were
62% working population
(Census 1971)

TABLE 4.4

University Participation by Social Class 1967-1979

N_e = Number of University (Home Entrants
N_a = Number in 18+ age group
Total N.M. = Total Non-Manual (Class 1-3)

Class 1. Professional, Technical, Artistic
Class 2. Managerial, Senior Administrative
Class 3. Clerical, Junior Administrative
Class 4. All Manual Workers

	Total Home Entrants N_e (000)	Total Age Group N_a (000)	Class 1		Class 2		Class 3		Class 4		Total N.M.	
			N_e	N_a	N_e	N_a	N_e	N_a	N_e	N_a	N_e	N_a
1967	55.9	790	16.8	64.3	7.8	48.9	15.7	172	15.7	504	40.3	286
1968	58.1	763	16.3	64.1	8.1	48.8	16.8	165	16.8	485	41.3	278
1969	60.3	741	18.7	63.7	9.0	48.9	16.3	159	16.3	470	44.0	271
1970	62.5	744	18.8	65.4	8.8	50.6	17.5	158	17.5	470	45.0	274
1971	63.6	760	19.1	68.4	8.9	53.2	17.2	160	18.4	479	45.2	281
1972	65.0	752	20.8	69.2	9.1	54.5	17.6	157	17.6	471	47.4	281
1973	65.6	752	22.3	70.7	9.8	56.4	16.4	157	17.1	468	48.5	284
1974	69.0	776	23.5	74.5	10.4	60.1	17.3	161	17.9	480	51.1	296
1975	73.1	880	25.6	86.2	11.7	70.4	17.5	182	18.3	541	54.8	339
1976	74.8	822	26.2	82.2	12.0	67.8	18.0	169	18.0	503	56.8	319
1977	77.8	831	28.0	84.8	12.4	70.6	18.7	171	18.7	505	59.1	326
1978	81.2		30.0		13.8		18.6		18.6		62.4	
1979	83.6		30.9		14.2		19.2		19.2		64.3	

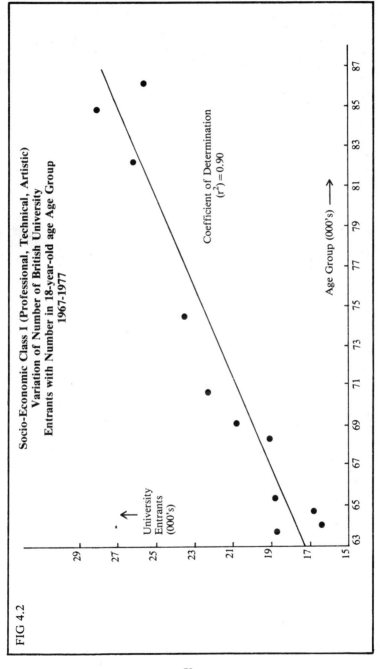

FIG 4.2

Socio-Economic Class I (Professional, Technical, Artistic)
Variation of Number of British University
Entrants with Number in 18-year-old age Age Group
1967-1977

Coefficient of Determination
$(r^2) = 0.90$

Age Group (000's) →

University
Entrants
(000's)

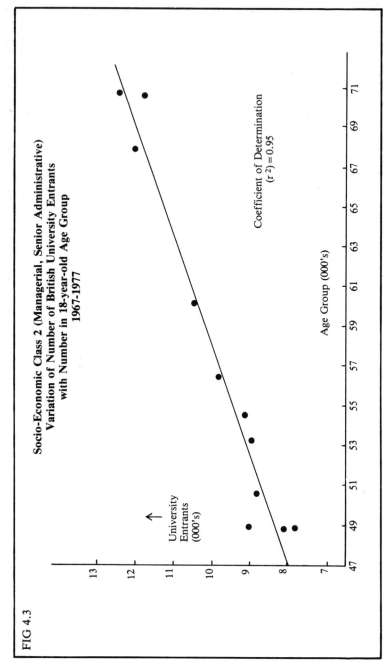

FIG 4.3

Socio-Economic Class 2 (Managerial, Senior Administrative)
Variation of Number of British University Entrants
with Number in 18-year-old Age Group
1967-1977

University
Entrants
(000's)

Coefficient of Determination
$(r^2) = 0.95$

Age Group (000's)

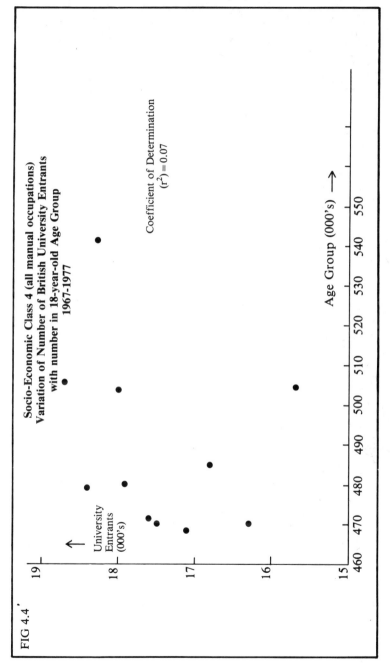

FIG 4.4

Socio-Economic Class 4 (all manual occupations)
Variation of Number of British University Entrants
with number in 18-year-old Age Group
1967-1977

Coefficient of Determination
$(r^2) = 0.07$

University
Entrants
(000's)

Age Group (000's) →

Reasonable estimates are available over a long period from 1925 to 1977 for the proportions of University entrants from children of non-manual and manual workers, and these are shown in Fig. 4.1a. This shows that the sharp escalation in numbers of students in the period from about 1955 to 1970 which we have described in Chapter 3 was not accompanied by any closing of the gap between manual and non-manual workers. This means, of course, that the great majority of the increased flow of students came from the same social classes as before.

In Table 4.3 are given the actual proportions of University students from each of three main divisions of non-manual workers and for the manual workers for each year of the decade from 1968 to 1978. In spite of the slow-down in the rate of overall expansion, the proportion of University students from the professional and managerial classes expanded rapidly, whereas the much smaller proportion from the children of manual workers correspondingly declined.

Table 4.4 and Fig. 4.1b show the actual steadily continuing expansion of students from the upper two classes, professional and managerial, during this latest decade, compared with the virtually static position of students from manual workers' families.

It will be seen that the continued growth in number from the former classes is a product of two factors; firstly, their steadily increasing share of the total entry numbers and secondly the fact the number of young people in these classes is also steadily increasing as we observed above.

Finally, we show in Figs. 4.2, 4.3 and 4.4 the way in which the number of students in each class is related to the number of young people of 18 years of age in the same class. It will be seen that in the professional class and also in the managerial class there is a good correlation between the numbers of students and the total numbers of young people. This is expressed by the high coefficients of determination which have the significance described in Chapter 2. On the other hand, in the case of the children of manual workers, there is apparently very little correlation. In other words, there is little connection between the number of students and the number of young people of University age. The census data available is too limited to be sure of the accuracy of the coefficients of determination in Figs. 4.2-4.4. Nevertheless, they are consistent with the more general fact that we have noted earlier that little connection can be found between the long-term rates of expansion of student numbers and the ebb and flow of the total number of young people of University age, since the latter will be predominantly influenced by the numerically predominant numbers in the manual working class.

The evidence is also consistent with the explanatory model we developed above for the nature of the growth in higher education. In the classes such as the professional and managerial, where the perception of the possibility of entering higher education is high, it would be normal for young people of University age to be in a position of choosing whether or not to enter and the numbers of such young people in this position would be a very high proportion of the total. Hence, the number of possible candidates for entrance would be expected to be a constant high fraction of the total. The proportion who actually entered would then depend almost wholly on the valuation, V, attached to University education as we have suggested above, and provided that this remained fairly constant throughout the decade, the high degrees of correlation shown in Figs. 4.2 and 4.3 would be expected. If we re-examine Table 4.4 it will be seen that, nevertheless, the proportion of those entering from the managerial class is considerably less than that from the professional. This may reasonably be attributed to the fact that the valuation by the former is still less than that by the latter, probably because the children of the managerial class, at least in Britain, still consider a number of alternative status preserving courses of action as equally or more attractive than higher education. Thus, although the correlation shown in Fig. 4.3 is as good as that in Fig. 4.2 showing an equal perception and consciousness of the possibility of higher education in the two upper strata, the different participation rates probably reflected a difference in the relative valuation of it.

On the other hand, the situation among manual workers is completely different. Here, the random scatter shown in Fig. 4.4 is consistent with the picture we have put foward of the abnormal, unusual nature of higher education in this class. Only a small fraction of young people of University age would be in a position to envisage it as a possible future and they would have attained this position, not by a steady process typical of young people around them, but rather by the fortunate chance of what we have described as patronage. There is no reason to suppose that the numbers of unusual children in this fortunate fraction should be a fixed proportion of the total number of young people in the class since the unusual perception which marks them out is not formed or cultivated by the usual social and cultural ambience in which they live, as is the case for the upper social classes. It is formed principally through contact with influential adults who are not typical of the normal adult members of the class, who have some prior contact with higher education, some special knowledge of its potential and some know-how of the methods of entry to it.

This favoured fraction of children of the manual working class nevertheless has a considerable significance for the long term expansion of higher education. Because of the large proportion (currently over 60 per cent) which manual workers form of the total population, students from this class form a significant fraction of the whole, currently about 20 per cent. They, together with those from the lower levels of non-manual workers, form an important source of the steady expansion of the proportions of the professional classes, particularly as these latter become more and more recruited from higher education.

As we have seen, the rise in participation by manual workers' children during the decade of general escalation of the 60s is parallel with the simultaneous rise in the much greater participation from non-manual sections, especially from the highest professional section. In this latter section, the very high percentage reached (over 80 per cent of the children of senior professionals) must be near what is termed the logistic limit when the flow of students must follow the pattern of the group of student age. As we have seen, this does not mean that expansion from this social sector ceases, since it is a continuously expanding section of the population. It is interesting to note, however, that precisely at the point where the participation rate of the senior professional group reaches this high saturation value of about 80 per cent, the participation rate for manual workers at its much lower value of about 7 per cent ceases to expand (see Table 4.4). It is as though the increase in the proportions of manual workers in higher education was not an independent process, but a side effect of the numerically much greater increase in the proportion of the non-manual and especially the professional classes. To put it another way, the tidal wave of expansion in the upper socio-cultural layers carried with it a certain expansion of the participation of workers' children with it, but this secondary movement ceased as the main wave ebbed.

This would strongly suggest that even the increase of the participation in higher education from manual workers' children, which took place from about 1955 to 1970, did not result from any real extension of the franchise. The small fraction which abnormally acquired a sufficiently high perception, P, to be in a position to decide whether or not to enter higher education was probably not increased, but a larger proportion of that enlightened group did so decide. In other words it was not due to an extension of the number of workers' children who had the necessary high perception, P, but as in the case of the professional class a parallel increase in the valuation, V. We shall see evidence below which tends to confirm that those few from manual working backgrounds who do filter up to those levels of secondary school preparation which immediately precede entrance to higher education, do, in fact, tend to behave similarly to the members of their new peer group. They have by then become as it were, almost associate members of the upper social classes they are being schooled with. They tend to follow behaviour patterns and adopt values which resemble them rather than those which would be typical of their age group in their original social backgrounds.

On the other hand, this adoption by the minority of children of manual workers of values and aspirations which differentiate them from the majority of young people from their own background may well be a factor which helps to deepen the alienation of those that are left, from the whole idea of higher education. Even those of their peer group who could give them some contact with (a sort of diluted form of that cultural reinforcement which is a continuous part of the daily lives of those from the professional sectors) are more or less removed from social contact with them and absorbed into the separate culture of the social layers of their new school groups. This is clearly more likely to be the case when school progression to the groups which are staying on to prepare for higher education means changing schools, and to an extent which may be comparable, when moving to a sharply and completely separate school stream. In the former case the rump schools which are left may have lost virtually all contact with the experience of higher education among their pupils and this is likely to be reinforced by the lack of graduate teachers who are drained off to cater for the academically "brighter" or "more gifted" of the age group who are so concentrated in the grammar schools or grammar school streams. In this way school separation reinforces, and even produces, a corresponding social separation which rapidly magnifies the effects of the original differences of educational perception.

A series of national surveys in the 50s, including the report on *Early Leaving* of the Central Advisory Council for Education in 1954 and *The Crowther Report* of 1959 on the education of children of ages between 15 and 18 highlighted the social differentiation which was persisting at secondary school level. *The Crowther Report* summarised the situation: "Most of the boys and girls between 15 and 18 were simply not being educated . . . . If we are to build a higher standard of living — and what is more important, if we are to have higher standards in life — we shall need a firmer educational base that we have today. Materially and morally, we are compelled to go forward . . . ." The Report showed that among manual workers' children it was the exception for any child to continue with education after the compulsory leaving age of 15.

For example, in the case of unskilled workers' sons, well over 90 per cent were leaving at the minimum age of 15, or even before, whereas less than 25 per cent of the sons of professional and managerial classes left at the minimum age.

The report on *Early Leaving* showed that 44 per cent of the children in Grammar School sixth forms came from families where the father was from the professional or managerial classes, whereas only 1.5% of them were the children of unskilled workers. The fact that this could not be explained by a difference in innate ability was shown by the Report's finding that children from professional and managerial families improved their scholastic performance throughout the school so that a majority of even those who had the lowest level of attainment on entering the school had passed to the top academic groups before they left. The reverse was the case for the pupils from unskilled workers' homes. The majority of those who were in the top selection group on entering the school had passed to the bottom group before they left. The report concluded that compared with the children of professional workers, the child of equal ability whose father was an unskilled or semi-skilled worker was handicapped in making the best use of grammar school education and this was due to the less favourable social circumstances of the latter.

They went on "We have been impressed above all with the far reaching influence of a child's home background. We have traced the school records of children in different social groups and we have found that from the children of parents in professional or managerial occupations at one extreme to children of unskilled workers at the other, there is a steady and marked decline in its performance at Grammar school, in the length of school life and in the academic promise at the time of leaving: This is not a mere development of the better performance at the age of 11 of children in certain groups; it reflects a widespread changing of places in academic order between 11 and 16 or 18."

One may only comment that if the favourable or unfavourable influence of family circumstances and the social environment associated with them can be so marked between the ages of 11 and 16, it must be even more likely to have produced an even greater changing of places in favour of the privileged children in their even more impressionable ages from birth to 11 years. Indeed, the evidence of these reports and other research conducted at that time showed that the earlier, formative, period of childhood was the most drastic in its partitioning of education along the lines of parental social status. At the ages of 11 to 13 a professional and managerial family's child already had nine times the change of entering the kind of school that then prepared for higher education (Grammar or Independent) as the child of the unskilled worker. At 17 he had thirty times as high a chance as the other of still being at school.

However, if a working class child survives in school to the point of achieving the standard for entrance to higher education, then all researches showed that he was almost as likely to proceed to higher education as one from a family of one of the higher social classes. This was particularly the case for boys, though rather less so for girls. The sex differentiation at this point is probably because of the particular opportunities and hence competitive values of careers for girls, for example in secretarial or other sub-professional occupations at this age point. The latest statistics have shown some recent fluctuations in the ebb and flow of children at the age of 18 + into higher education. Indeed, after the great escalation of the 60s there was some decline in the proportion of school leavers with qualifications for degree level education who actually proceeded to it. However, these fluctuations were not particularly different for the different social classes, except only that those from the working class more usually set their sights on the less socially prestigious areas of higher education such as teacher training. This finding bears out the analysis we have suggested above. The dominant professional and managerial class children have almost over-reached their interest in higher education. At as much as 80 per cent participation there sets in that unsteadiness characteristic of processes of growth which are near their maximum. As for the children from manual workers' families who have survived the educational race so far, though their participation rate is, of course, much lower, their behaviour will follow the pattern of their new peer group of which they have become associate members.

An analysis of all the factors which researchers have suggested has influenced the social differentiation of achievement in primary and secondary education is beyond the purpose of this book. We can only be concerned with the overall effects on the persisting social apartheid in higher education. In the post-war period mandatory maintenance grants have been available for all children accepted on full-time courses in higher education and fees have been paid by Local Education Authorities. In periods of relatively full employment most children who reached the necessary level of examination attainment by the age of 18 were not held back by the economic position of their families. On the whole, the evidence is that among the small proportion of working class children who survived the education rat race so far, the proportions who took up higher education were not much less than that from the upper social classes. (The situation may well be much different in the immediate future as we shall discuss in Chapter 11). The social segregation was not mainly a consequence of any special economic barrier at the immediate point of entry to higher education. It had been imposed more gradually over many years of school and preschool conditioning. At each stage in secondary education there has been a successive reduction of the proportion of the working classes who pass successfully to the necessary levels of "attainment" or even survive to remain in the stream destined for higher education. As the official reports showed, this was still overwhelmingly the case, even if comparison was restricted to those children who were in the same "ability stream" when they entered the secondary school. When we consider that well before that age, the attainment of that level of "ability" was already heavily prejudiced in the favour of those coming from backgrounds where books, study and the company of the educated was a normal feature of daily life, the point becomes even plainer to see.

On the other hand, the nature of higher education and its aura of élitism and separation from the life and culture of the majority of the people, and even the nature of its entrance tests do cast their shadow before them in a different way for different social sectors of the population. It exerts this influence, not at the point of entry after surviving the selective streaming of secondary education to the age of 18, but more directly on the social and cultural life of the different classes in which the pupil grows up from his or her earliest years. In the case of the professional classes it is a friendly and familiar influence bringing expectation of the continuance of status and privilege. In the case of most of the manual workers it is strange and somewhat alien, even dangerous. Much research has shown that many of those who do break through this barrier have already some unusual connection with higher education which differentiates them from the majority of their class. In the first place they come mainly from the families of the most highly skilled workers. These have the closest work connection with the strata of technicians and even professional workers who are in many cases as we have seen in earlier chapters their lineal descendants. Then a much larger than average proportion of manual workers' children who survive secondary education to the highest level and proceed to higher education have one parent or grandparent or close relative who has more than average education herself (or less frequently himself).

The progressive expansion of opportunities of education of a Grammar school type has increased significantly since the Education Act of 1944. However there is little evidence that it has changed the social division in secondary education. It has, in fact, increased the participation in Grammar School kind of education from all social classes, so that the social division has probably remained as high as before. Indeed, if we consider the proportions of each social class not proceeding to Grammar School type of education, then by the mid-50s this had been reduced from nearly 70 per cent to less than 40 per cent for the non-manual classes, but still stood at the level of over 90 per cent for semi-skilled and unskilled workers' children.

The data we have given above in this chapter for the actually widening gap of class participation in higher education in the period since the late 50s would indicate that the spread of comprehensive education has not yet had much further effect in reducing the class division of those who survive the full range of secondary education to the age of 18.

Nevertheless, it is too early to say whether the comprehensivisation of secondary education will in itself have any significant effect on the ultimate broadening of the social base of higher education. As we have suggested above for higher education, the institutional character of a system of education, its entrance barriers or tests, its objectives, goals, subjects of study, social manners, even the financial aspects of it such as levels of financial support available for students who proceed further in it, may nevertheless not exert their social influence directly on those who have already reached the point of being able to choose. They rather form part of a backcloth to the stage of education which can be clearly perceived well in advance by those whose social upbringing has trained their eyes to see it but remains dim and unreal to those for whom it is a strange and unknown world. We might tentatively conclude at this point that the reforms in the entrance conditions and availability and financial assistance for successively higher steps on the educational ladder are necessary but not sufficient to cause any significant changes in the divergence of social participation.

Earlier in this chapter we outlined a theoretical model which seemed to account for the main features of the expansion and social division in higher education over the past century. We can now see that the necessary perception of the possibility of success in entering higher education, P, is the end point of a process of survival through the many stages of previous preparation and education. Failure to make the requisite attainment at any of the preceding stages means in most cases that the precious time lost can never be regained. Except for those few in any social class whose highly individual cast of interest and talent takes them directly into contact with the rather abstract stuff of post-primary education, the necessary growth in perception is clearly highly susceptible to the influence of family and social environment. It is not as difficult as many researchers in this field seem to find to grasp why this should be so. For most pupils the abstractions of education are only given their strongest significance because of their known connections with the individual's future, particularly his or her future career. For children of the professional class the career desired, envisaged, expected and anticipated, is at least survival at the same status level. Every force, encouragement, admonition, and if necessary the force feeding of special tuition constantly reinforces that vision. Eighty per cent of the children make the expected response. One has to be very stupid or wilful not to.

At the other end of the socio-cultural spectrum, the strange irrelevancies of formal education have little or no connection with the realities of life. Every child knows that the adults in their community have lost no time in forgetting most of it as soon as leaving school. After all what use would it have been in the work which is available for most of them. Many parents do, of course, have ambitions for their children, but these, sensibly, do not usually extend beyond the next rung in the ladder of occupational hierarchy for which further formal education is often equally unecessary. Indeed, in the minority of cases where it is seen as necessary it is often of the special technical kind which leads to careers in the more socially accessible technician or secretarial levels which are not entirely foreign to the adult world of the child.

It follows from the above that we consider that increase in the formal opportunity to enter any stage in education for which the pupil is qualified and willing does not in itself guarantee any diminution of social privilege in education. Nor, indeed, does it necessarily lead to the development of even that talent among the underprivileged which has proved itself present, still less of the abilities which never rise above the surface of local social cultural apathy or hostility.

Even the changes in the balance of students between the Universities and the public sector of higher education which have resulted from government policy in the most recent period, do not appear to have increased the participation of children from the manual working class.

The most significant development has been the increasing proportion of degree level students in the Local Authority College sector and the large majority of these are in the 30 or so Polytechnics which have been designated and designed to give an equal but different form of higher education to that in the universities. It might have been expected that these Colleges, with their supposedly more technical bias, their closeness to local communities and their recent evolution from Technical Colleges, would have attracted a larger proportion of manual workers' children.

A detailed year by year analysis of the social division among their degree-level students is not available, but an overall survey has been made for the entry year 1972-3.

Table 4.5 compares this with the statistics for the same year in Universities. It will be seen that the proportion of manual workers' students in Polytechnics was apparently the same as those in Universities.

TABLE 4.5

Comparison of approximate social class of British entrants to Universities and Polytechnics 1972

Approx. Occupational Social Class of Father	Census 1971 % males aged 45-59 in working population	Universities	Percentage of Total Enrolments Polytechnics	
			Degree Students	Total Students
Professional & Managerial	16	45	52	49
Clerical and Junior Admin.	21	26	20	20
Total Manual Workers	62	29	28	31

Note:
The data for Polytechnics are obtained from a slightly different classification system from that availble for Universities, so the above class comparison is only approximate.

Sources:
1. Conference of University Administrators. Group on Forecasting and University Expansion. Final Report. University of East Anglia. 1978.

2. UCCA Statistical Supplement. UCCA Cheltenham. 1971-2.

It would appear that the main net effect of the rise of the public sector is similar to that of the rise of the Colleges of Advanced Technology in a previous period. It has acted as a reserve to University capacity, taking the overflow from it without affecting appreciably the social composition. One may conclude tentatively that had the alternative policy of expanding the existing Universities been pursued the total numbers of students and their social composition would have been much the same, though the balance between pure science and arts and applied studies might well have been different.

In the last chapter we demonstrated that the Robbins Report was hardly to blame for the rapid expansion in higher education of the 60s which is frequently associated with his name. Now we must come to the conclusion that government's adoption of the Robbins principle that "Higher Education should be available to all those with the necessary ability and attainment and who wish to pursue it" was, after all, unlikely to change anything. It is rather a formula which describes precisely how social privilege in higher education works. Doubtless it might get even worse if the principle were abandoned, and for that reason it is necessary to defend it from attack, as we shall see later. But in itself it does not guarantee any change in the proportions of the different social classes entering higher education, nor does it promise to release the wasted ability and talent among the less favoured of them, for which Robbins found ample evidence.

CHAPTER FIVE

A Crisis of National Confidence

In Chapter 1 we gave a preliminary definition of higher education. We suggested that it was that level of education which is associated with the professional function in modern society. We have seen that its expansion over the past century runs parallel with the expansion of the professional and managerial classes for whom it becomes the major source of provision of new recruits. This does not mean that all higher education is directly tailored to a specific professional or managerial function, but it is nearly all conducted in Institutions which have a near monopoly of professional level education. Indeed, it is characteristic of some professions that they will accept a wide variety of degrees, incuding degrees in the Arts and Humanities as suitable for entry to their professional grades, the cadre of employees who are groomed for decision-making and management. This is true for example of most of the senior branches of the Civil Service in Britain. Then, of course, the full recognition of teaching as a senior Profession has largely been restricted to those levels of teaching which have required degree level higher education.

We also noted that at any moment there may be a number of minor professions which have not yet received that degree of recognition which is accorded to the senior professions. Again, although the division between them is not, at any rate in Britain, a matter of exact definition, there is little actual public uncertainty about where they stand. They do not receive the same recognition of their independent decision-making, autonomous role. They are not yet associated with degree level courses in Institutes predominantly dealing with higher education, though of course they may be pursuing ambitious plans for the former, usually by first insisting on the latter as a new condition of entry for new members.

The same is broadly true throughout Europe, except that in most of the countries of Continental Europe, the practice of the independent, decision-making professions is even more closely tied to formal higher educational programmes than in this country and in general is so specified by legal statute. Hence the meaning of higher education has a similar basis in social status through most countries of Europe. As for academic status, it has always moulded itself in practice, around the requirements of the professions, even though the pure, "non-professional", academics have attempted to suggest the existence of absolute standards characteristic of the abstract disciplines of study. Unfortunately no-one has ever been able to give more than an arbitrary account of them. Even entry to the so-called pure scientific professions is, in fact, controlled by a social consensus which is parallel to and must be closely related to the social consensus of the applied, public and statutory professions.

This means that we can accept for each country the definition of higher education current in that country at the time concerned and regard it as socially comparable with that in the other countries. At least this is reasonable in a Continent such as Western Europe with a common inheritance of most of the professional functions and more recently a common concept of managerial responsibility. It is worthwhile noting that all European Universities are lineal descendants of the first two at Bologna and Salerno in the 11th century, whose studies were virtually confined to law and medicine respectively, the two oldest learned professions. It means therefore, that higher education as it is normally understood within each of the countries, represents broadly the same level of social status. The decision to enter higher education in each country represents the same attempt to consolidate, or less often, to climb to a higher, social status. Full-time education is precisely a major commitment of the individual concerned to that goal which, for the time being, largely excludes alternative individual purposes.

In all the statistics for full-time enrolments in higher education that we have given in the previous chapters, we have therefore accepted the definition of the country concerned and used the National basis concerned for the definition of higher education and the National records, supplemented by our own direct researches where the latter were incomplete. For the reasons given above we hold that figures collected on this basis give the most meaningful comparison between the different countries. They enable us to compare the commitment to higher education in different countries in terms which are most relevant to its impact on society. They do not attempt to measure the relative cultivation of genius or even intellectual brilliance, however those qualities might be construed. In any case the number of students ever recognised by their peers or superiors as having achieved these elusive qualities would, on any count, be a very tiny fraction of those in any country.

They do measure the extent to which the young people are committed to participating in educational preparation for their hopes for positions of social leadership (or at least independence) and the extent to which their society is committed to finding a place at the top or near the top for them. They measure the potential flatness of the top. They also measure the extent to which the education system is preparing consciously or unconsciously for processes of production and service which require the employment of more knowledge, independence of judgement and participation in management.

We have given this detailed elaboration of the concept of higher education developed earlier because as we move into a critical inspection of the current period, we are most likely to meet the special pleading that our increasing shortfall in student numbers in Britain is balanced by considerations of quality. It is, as we have said, difficult to give any comparative meaning to the mystical question of academic quality, but there is certainly no evidence that it has improved more rapidly in Britain compared with its Continental neighbours during the recent decades and years that will now be our concern. In any case, the professional, economic, social and status relevance of higher education has certainly not become more significant in Britain than in her neighbours. By standards of relative salaries or representation of graduates in top management it has rather lagged behind.

With this background in mind it is salutary to compare the rate of increase of the student population in Britain with that in the major European countries since 1970, the end of the period reviewed in Chapter 2.

TABLE 5.1

Proportionate Increase in Number and Ratio of Full-time Students 1964-70 and 1970-76

N_s = No. of Full-time Students in Higher Education
N_p = Total Population
R_s = Ratio of Full-Time Students to Total Population N_s/N_p

Country	% Increase 1964-70		% Increase 1970-76		R_s 1970 per thousand inhabitants	R_s 1976
	N_s	R_s	N_s	R_s		
Great Britain	66	62	16	15	8.3	9.5
France	79	71	27	21	14.1	17.1
Italy	89	81	41	36	12.5	17.0
W. Germany	55	49	66	63	8.7	14.2
Little Europe	74	67	42	38	10.1	14.0
USA	60	50	39	34	38	52.0
Japan	70	59	—	—	16	19.0 (est.)

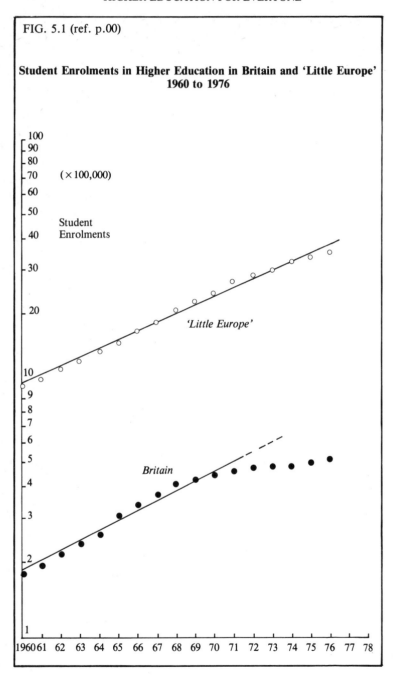

FIG. 5.1 (ref. p.00)

Student Enrolments in Higher Education in Britain and 'Little Europe' 1960 to 1976

Table 5.1 sets out the actual course of expansion of higher education in the main countries of Europe since 1970. It will be seen that in every case (except that of West Germany) that there has been a decline in the annual percentage increase compared with the figures given in Table 3.2 for the period of rapid escalation from 1954 to 1970. But the relative decline in Britain has been much greater than in any other European country or in the other advanced countries, USA and Japan, which are included for reference. In this table are also listed the values of R_s, the ratio of the numbers of students to the total population. It will be seen that in 1970 these were not very far different for Britain and Europe as a whole, though both were much less than those for the USA and Japan. But by 1976 the gap between Britain and Europe as a whole and between Britain and individal other European countries had widened very considerably.

Figure 5.1 shows this graphically. In the case of Britain, the curve of expansion slowed down considerably in the period from 1970-76 to a rate of annual increase of 2.5 per cent, which is actually less than that of the long period from 1860 to 1955, whereas that for Europe is only slightly reduced to a value of about 5 per cent midway between the very fast rate after 1955 and the long term rate before that. The significance of this relatively severe decline in Britain cannot be explained by differences in the definition of higher education in the different countries both for the general reasons given earlier in this chapter and, more specifically, since the base of the statistics has not changed since the decline set in. It is rather that a certain degree of failure of confidence in education, which has succeeded the euphoria of the 60s in the advanced countries has been most severe in Britain. As we shall see later, this failure of confidence led in the late 1970s to an absolute cessation of expansion and the onset of a net decline in student enrolments. We may note here that this failure of confidence may be typical of a faltering capacity to cope with the impact of the most recent advances of technology and the knowledge explosion on the industry, economics and services of the modern world. Again though, there is a general international decline in the optimism of the previous two decades, the most severe loss of momentum and the greatest decline in relative position among the advanced countries has probably been in Britain.

The student revolts of 1968-70 were an excuse for a general reappraisal of the role and scope of higher education throughout Europe and to some extent internationally. The decade which followed might be called the decade of cost accounting. Expenditure on higher education had risen rapidly, indeed at an even faster rate of annual percentage growth than that of student numbers. Table 5.2 shows the average annual growth rates in real terms for expenditure on higher education in the countries we have been reviewing. Reforms in the structure of Universities and other higher education institutes were a reaction to the social instablility which had spread through academic life. A rapid growth of concern with the techniques of financial control and Institutional management were a response to the rapidly mounting costs. Both resulted in a much greater measure of State intervention and planning. Both represented potential threats to the previous degree of control of University and College programmes and even teaching methods and administration by the academics themselves. The role, function and societal relevance of higher education became a major concern by Governments. The University and Higher Education world which "had never had it so good" in the decade of escalation was now being called to account by its paymasters.

TABLE 5.2

Trends in Total Expenditure on Higher Education

Country	Period	Annual Growth per cent
Great Britain	1953-65	11.9
France	1958-68	12.4
Italy	1950-65	15.0*
Germany	1957-66	13.9
Belgium	1958-67	9.1
Netherlands	1950-68	14.5
USA	1955-67	10.2

*current expenditure only

Source: Trends in Expenditure in the OECD countries.
Organisation for Economic Co-operation and Development, Paris, 1978.

The reforms in the internal structures and academic programmes need not concern us too much at this point since it is no more likely than in the past that they would have a great effect on the flow of students. They involved some formal democratisation of the internal control of Universities, particularly in the larger countries of Continental Europe. In some cases the changes appeared striking. In German Universities students were given a large measure of representation on the Governing councils of the Universities and participation was also extended among the junior academic staff and initiated for the non-academic staff. It is by no means clear yet whether this represented a permament reduction in the previous supreme concentration of internal University power in the Professoriate. More significantly, they represented an assertion by the State Governments concerned of their intention to intervene in the internal government of the Universities. Similar concessions to student demands for participation in University management were made in the other European countries, even eventually in Britain, though here the changes were much more muted (as indeed the trouble had been) and little was done to involve the rapidly growing numbers of technicians, administrative and ancillary workers.

Of more significance was a general tendency to diversify higher education. As we have seen, in Britain this meant that the so-called public sector represented by the polytechnics increased more rapidly than the Universities. In the European countries there were parallel developments of non-University institutions of higher education. In general these developments were supposed to be in line with the new degree of concern with the possible direct pay-off from higher education since they were formally supposed to be more concerned with the studies of direct application to the economy. In Germany and France particularly, the degree of State control imposed on these alternative forms of higher education probably had that effect. In Britain, it is less likely that the changes made much difference to the "relevance" of higher education to the supposed targets of economic growth. We shall be looking at the reasons for this later in Chapter 7. Here we may just record that the flow of students to the supposedly industrially important fields such as Engineering, generally lagged severely behind target in the decade of the 70s, not least in the specifically designated Polytechnics.

Indeed, in their enforced role of taking up the overflow from the Universities, their most rapid rate of advance was in the various social sciences, where demand for places tended to exceed National supply, and sociology, the science of behaviour within and between the various groups or classes that form themselves in society, became the boom subject in higher education. This was much to the frustration of industrial employers and leading politicians who professed to believe that the main employment need was still for graduates in the hard sciences and the older technologies which had sprung from the industrial changes of the last decades of the previous century. As the closing years of the decade lapsed more and more into the paralysis of industrial social strife and as industry found itself less and less capable of handling its social problems, even those associated with the previous levels of technology, the instinct of student demand seems to be at least as justified as the rather obsolete mechanistic concepts of industrial relevance of the planners. We shall defer further consideration of the significance of the "relevance" of higher education to its future expansion till later, and pass to a consideration of the rapidly increasing concern with costs and hence with possible controlled planning of numbers and cost control which have increasingly dominated official "policy" since 1970.

By the end of the 1960s, public expenditure on higher education had reached a level which, for the first time, was becoming comparable with other sectors of public spending. Although in Britain, for example, it was still only about 18 per cent of total educational expenditure it had been expanding at more than one-and-a-half times as fast, though, as we shall see later, the precise meaning of these figures is doubtful because Universities are not solely educational institutions, but produce other products such as a research which probably take more than half their budgets. And educational expenditure as a whole was becoming the most rapidly increasing single section of National public expenditure. The same trends were present in most advanced countries and provided justification for a rapidly mounting production of researches, conferences, plans, rules and specialists on cost control and institutional management.

Again, it is not our intention in this book to survey this new industry in detail. It is in fact, quite simple to make economies in higher education. All that is necessary is to make less money available. The problem is to determine what effect this will have on either the number of students that can be educated or the quality of the education they receive and of the other products of higher education. The difficulty that has beset the attempts at cost benefit analysis has been to get any kind of consensus among those operating on the higher education systems and those operating within them on the meaning of benefits and to some extent even on the meaning, and certainly of the allocation, of costs. Unfortunately higher education produces a multitude of products, some of which are fairly readily appraised, while others bear fruit, like most long range research and many schemes of study, generations later. An analysis of profitability is not so simple as examining the last line in the accounts of an industrial company to discover the annual profit. This does not mean that we should be complacent about the costs of higher education, but is rather to emphasise that they can only mean anything definite in terms of what we want from it and whom we want to participate in it, a subject to which we will be returning in Chapter 7.

Nevertheless, the increasing preoccupation with finance is, perhaps, part of the explanation of the extraordinary games of guesswork which have apparently preoccupied the other aspect of official intervention in recent years, that of projecting future student numbers. We have already mentioned the great forerunner of recent projections, the Robbins Report of 1963. We have shown in Chapter 3 that the escalation which this report is popularly reputed to have unleashed actually started some seven or so years before the report was published and was more than half over before it was adopted as government policy. We have also mentioned that the report so seriously underestimated the actual immediate course of student expansion as to provide a worse forecast than any reasonable extrapolation of the previous five years.

The projections which follows have all been based on variants of the methodology of the Robbins Report. None of them have attempted any serious analysis of the actual course of expansion of higher education during the last century, of its social division, and particularly its dominance by the "educated classes" nor of the social inertias which lie behind the statistically low participation from the children of the majority of the population. The range of forecasts that have been made in successive official papers is shown in Table 5.3. Two things are noteworthy about them. The first is that each successive attempt does not appear to have wasted time in analysing what went wrong in the previous attempts. The second is that the variation from one forecast to another is somewhat larger than anything that might have been accomplished one way or the other by any except the most destructive or the most apparently foolhardy of government policies. Indeed, it would have been impossible for any planned development to follow the rapid fluctuations of the projections.

TABLE 5.3

Some Official Projections of Student Numbers in Higher Education in Britain

(thousands)

Date of Projection	1963* Robbins' Report	1970* DES Planning Paper No.2	1972 Education A Framework for choice	1978 Higher Education into the 1990s	1979 Command 7439	Actual Student Number
1968	322	—	—	—	—	410
1971	350	506	—	—	—	464
1973	390	—	—	—	—	481
1976	445	648	—	—	—	519
1981	586	843	750	564	544	—

*Estimated from Projections for England and Wales.

101

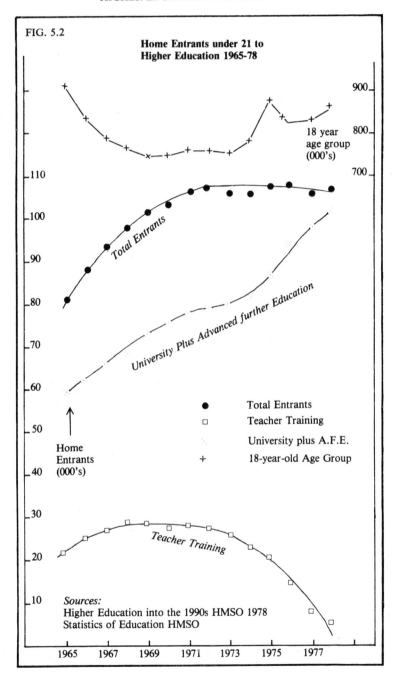

FIG. 5.2

**Home Entrants under 21 to
Higher Education 1965-78**

Total Entrants

University Plus Advanced further Education

18 year
age group
(000's)

Home
Entrants
(000's)

●   Total Entrants
□   Teacher Training
     University plus A.F.E.
+   18-year-old Age Group

Teacher Training

Sources:
Higher Education into the 1990s HMSO 1978
Statistics of Education HMSO

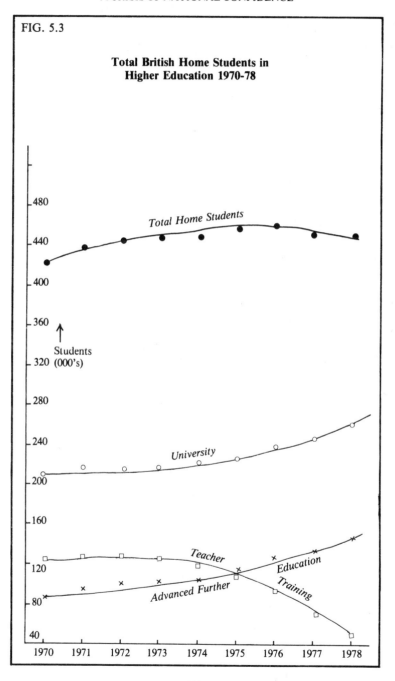

FIG. 5.3

**Total British Home Students in
Higher Education 1970-78**

In order to study the internal factors which have affected student enrolments in the most recent period, we show in Figs. 5.2 and 5.3 the trends in Home (British) student enrolments under the age of 21 and also the variations in the 18-year-old age group. The first thing to be noticed is that neither the total entrants nor those in the separate sectors have been noticeably affected by the size of the total age group. This confirms the analysis we made in Chapter 4. It may be noted in passing that all the evidence available indicates the same lack of dependence between entrants to higher education and the size of the dominant age group in the majority of European countries. The second fact is that when we confine our attention to Home (British) entrants, i.e. after subtracting from total new enrolments the slowly rising proportion of overseas students, expansion has not merely ceased, but is being transformed into absolute decline.

On the other hand, both the University and the advanced further education sector (nearly all of which was in the Polytechnics) continued to expand at a rate of over 3.5 per cent per annum, which, while below the extremely rapid acceleration of the period from 1955-70, was significantly above that of the long period prior to 1955.

The main reason for the flagging bouyancy of enrolments in higher education as a whole was clearly in the area of teacher training where total student numbers declined from about 125,000 to less than 50,000 in eight years. This was a result, not of any decline in demand for places, but of deliberate government cuts in the number of places available. The extreme severity of these cuts is shown in Fig. 5.2, where it will be seen that new entrants to teacher training were reduced from over 28,000 per annum in 1972 to just over 5,000 per annum. But the Robbins Committee report showed that the proportion of manual workers' children in teacher training courses in College of Education was about 60 per cent higher than the proportion in University undergraduate courses and a similar result has been obtained by A.H. Halsey and his co-workers in recent research. Thus, the cuts in teacher training will almost certainly have increased much further the widening social apartheid in higher education and led to an absolute decline in working class participation. We can now construct a reasonably comprehensive explanation for the apparently mysterious change from the headlong acceleration of enrolments of the period 1955-1970, through the gradual slowdown of the early 1970s to the onset of actual decline at the end of that decade.

As we saw in Chapter 4, higher education has always been dominated by the children of the professional and managerial classes. The mainforce behind the escalation of the 1960s was the multiplication of demand from this sector and the porportion of places they took in the Universities was maintained and eventually increased. From the limited statistics available (e.g. Table 4.5) the same trend is most probably true for the other major source of degree level courses, the polytechnics.

This expansion of demand from the upper socio-economic groups was compounded of two factors, firstly their steady gradual growth as a proportion of the active population at about 2.5 per cent per annum and secondly by a relatively rapid rise in their valuation of higher education and hence of their participation rate. By 1970 the second factor had reached the extremely high figure of over 80 per cent for the trend setting group of senior professionals and hence future enrolments from this sector must have reverted to the somewhat slower rate of expansion of the class itself. It is however, likely that this expansion, enhanced by the high graduation rates of some two decades before, would commence to rise towards a higher annual rate of increase. The same tendency towards a logistic slowdown in the expansion of participation rates was evident in the other main social sources of student expansion, the managerial and administrative workers' children, though in this case some further increase was evidently possible (see Table 4.4). But again, the continued expansion of these sections as a proportion of the population ensured their continued expansion in higher education. Together, these upper socio-economic sections continued to provide a source of student enrolments expanding throughout the decade of the 70s at a fairly regular 5-6 per cent per annum.

On the other hand, the much smaller proportion of manual workers' children who reached the possibility of applying for degree level courses was, as we have seen in Chapter 4, almost independent of the numbers in their total age group. And it is most likely that by 1970, the majority of these would follow the participation slow-down of the dominant social groups in their level of secondary education; at any rate, the available statistics show that their participation rates in degree level courses had ceased to increase and had in fact begun to decline by the late 1970s.

But, as we have shown above and in Figs. 5.2 and 5.3, the main location of the decline in enrolments in higher education after 1973 has been in the teacher training sections of the Colleges of Education, and these would inevitably have occurred mainly at the expense of entrants from children of manual workers, who formed the major porportion of those with lower entrance qualifications. It is unlikely that any significant proportion of potential entrants from this source would have been able to persist in preparatory education to transfer their applications to degree level courses which were expanding in the Universities and Polytechnics, as their actually declining proportions in the latter confirm. The history of the decline in higher education in the decade since 1970 is therefore a story of even more social inequality than before. Students from the professional and managerial classes have continued to expand even more rapidly as a proportion of the whole and with an absolute annual rate of increase appreciably faster than that of the long period before the once-for-all escalation of the 1960s. There is no reason to believe that the restrictions of the late 1970s had any significant effect on their prospects of entry to higher education.

On the other hand, entrance to higher education from children of manual workers commenced an absolute decline. While this was perhaps to some degree occasioned by a fall in effective demand as a result of increasing economic difficulties in working class families (an aspect we shall return to in Chapter 11) it was more probably mainly due to the severe cuts in student places in the traditionally most working class sector of higher education, the teacher training Colleges. Thus, for the first time in recorded British educational history, certainly in the post-war period, the provision of student places was deliberately reduced below even the effective demand by direct Government restriction.

This was the overall result; a process of falling student enrolments almost unique among advanced countries which characterised what we have termed the Decline of National Confidence in Education.

It is therefore not difficult to understand the irrelevance of previous official projections of student enrolments to the actual course of subsequent developments. In the first place the overall projections of future numbers of people of the age to enter higher education have been treated as an undifferentiated whole. They have concealed the complete different trends in the growth or decline in the age groups concerned within the different socio-economic classes, and particularly have neglected the steady exponential expansion of the professional and managerial classes which has under-pinned the whole expansion process in higher education. Secondly, in their speculations about overall participation rates among young people of higher education age, they have failed to explore the completely different factors underlying the participation in higher education from the different social classes and particularly the difference between those classes, already familiar with higher education (the professional and managerial classes) and the majority of young people coming from the families of manual workers. Finally, they have failed to analyse the recent effects of deliberate government restriction on the numbers of places in one major sector of higher education, particularly in its differential impact on the different social classes of potential entrants.

In 1978 the latest of the official projections, optimistically entitled *Higher Education into the 1990s,* became the first in the postwar period to suggest that future provision should be deliberately held below the effective demand for higher education and to contemplate the abandonment of the sacred Robbins principle that places should be available for all those able and willing to take advantage of them. This was in spite of the fact that the record of social stratification, by then accumulated over the previous 10 years by the Central Council for Admission to Universities, provided ample evidence for the fact that the principle itself was operating to widen the social gap in University admissions. Once again the projection was based on calculations of overall demographically determined numbers of young people of the 18-year-old age group. This time it was admitted that "past experience has shown how difficult it is to predict the age participation rate". Nevertheless it was assumed (logically enough) that it would either remain the same as in the immediate past or rise above or sink below that value. These three obvious but unilluminating possibilities were somewhat arbitrarily projected into the future 15 years or so, unfortunately without any justification being offered to support one guess of future demand for places as against either of the others, and became the basis for the 'high', 'central' and 'low' projections of future student numbers. However, each of these variants assumed that the demographic bulge in the number of 18-year-olds in the mid-80s would cause an upsurge of student demand to be followed by a low ebb because of the demographic fall in the number of 18-year-olds expected in the mid-90s. On this basis three model policy variants were constructed. The first was to expand higher educational facilities to meet the high expected demand of the mid-80s and to contract them later. The second was to abandon the Robbins principle and contract supply of places below demand in the 80s in order to avoid over-provision in the 90s. The third involved temporary expedients which could be more easily discarded later.

The absence of any rational basis for any of these random speculations was perhaps unimportant as it became clear that this and other contemporary official projections were no more than apologia for a new trend in Government policy to achieve cuts in educational expenditure at all costs. In the end, as we shall see in Chapter 11, the Government of 1980 solved the problem by disregarding all three alternatives and by simple imposition of massive financial cuts. It was left to the Select Committee on Education Science and the Arts in its report on "the Funding and

Organisation of Courses in Higher Education" in 1980 to note that "the proportion of young people in the United Kingdom participating in Higher Education has been falling and that comparisons with other Nations are somewhat disturbing". It went on to recommend "that positive steps be taken to improve the age participation rate, particularly in those regions where is is low". But the Secretary of State for Education and Science had already confessed that he was not concerned with the age participation rate because its present level was about the figure at which it had been levelling off naturally. His solution to the question of increasing the proportion of working class children in higher education was the restoration of the Direct Grant School. It may only be commented that the proportion of working class children in Direct Grant Schools has always been much lower, even than the proportion in Higher Education; the selection process which operates at each stage to screen out working class children from the streams leading towards higher education, operates, *a fortiori,* in this most selective section of the whole of Secondary education.

The final example of the loss of National confidence in the British Higher Educational scene consisted of a uniquely British retreat from an ancient principle of internationalism in European higher education.

This might be called the disgraceful episode of the overseas students' fees. Universities have always been traditionally international bodies. One of their main products, new knowledge, which proceeds from the research, which in Britain takes more than half their cost, has always been recognised as an international product freely published for all to know. Most of the current content of the teaching syllabuses of all institutes of higher education have been discovered in the Universities of foreign countries. This internationalism is the necessary condition for the advance of knowledge. It was precisely the birth of such an international network of scholars in the fifteenth and sixteenth centuries which set off the new expansion of science and scholarship which has advanced exponentially ever since. In Europe, where it received its new start some three to four hundred years ago, the tradition was created of the free movement of students and scholars from country to country and College to College. Even today the vast majority of European Universities either charge no fees or the same small fees to their own and foreign Nationals.

It was largely with the aid of the technology arising from this knowledge that Europe colonised the world, and became rich partly by exploiting the cheap labour and by buying cheaply much of its food and raw materials from the colonial world. During this century the less developed countries have sent their students to Europe to learn how to catch up. Table 5.4 shows the number of foreign students in the main European countries in 1970 and 1975. It will be seen that though the number in Britain had become 6.8 per cent of the total in 1975, it was no larger than in a number of other European countries. But it was Britain alone of all the major European countries that broke the tradition of centuries in the late 60s in order to make a trifling possible economy by charging higher fees to overseas students. Already by the early 70s this was having the effect of concentrating the entry of overseas students among the wealthier foreign countries such as the oil producing ones at the expense of students from poorer countries such as India and other ex-colonies.

TABLE 5.4

Foreign Students in Higher Education Institutions in some European Countries in 1970 and 1975

Host Country	Numbers of enrolled foreign students		Per cent of foreigners in total enrolment	
	1970	1975	1970	1975
United Kingdom	24,606	49.032	4.1	6.8
France	34,500	93,750	4.3	9.0
Italy	14.357	18,921	2.1	1.9
West Germany	27,769	47,298	5.5	5.7
Belgium	8,611	9.748	6.9	6.1
Austria	8.753	10.320	14.3	10.7
Switzerland	9.469	10.113	18.4	15.6

Source: Higher Education in Europe. UNESCO, Bucarest, April-June 1979.

It was ironical that these poor countries were at the same time educating for Britain a large proportion of her hospital doctors at their own cost. In the late 70s this area of government economy passed into the nonsensical stage of charging full economic fees to foreign students. These are defined as the cost of the annual budget of the Universities and Colleges concerned divided by the number of students.

This is trebly dishonest. Firstly, it neglects the fact that Universities do not pay at all for their most important input, the continually growing fund of new knowledge, which is freely available because of that very international tradition which the new policy denies. Secondly, it neglects the fact that about half the cost, at any rate of Universities, goes to pay for their research output and it is dishonest accounting to make students pay for it, since it is available to all, particlarly to those who apply it in industry and commerce and public services. Thirdly, it neglects the fact that a large fraction of the foreign students are actually junior research workers who have already completed their first degrees in their home countries. They do virtually the same collection and collation of research data as paid research assistants. The research work of the Universities would, in many cases, collapse without them. In some Continental countries the majority of such junior foreign research workers are salaried employees. Finally, it neglects that many British students, especially those studying a foreign language, are enrolled without fees or with smaller fees in foreign Universities (Table 5.5). A narrower aspect of this dismal business, but one of

TABLE 5.5

Foreign Students in Higher Education by country of origin within Europe (1971)and within UNESCO European Region (1975)

Country of Origin	Within Europe	Within UNESCO European Region
United Kingdom	4347	16323
France	3790	7220
Italy	7053	7315
Germany	6588	10253
Belgium	905	1872
Austria	1714	3043
Switzerland	1635	2758

Source: Higher Education in Europe, UNESCO, Bucarest, April-June 1979.

potentially great danger to the future economic position of Britain, is the loss of goodwill and of the almost certain damage to those trade links which in the future, even more than in the past, will follow the transfer of modern technology and the training of modern technologists. It is not even clear that the vast increase in fees of foreign students will save any appreciable fraction of the cost of higher education. Indeed, if a major reduction takes place in the flow of foreign research students, then either they will have to be replaced by expensive salaried research assistants or our resources for research, the major lever to an advanced economy, will be wasted and dispersed. It is worth while noting in passing that almost every great scientific breakthrough, particularly those in which Britain has played a leading role, such as nuclear energy, antibiotics, molecular biology and micro-electronics, has owed a great deal, sometimes critically so, to young foreign research workers in British Universities. We may well regard this deplorable measure as another sign, not only of the loss of confidence in higher education which has overtaken administrations in this decade, but even more of a failure of nerve in the face of the challenge of the new age of communication which the knowledge revolution is bringing into existence.

Perhaps the hallmark of this loss of confidence is the retreat of government policy to the hard line from which education, including higher education, is regarded as an article of consumption to be sacrificed to the extent necessary to permit the tax cuts which will release consumption elsewhere. During the general optimism of the previous decade it was almost accepted nationally as well as internationally, that education was a necessary form of social investment and that for advanced countries, higher education was an essential ingredient in economic investment. We shall suggest in the next chapter that this is only ever the case for those countries, classes and peoples who have the vision and the will and the common purpose to make use of it. The question will arise whether Britain has lost the will to do so.

CHAPTER SIX

Levers of Economic Growth

In the decade since 1970 the administrators and paymasters of
higher education have become increasingly preoccupied with its
costs, and to a lesser extent, with its calculable benefits. It is virtually only in the post-war period that the economics of education
as a whole have become a special subject of study. The main centre
of interest has been the Third World where the elimination of il-
literacy has emerged as a necessary part of the strategy of attacking
its abject poverty.

For the most part of the hundred years during which the advanced world has moved steadily towards increasing affluence, elementary education has been assumed to be a simple human right in the
Western democracies. On the other hand, higher education has in
practice been available for those few whose social and cultural
background gave them the necessary preparation as well as the
motivation to pursue it. However, once education as a whole
became apparently susceptible to economic analysis it was inevitable that special attention should be paid to its most expensive
section, the Universities and Colleges. It is significant that the concern with the costs and benefits of higher education began to arise
precisely when the upward escalation of the 1960s excited the vision
of mass higher education. The possibility of higher education
becoming a similar universal human right to elementary education
seemed to be on the order of the day. In the remainder of this book
we shall seek to show that this question is indeed the major strategic
question, not merely for higher education, but for the future of the
continued progress of both material and social well-being.

However, the question was not to be begged. The possible transition to mass higher education has, in fact, been halted, at least in
Britain, at a point which leaves unchanged its privileged and
meritocratic character. And the halt has been called mainly on the
question of cost. At the point where the participation rate of the
professional classes has reached over 80 per cent, and where we saw
in Chapter 4, the corresponding expansion from the other
managerial and 'educated' classes is climbing faster than ever
before towards the same upper limits, the Departments of State
begin to reassess the limits to growth. While enrolments from
manual workers' children to Universities actually shows a steady

decline over the past decade, the question of how much further expansion of higher education we can afford is suddenly realised to be highly important.

Public expenditure on higher education has until now been mainly for the benefit of the children of the richer sections of society. A.H. Halsey has calculated that ever since the Second World War the average son of a professional or managerial family has had approximately six times as much public money spent on his postschool education as the average son of an agricultural labourer. This is the situation which the current freeze on the expansion of expenditure on higher education seeks to freeze.

Until higher education is regarded as a normal human right it is presumed to compete with other goals for private or public effort and expenditure. In this competition for support it may be regarded simply as an article of consumption or a factor of private or public investment. The economic evaluation of higher education attempts to compare the returns from it with the costs. Both returns and costs may be regarded from their general, social, national or even international aspect, or from the point of view of the individual or those classes who predominantly possess and use higher education. Whether social or private, the returns to higher education express the values which motivate the pursuit of it and which we have seen in Chapter 4, together with the simple perception of it as a real possible future, constitute the force behind its expansion.

In the following we shall be concentrating temporarily on an assessment of the economic value of higher education, that is the value that may be assigned to it as a factor enabling either the individual or society to increase possession of those goods and services which are commonly subject to the market, i.e. which are bought or sold. However, behind these common denominators of exchange value are the more fundamental use values, the cultural, intellectual, spiritual, social, aesthetic. The fundamental quality of education which unites this broader range of values, both for the individual and society is its role in enabling us to move from being the blind playthings of forces beyond our control to becoming the creators of our own future. Only knowledge can deliver us from complete subservience to "Chance and Nature's changing course". In modern society only that section of the population whose education takes them to the point of comprehending and use this role of knowledge, can enjoy fully that increased freedom to determine their own lives which is made possible by cultural and technical progress.

It is, of course, this broad range of the real uses of education, its potential capacity to effect significant changes in the quality of life as well as the material environment of societies which gives its economic value. But it is important to note that the reverse is not true. The economic value of education, especially higher education can only account for those results which are subject to the economic market, i.e. which can be measured as objects of exchange. These are only part of the value of education. A great deal (in the future perhaps most) of its value cannot be subject to this cash calculation. Perhaps the most striking example of this is the social value of the education of those women who spend most of their lives working for their families. Like their work, their education cannot be economically measured by the mechanism of the market. It is not bought or sold. Its value to society is arguably the most important return that society receives for all its effort in providing education services. It is the source of constant renewal of human culture and co-operation. It is the most important of all educational investments in a civilised human future.

The economic costs and benefits of education, especially higher education, are an aspect of the economic role of the growth of knowledge. Higher education especially, is concerned both with the creation and application of knowledge which is continually growing and changing and coming into new application. The exponential growth of knowledge and of the material wealth of the world in modern times both arose from those revolutionary changes in the vision of the relation of man to nature which arose in 17th century Europe.

In the three hundred years which have followed both knowledge and its application to control over nature have expanded with that undeviating acceleration which is the hallmark of the self-generating, exponential process. In the case of knowledge the carriers of the momentum of ever-increasing speed have been the scientists, or in more general terms, the highly educated, each of whom on the average, generates new possibilities and problems which require more than one successor to pursue. The capacity to create material and economic wealth is multiplied by the accumulation of physical and human (cultural) capital. The two parallel expansion processes of knowledge and production are united and fastened together in their interdependence by technology. This is the source of the new forms of material capital. But for its development it requires constant new investment in the application of knowledge, and hence, in education. By technology we mean all the applied knowledge necessary to both initiate and control new methods of production, and not merely those aspects which fall within the branches of engineering or physical science. Indeed, although these latter may predominate in the initial stages of innovation of new methods of production, they usually form only a minor part of the total range of new knowledge involved in their full development.

From a short term point of view, or in the restricted conditions of a particular country, it may appear that almost the only direct factors in accelerating the growth of production are investment in capital and employment of labour. The production of new knowledge and education may then be regarded merely as optional extras, perhaps disposable, maybe even luxury factors. Indeed, the term "Residual factors" has been invented to attempt to bring them into economic calculation.

But it is precisely these knowledge encapsulating changes which are almost the sole source of the most fundamental, i.e. irreversible changes in productivity. To put it another way, although the social mechanism for economic growth has clearly depended at each stage on other political and economic factors, particularly the foregoing of consumption and the resultant accumulation of capital, the consequent resultant changes in the nature of production may be rapidly re-created from the knowledge embodied in them. Indeed this has been proved to the cost of the Victor Nations in the two wars, especially Britain, when their former enemies, in spite of the physical destruction of their capital, built up slowly over centuries of slow growth, were able to climb rapidly back to, not merely a competitive, but in fact a greatly superior productive position, within decades. This they were able to do because they used the knowledge, generally available, of the best modern technology. From this point of view knowledge and education is not merely one form of investment, but ultimately the most fundamental factor of investment underlying all others. This, however, is seen even more clearly and indeed, is only fully applicable at all times on the world scale, or the scale of great semi-independent regions.

Figure 6.1 shows the parallel exponential processes of industrial production and higher education since 1870. Since the earlier total world estimates for higher education are not yet available the figure comprises the totals for the USA and the main countries of Western Europe which together dominated world industrial growth for most of the period. Until about the middle of the 19th century this group accounted for about 85 per cent of the estimated world industrial production, and even today they still produce about 55 per cent of the whole. Since about 1880, of course, the USA has been the dominant force, and in the century since then has been responsible steadily for about one third of the world's total industrial production. It is probable that it has also accounted throughout most of the period for a similar proportion of the world's higher education.

The overall similarity in the growth curves of industry and higher education are striking. On the whole the latter has grown slightly faster than the former, with an average doubling period since 1870

FIGURE 6.1

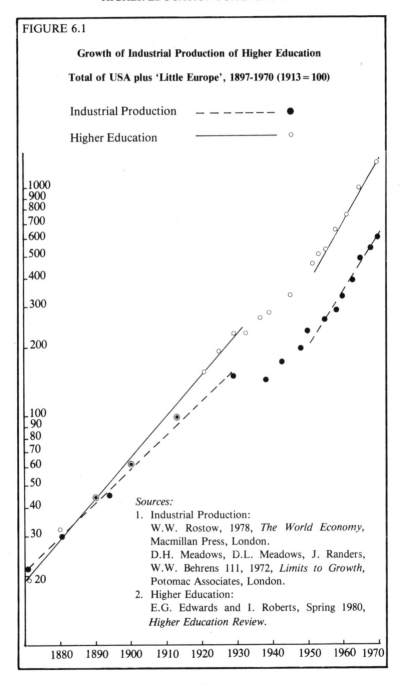

Growth of Industrial Production of Higher Education

Total of USA plus 'Little Europe', 1897-1970 (1913 = 100)

Industrial Production — — — — — — ●

Higher Education —————— ○

Sources:
1. Industrial Production:
   W.W. Rostow, 1978, *The World Economy*,
   Macmillan Press, London.
   D.H. Meadows, D.L. Meadows, J. Randers,
   W.W. Behrens 111, 1972, *Limits to Growth*,
   Potomac Associates, London.
2. Higher Education:
   E.G. Edwards and I. Roberts, Spring 1980,
   Higher Education Review.

of 16 years, compared with 20. In each case growth starts accelerating to its modern levels in the early 19th century. This process reaches a point of new take off at about 1870. From then on the technology of production becomes increasingly dominated by a series of inventions which underlie modern industrial civilisation and lay the basis for mass production and consumption. Examples are Bessemer Steel about 1860, electric light about 1870, synthetic chemicals in the 1870s and above all, the invention of the automobile in the 1880s. The next century of industrial expansion may be regarded as the steady accumulation of productive capabity and diversity based on the pattern established in that period of the closing decades of the 19th and early years of the 20th century. It became the century of mass prodction. In a closely analogous way, the modern pattern of higher education was developed in the same period. In very strong contrast with the preceding centuries it became dominated, as we have already mentioned in Chapter 2, by the new highly specialised methodologies of the separate sciences. Even the humanities and social studies such as history and political economy had to seek respectability by adopting the new look and the new goals. These goals were, briefly speaking, the accumulation of facts; the mass production of knowledge.

The steady acceleration of industrial production was more affected than the parallel growth of scientific and technical knowledge and of higher education by the great wars and the great depression. Nevertheless, it seems probably from the American experience that even without these disturbances the latter would have grown with a rather more rapid acceleration than the former. This is because, as industry becomes more increasingly dependent on knowledge inputs, on research and development and on scientific management, a prior increase in qualified personnel becomes a precondition for that continued growth of productivity which is necessary for overall industrial expansion.

The escalation of both industrial production and higher education to unprecedented rates of annual increase in the period from 1950 to 1970 is strikingly parallel. Both are in a sense to be linked with the ultimate success in material terms of the preceding period. The productivity of the mass production industries and parallel with them of the basic food producing technologies has given rise to mass consumption in the fortunate advanced economies. They provided the economic base for both the expansion of higher education and that of a new phase in industrial development, the rise of the service and knowledge industries. The basic motivation behind the upsurge in higher education (in the light of its social partition) is to be understood as arising from the new challenge of this emerging latest phase of industrial development rather than merely from the surplus resources released by the previous period. It is still from the dominant professional and managerial classes that the swell of new enrolments in Universities proceed. It is for them basically an investment in their future status, an intelligent anticipation of the pre-condition for future development that higher education mainly represents.

We have mentioned above that growth arises mainly from changes in productivity. Indeed, almost all economic expansion per employed person may be so regarded. Higher productivity is again mainly characterised by technological change, understanding the latter to be expressed not merely by new types of material machinery, but by new methods of management and labour organisation that arise from new application of knowledge. It results from such changes, not merely in industry, but also in the infrastructure of essential services and means of communication, as well as parallel changes in the institutional structures of political, social and cultural life and, of course, from improvements in the technology of agriculture. W.W. Rostow in his epochal survey of the World Economy since 1700 concluded that the generation and absorption of new technologies in all these fields was central to the processes at work in its steady exponential growth.

As we turn from the world scene to that of the individual nations the picture of growth becomes less uniform. On the world scale, if we looked forward from the 18th century we would see the relatively uniform steadily accelerating uninterrupted processes of economic growth and the growth of knowledge and higher education that we have represented in Fig. 6.1. But, in the case of individual nations the deviations from the regular pattern, both of economic growth and its interconnection with knowledge and education would be much more pronounced. Whereas, in the case of world growth, there is a certain degree of apparent inevitability in material expansion and in the harnessing of science and technology to its continuous acceleration, in the case of the separate countries their share in the production of wealth has to be deliberately struggled for. The latent connection between knowledge, higher education and economic progress may be obscured for relatively long periods.

In large part this is due to the fact that although new knowledge and new technology is the ultimate fundamental source of most advances in productivity, the gains in the latter may not accrue immediately to those who create the new knowledge, but rather to those who have the skill, power and, above all, the will to apply it. The basic advances in scientific, and even technical knowledge, that have accumulated with accelerating speed over the past three centuries are largely a common world possession. Although the more applied aspects may be protected by simple secrecy or by the Patent Laws for a short period, it is doubtful whether such protection gives more than a slight and temporary advantage. And as for the more fundamental aspects of new scientific knowledge which always have ultimately the most far-reaching effects on production and social life, they are outside the economic market, international common property of those who can understand them.

Indeed, it is this international freedom of access to the most fundamental advances in human knowledge that has been the indispensible condition, not only for its exponentially rapid advance since the Rennaissance but for the very methods which it has evolved to verify its truths. On the other hand, higher education produced also the scientists, engineers and experts in all fields who both produce new knowledge and apply it. But it can be only applied to industry in individual countries according to the state of technology already achieved and capacity of the country concerned to sustain the material investment and to provide the labour of the quantity and quality required. This in turn will be deeply affected by the political, social and cultural conditions prevailing both externally and internally. It is therefore not surprising that in the history of the long period of economic expansion of the world, different countries in turn have taken the lead and have been in turn the introducers of new technologies and new dominant industries. It follows that we should hardly expect that higher education and its attendant process of knowledge creation would always, and in the short term, be a simple measure of the actual position of individual countries in the hierarchy of world material progress. The contrary examples are well enough known. India is among the poorest of countries, but has a proportion of higher education students in its population which is not far short of some immensely richer European countries.

Nevertheless, although there are outstanding exceptions of this character, among the poorest countries of the world it is usually not difficult to discover the factors which have thrown the country off balance. In the case of India the tradition of consumption of higher education among the upper classes derives its unreality, its isolation from practical application and its fundamental imbalance with the ignorance and primitive economy among the vast majority of Indians, largely from its recently colonial past.

Among the advanced countries and the moderately developed newcomers to economic take-off there is evidence of a broad correlation between the rate at which productivity is developing and various measures of the penetration of education, including higher education into economic application. Rapidly developing countries such as Sweden, and above all, Japan, may depend initially on their skills in borrowing and assiduously applying technology developed and perhaps neglected elsewhere, and in this stage of their take-off may depend on favourable political and social factors. But the evidence accumulates that their passage to sustained growth is marked by the acceleration in innovation and that reliance on the knowledge and education factors in the growth of productivity which is typical of large regions.

Japan is obviously an outstanding case in this respect. In the late 1950s Japan was still only at an intermediate position in economic product per capita. The average income of its workers was significantly lower than the European average and its productivity per worker employed in industry was also lower. On the other hand, Japan had by this time a ratio of students to population which was already twice as high as Europe, as a result of a deliberate policy of accelerated growth. The indices of the proportions of more highly educated personnel employed in the managerial, technical and executive positions in industry were also high compared with much richer European countries. In other words Japan was not merely accelerating its production of graduates, but accelerating equally its employment of them in production. The general conclusion of some economic analysts of the connection between productivity and education of the work force in the 60s, was that Japan was an example of a country which was over-educating its people beyond the point of economic return for educational expenditure.

However, during the next decades Japan rose rapidly to the position of the third industrial power in the world, in spite of its relative lack of raw materials, its virtually complete dependence on external energy supply, particularly oil, and an agricultural base inadequate to provide sufficient food for its growing population. The only resource it had to exploit was the potential talent of its people, and this it did. Initially the major part of its extraordinarily rapid growth since 1950 was a result of an even more intensive application of existing mass-production technologies than that which characterised the somewhat slower growth in Western Europe. This clearly stimulated the demand for, and supply of, highly educated personnel, and particularly of highly educated management. However, the latest developments in Japan show that its outstanding investment in higher education during this period placed it in a commanding position to pass from imitative technology to the leadership of several branches of the newest and most innovative fields. Among these, the most significant for the future is its rapidly growing dominance in the key area of micro-electronics and micro-computers. The example of Japan demonstrates the fundamental (but not inevitable) connection between investment in human educational resources and economic growth. The question as to whether the connection is actually realised in practice in a particular country depends on its will and confidence to take advantage of world trends in the application of knowledge to material progress.

Thus, the steady unfolding of the expansion of the world economy and the equally steady growth of knowledge and its incorporation into that succession of ever more complex technologies that successively multiplied productivity conceals a much more uneven process at National level. Different Nations have seized the lead from time to time. For the century until 1870 Britain accounted for the largest single proportion, and indeed, throughout the latter part of the period, its share increased from about 22 per cent to about 30 per cent. But since the turn of the century the USA reached a one-third share of the world production and has maintained that proportion ever since; whereas that of Britain has steadily declined to a present level of between 3 per cent and 4 per cent. In Europe, Germany passed Britain by the outbreak of the First World War, and several other European countries such as France, Italy and Scandinavia, have now reached about the British level in volume of production, and passed it in productivity. On the world scale the USSR has emerged since the beginning of the Second World War as the second industrial power, and in the postwar period Japan, with the fastest growth of all, has climbed from a position of minor power at the beginning of the century, to the third most productive nation at the present day.

This change in the hierarchy of nations has gone parallel with the change in importance of different sectors of industry. Apart from the food industry, the earliest industries to appear in countries which have begun the march to industrial take-off were such basic sectors as textiles, iron and railroads and mining; these were overtaken in importance by steel, basic chemicals and electricity, petroleum, and a wider range of consumer products, and then by automobiles; and in the latest period by synthetics, electronics and all the mass-production industries supplying the mass consumer market. The final stage, into which the economy of the USA is rapidly passing (soon to be joined by Japan) is that in which the production of services, such as education, begins to take over from manufacturing industry, the major share in the gross National Product.

Between 1947 and 1967 the total employment in the USA rose from 57 to 74 million. Virtually all of the net increase occurred in institutions that provide services such as schools, hospitals, banks, shops. During this period the USA became the first nation in which more than half the employed population is not involved in the production of tangible material goods such as metals, minerals and energy and all the consumer goods which can be made out of them, as well as food, clothing and housing. Each stage in the changing importance of different sectors of industry through the whole long period of economic growth has been characterised also by a change to ever more advanced technology, increasingly dependent for both innovation and maintenance and control on applied science and scientific management. This is indeed the basis for the exponential increase of the employment of the professional and managerial classes at a much faster rate of annual growth than the employed population as a whole that we have noted in Chapter 2 (Fig. 2.6).

Hence the main factor behind the changing leadership in the world table of relative growth has been the capacity of the succeeding nations to seize the initiatives released by the new technologies. With few exceptions it has only been possible for individual nations to pass from a lower to a higher stage of National Income per capita by participating significantly in that group of industries which were for the time being in the leading position, since these were becoming at each stage the main contributors to increasing the productivity of the world economy as a whole. By the same token such participation could, in general, only be assumed, or at least sustained, by developing on a national basis the innovative technology and hence the employment of highly educated personnel necessary for the continued development. A major reason for this is the more advanced the industry and the technology behind it, the more rapidly is it changing. The speed of obsolescence increases with the scientific content of industry since science itself is the most rapidly changing factor in an ever more rapidly changing industrial world. And as we have seen, it is the need for constant replacement of the obsolescent that demands the constantly increasing employment of the highly educated.

CHAPTER SEVEN

Costs and Benefits

It is in the light of the dynamic relationship between the growth of the economy and the growth of knowledge and its application by the highly educated that we must look briefly at the approaches to measure the costs and possible financial returns to higher education which are currently obsessing government departments, particularly in Britain. The decade of the 1970s closed with an audible sigh of relief from a new Administration bent on the reduction of public expenditure that the upsurge of demand for higher education was apparently slowing down to a half. If they had been aware of the warning signal this should have conveyed about the future position in the share of world economic growth from the experience of the interrelation between the two that we have outlined above, one would have expected rather an urgent call to renewed growth. This would have required an analysis of the social apartheid which is the main inhibitor of educational expansion as we have shown in Chapter 4. Instead, a kind of paralytic acceptance of the relative decline of Britain as an educated nation has seized, not merely the corridors of governmental power, but the quadrangles of academic privilege. We shall analyse the intellectual apologia for this inertia in the next chapter.

From an economic point of view it is compatible with a reliance on monetary remedies whose innocence of any knowledge of the new complex technological basis of the modern economy corresponds well with their derivation from the fundamental teachings of the economists of the first industrial revolution. In most of the intervening period Britain has relied on the political and financial status it achieved in that early lead. Though for a large part of the two centuries that have intervened its contributions to research and its expansion of higher education have given it the potential to remain in the leadership of economic advance, it has left a succession of competing countries to take advantage of the technological changes and corresponding changes in the centre of gravity of industrial advance that have intervened.

It is hardly surprising that in Britain there is a marked scepticism of the economic significance of higher education, a significant doubt whether it is to be regarded mainly as an article of consumption to be pruned in hard times or an essential investment. It might well be argued that since Britain's economic position has continued to rely on a political and financial status belonging to its imperial past, its higher education system has indeed been a largely political luxury serving more to strengthen the self-confidence of its élite in their natural right to leadership than to renew its productive economy and its social structures.

In the economic calculation of the costs and benefits of higher education on the national scale, only those factors which are directly subject to the market can be taken into account. The inputs into higher education are of two main kinds: knowledge and the instruments for its transmission. Both require resources of capital and labour. Knowledge is a product of research and scholarship and experience. On a worldwide scale its production absorbs probably more than half of the total resources that are consumed by institutions of higher education and research. On the other hand, it is available for the purposes of input into higher education institutions in particular countries at a small fraction of its total cost. This results from the tradition of free exchange in fundamental knowledge of the three centuries since the seventeenth.

On the other hand, any national analysis of the costs of higher education disregards the value of this relatively free input since it is not subject to buying and selling. In effect this means that a reduction in the scale of higher education in a particular country represents the waste of its potential share in a vital expensive asset which has largely been paid for by the world as a whole.

The national costs of higher education are usually reckoned by summing the wages and salaries of all the staff involved and the costs of the various capital inputs and by adding the cost of the foregone productive income of the students. On the other hand, the returns are usually calculated by assuming that they are to be represented by the increased income of the graduates which may be ascribed to their higher education. Such calculations that have been made on this basis have yielded social rates of return to higher education in advanced countries of between about 12 per cent and 20 per cent per annum, generally significantly higher than those available for most alternative social investments. Nevertheless, the inadequacy of such calculations again stems from the fact that just as a large part of the input cannot be costed, so a major part of the output is not subject to market calculations. As we have already mentioned, this includes that very large contribution of higher education to the work of the unpaid but essential workers in modern society such as the housewives, and also the voluntary workers of all kinds. The calculation of the returns also undervalues all those occupations for which higher education is essential, but which for various reasons, do not attempt to realise their potential market selling price. An obvious example is priests of religion who, in terms of salary return, clearly represent an unjustified waste of educational expenditure.

Finally, the research output of institutions of higher education, though it may be regarded as absorbing about half their costs cannot again be evaluated on the market since, in the main, it flows freely into the information system of the world through the scientific and scholarly journals. Far from being a source of income to the researcher he usually has to contribute to paying for their publication. On the other hand, the fundamental research contribution from higher education is, as we have seen, one of the major factors in raising the ultimate level of world productivity of goods and services. Its free availability to the highly educated world does not detract from the possibility of its especial benefit to the country of its origin, since potentially, its application could occur there most rapidly and most easily under the guidance of its discoverers. However, this potential benefit is again not susceptible to economic analysis using the usual techniques of fixing costs and returns. It depends not on some prior equilibrium state of the market, but rather on the reverse, the capacity and will of the country concerned to exploit its potential advantage, to distort the previous world market to its advantage by pioneering new technology and new industry.

Of course, investment in higher education, like any other investment, can only be realised if the other social and political and economic conditions permit. Balance is vital. The point we have been making above is that balance in the various factors which contribute to economc growth is a dynamic rather than a static state, and that the fundamental source of dynamic movement is precisely the growth and application of new knowledge. The problem of balance rises most sharply, as we have seen, in the most recently developing countries or those whose colonial past has divorced the pressure for higher education most completely from the surrounding social reality; converted it to being the object of status without realisable productive function. In such cases it is a not unreasonable objective to seek an economic appraisal of the balance between the return to the different stages of education in the light of the phase reached in overall economic growth and potential development in the short term. Such a semi-determinist appraisal is possible because the country concerned is at an early stage of development and some guidance can be obtained from the known historical experience of those who have gone through it.

In the case of advanced countries such as Britain, the problem of balance between higher and normal education is not so significant since, in the main, the latter is already compulsory. Though more expenditure on it may improve performance, and indeed, as we shall stress later, may be politically and socially of key importance to higher education itself, it does not compete significantly with the former for scarce resources.

Indeed, in advanced countries the linkage is so close between the different stages of education that any increase of expenditure on one stage automatically produced a multiplying effect in the other, and vice versa. Thus, the reduction in expenditure on higher education in Britain during the closing years of the 70s will have its most disastrous effects on the quality of primary and secondary education through reducing the flow and quality of teachers entering them and hence, in reducing also the resources allocated to them.

Within higher education itself attempts at assessing the balance of expenditure have revolved around the assessments or forecasts of the future needs for highly educated personnel in employment, the so-called manpower projections. Apart from attempting to decide the proper proportions of experts of various kinds, to give the right mix in the pool of so-called qualified manpower, these projections raise the question fundamental to the subject of this book — how many highly educated people do we need? Although they only deal with one dimension of need, that which can be measured against the demands of the employment market and hence neglect the non-marketable but socially vital other needs for higher education, it is necessary to make an examination of the broad principles which underly them and the extent to which they have given guidance to future trends. In principle we are dealing with the question not merely of the size of higher education, but the extent to which the emphasis on this or that subject of study can be left to the spontaneous demand of the student or to the special enthusiasms of the academic taff, or on the contrary, should be subject to national direction in the light of the different needs for different kinds of highly educated experts. The main features of this latter question will overlap into the next chapters. Here we will accept for the moment that it is a legitimate objective that higher education should be linked with social needs.

However the methodology of succeeding attempts at manpower projections has incorporated basic misconceptions about the nature of this linkage. It must be explained the basis of such surveys has been to seek information from representative samples of employers of all kinds of their future needs for various specific categories of highly educated experts, most usually graduates or professionally qualified personnel in the various highly specialised fields of science and technology.

Since the projections started in the early post-war period they have almost all yielded results of little, medium or long term value.

In some cases had they been used as guidance the results would have been so disastrous that one can only be thankful that little attention was paid to them. For example, in the late 1950s, the official survey for the future needs of graduate mathematicians found that Britain was already producing 25 per cent more per annum than could be found suitable employment. Fortunately the enrolment of students in this field was not curtailed, but neither was it increased. In the following years of the 60s, the demands from employers, particuarly in industry, rose so sharply that the schools were starved of qualified mathematics teachers for almost the whole decade and, indeed, even now, the supply is completely inadequate. It was this lack of qualified teachers and not some mysterious effect of progressive new teaching in the schools which led to the deterioration in performance of school children in this subject and produced the relative dearth of entrants to higher education in the whole range of hard sciences and engineering in the decades which followed.

The various projections of demand for engineers of various kinds have fared no better than chance guesses would in predicting the ebb and flow of demand in those specialities. This is not surprising since the direct public pronouncements of the leaders of industry have usually reflected no more than the market situation of the moment. The reaction of the Confederation of British Industry to the 1978 discussion paper of the Department of Education and Science on Higher Education into the 1990s was typical. As we have mentioned in Chapter 5, the DES paper itself represented an extreme retreat from all previous estimates and policies and was based on an assumed relation between enrolments and birth rates for which there is no evidence. Even so, the paper offered three alternative projections which might be described as ranging from the merely pessimistic to the disastrous. We have suggested above that this paper represented not so much a projection as an apologia for the reduction of expenditure, a confession of a lack of national confidence, not merely in the future of higher education, but in the future of the economy in the approaching period of the dominance of micro-computer and the knowledge industries. However, the Confederation of British Industries were doubtful about even the most pessimistic variant and the main thrust of their commentary was to demand an even more searching exploration for further cuts in educational expenditure.

In the light of the dynamic relation between new knowledge, technology and higher education outlined in Chapter 6, the reasons for failure of manpower forecasting are not difficult to understand. The primary shortcoming in all such official attempts has been the assumption that for each subject of higher education there is a fixed number of graduate jobs to be filled. The sum of all these are conventionally known as the "traditional opportunities for graduate employment". Once these are filled it is assumed that graduate unemployment will result from any expansion of higher education. The calculated numbers required in each field are based on the experience of the immediate past. In times of depression the forecasts are always low, often lower than the current output from higher education. Within a few years, if the economic situation in an industry has improved, the same employers will be complaining that their special interests are being neglected.

We have already mentioned the systematic underestimation of the need for engineers in Britain in the projection of the 1950s (the Hankey reports). Yet again, in the mini depression of the early 70s, the industrial demands for engineers were again depressed below the numbers graduating and a large proportion turned to employment in non-technical fields. As we shall stress below, this is not necessarily a bad thing. However, the point is that at that time the representative leaders of the engineering industry in their meetings with the heads of Universities and Colleges stressed that the lack of employment prospects for graduate engineers was likely to persist into the indefinite future. They could see no prospect of a major revival of demand. Before the end of the decade a committee under Sir Monty Finneston had once again reversed the position and concluded that "future demands would be for significantly greater numbers of engineers than are currently available".

The main role of higher education in industry is, as we have seen, to prepare for future change, especially in technology and organisation which transform the whole nature of industry, including even its goals. It is precisely this kind of change which is almost never anticipated in the surveys of need for future qualified people. The existing managements which supply the basic information in which the surveys are based are precisely those whose outlook, methods and goals may be rendered obsolete by the influx of new knowledge and new technology. Their answers reflect the past, whereas the problem is to create the future. The example given above of the disastrous failure to anticipate the vastly increased numbers of mathematicians needed, coincided with the beginning of the computer era whose impact has still not been grasped by British industry.

This is hardly surprising since less than 12 per cent of those holding managerial positions have themselves been educated to degree level, nor is the deficiency being remedied by any systematic re-education of the majority of managers. Perhaps it is this relatively low level of the education of its managers that is responsible for the fact that Britain's position in the economic world was slipping below its main competitors even before its output and employment of graduates began to fall below theirs. The relatively high previous British contributions to the fundamental scientific discoveries that underlie modern technology were not exploited by an industrial leadership which continued to rely on the residue of the former British imperial political strength and the captive markets of the former British Empire. Evidence given to the House of Commons Education, Science and Arts Committee in 1980 was that even in the larger companies in Britain only 1 in 3 of managers was a graduate, whereas in Germany over three-quarters, and in France as many as 90 per cent of the corresponding chief executives were graduates. Most of the latter were engineers or technical generalists, while in Britain, the much fewer highly educated managers were generally classicists or arts trained.

Finally, the surveys of the needs for graduates and professionals normally neglect the flexibility of employment roles. They are coloured by the assumption of a close fit between higher education and its application in employment. This has never actually been obtained except in the closely controlled minority of the older professions, especially medicine and law, or in the institutionalised and artificially narrowed occupations of primary, and to a lesser extent, secondary, education, which are assumed to be controlled by forecasts of the numbers of children in compulsory education. The truth is that for the majority of students the concept of "the traditional graduate occupation" has always been a myth. The opportunities for employment of graduates and the roles they play in them have largely been created by the graduates themselves. They are rarely as specialised as the actual course of higher education which led to the qualification. They rarely stay within the vocational channels for which they have been created. Indceed, it is precisely this mobility of the highly educated, their capacity to move from role to role and to undertake their own retraining which gives them their central function in redesigning and transforming the nature of production and hence, of course, the nature of their own place in it.

All this means that the detailed breakdown of future needs of different kinds of specialised expertise has a very limited and very short term usefulness. But without such a detailed breakdown the methodology of manpower surveys loses its main focus. Instead, industries and nations are faced with the wider problem of anticipating how far their future survival will demand a labour force with the education necessary to adapt its functions more or less continuously to roles which cannot be foreseen, since they depend on as yet undiscovered or unrevealed technological and organisational change. The answer to the question of how much education expansion is necessary then becomes simply as much as possible. Indeed, in the age of the micro-computer, knowledge and education pass from the periphery of economic progress to its centre.

At the beginning of the 300 years of world development that we have been reviewing, the production of grain was still the central theme of human economic activity and the disposal of the small surpluses created by the labour of the vast majority of the population in agriculture was the basis of all trade. In the passage from stage to stage of increasing productivity, artifacts of increasing remoteness from the primary human needs of food, clothing and shelter have occupied the leading position and made the leading contribution to the total increase in material wealth. At each stage the "congealed knowledge" in the leading industries and their technologies assumed greater significance. In the latest stage knowledge itself becomes the central material which is fashioned into the objects of production, trade and education. This coincides with the rise to leading position in the economy of the "Service Industries" that we have referred to above. More than any of their predecessors the main product they provide is not a material artifact at all. It is a direct contribution to the health, education, entertainment, information, or other intangible element in the quality of life.

The role of the vast new potentialities of the micro-computer in this transition is, of course, to raise enormously the productivity of those other sectors of production which have previously absorbed most of the labour of modern society in providing the necessary hardware of civilised life or the machines that make it, and the mass of routine clerical type labour that has accumulated around it. It is the human effort released from these older forms of industry which will provide the vastly increased range of services, just as in the more primitive stages of economic growth it was the labour released from agriculture which set off the whole march of the expansion of material wealth. It need only be added that the previous successive stages of mass-production industries not only accelerated the need for highly educated experts, designers and managers so that this section became the fastest growing section of the labour forces. They also created the soul destroying function of routine mass-production work in which the machine dominates the human being and reduces him to a robot-like dependence.

The natural consequence of fully automated production controlled by the micro-computer is the replacement of human robots by mechanical robots. The service industries on the other hand can reverse the former dehumanising tendency. Education is a prime example of this new direction of development where each advance in technology can release the possibility of creative employment by the workers involved. As the more routine aspects of the organisation of information are taken over by the computer, the more fully human aspects of teaching, the mutual formation of judgement, taste and value can come to the fore and there is no natural limit other than that imposed by the competition of other equally creative work to the potentiality of employment. The same is broadly true of the whole range of the social services. At present only a small fraction of nurses, social workers, welfare and community workers or police workers have the benefit of higher education, but who can doubt that the complexity of their essential work of human service could not benefit almost indefinitely from the illumination of the human and social sciences.

This has always been recognised to be true for the first and earliest category of social workers, the priests for whose vocational training, together with two other service professions; the doctors and lawyers, the original Universities came into existence some 800 years ago. Finally, the creation and dissemination of culture and entertainment, recreation, the understanding of the world and the enjoyment of that understanding have already begun to occupy a major role in direct employment and the multitude of indirect services, such as catering and tourism, that they stimulate.

These again are labour intensive employments whose value depends enormously on the cultivated individual skills of those who provide them. Here again technology can remove much of the drudgery of these occupations. (It is no loss to the composer that he no longer has to copy out his score by hand or to the photographer that he has no need to mix his own chemicals). But it imposes no limit to the possibilities of growth of human creative effort.

These new service industries and professions, which are typical of post-industrial society and depend for their expansion on the production and application of knowledge as the main agent of economic development, differ basically from the mass production industries which they replace at the leading edge of development. Firstly, there are no externally imposed limits to growth. By and large they do not consume irreplaceable resources such as energy or raw materials and successive advances in technology can even reduce further their dependence on these with out reducing their intrinsic capacity for human employment. Secondly, the nature of their development is continuous innovation. In this their prototype is the creation of knowledge itself. The greater our understanding of the world, the more new things we find to understand. Thirdly, they ultimately pass beyond the structural limitations imposed by a market economy. By and large the process of buying and selling which has been both the lever of multiplication of all other products and which at the same time has imposed rigid limitations on their social diffusion at any given time cannot apply with the same rigidity to human services.

Their production for economic gain merges and overlaps with their voluntary production or their pursuit as direct objects of enjoyment. Indeed their most important expressions in the creation of art and science and in the relief of human suffering have never been pursued principally as objects of gain but have at their best been given freely. They lead naturally to a concept of the world in which work and leisure have largely merged and the distinction between them has become largely meaningless, in a word, to a human world. Their continued expansion no longer entails a constantly diminishing scope for creative human employment.

These are the prospective future economic returns to higher education, the knowledge it creates and transmits, the changes in the objectives of production that the application of knowledge can naturally lead to. They are not visionary. The prototypes are all there. But they will not happen in any particular country automatically, no more so than any of the previous stages of industrial, economic and technological development. Even on a world scale they are not inevitable. The misapplication of the very knowledge which makes them possible could destroy even the gains in potential human progress that have accumulated with accelerating speed since the start of the knowledge revolution in the 17th century. Even though the march forward of its successive stages now have the appearance of the inevitability which we have outlined above, it has depended at each moment of time on the will and determination of individual and collective human effort.

This is even truer for the future. In this book, devoted mainly to the perspectives for higher education in Britain, we have left aside the enormous concurrent task of redressing the balance between the poor majority of countries in the world and the small minority of advanced countries where the most advanced transformations of the economy outlined above may appear to be potential subjects for policy agendas. It must simply be mentioned that this task also depends critically on the extension of knowledge and education, but with a different temporary balance from that in the advanced countries themselves. The dynamics of this vital process are not the subject of this book: however, they are not incompatible with programmes of industrial transformation of the advanced countries outlined above. The inevitable lag in advance of the poor world cannot be avoided. The point is to devise that international division of labour and trade which will most stimulate their own efforts to make up this lag in their own ways and according to their own goals.

Such a development cannot take place while the rich countries dominate the basic and manufacturing industries and the poor countries are confined to the more primitive areas of production. But the redress of this balance would appear to threaten still further the employment of the working class in the capitalist world. Yet neither the transition to a predominantly service economy in the rich countries, nor the economic emancipation of the poor countries are technically or economically impossible. Neither the technical knowledge nor the material resources for their accomplishment are now out of reach. And the expansion of education would be a major source of the enhancement of human resourcefulness and capacity also required. These basic means are all now within reach. In this respect we stand, as a race, in an incomparably more favourable position than any previous generation. For the first time in history we have the knowledge of natural forces necessary to render us virtually the masters of natural hazard.

The resistance to solving these problems is a resistance to the surrender of privilege. In this book we have been concerned with the expression of privilege by the social apartheid in higher education. We have seen that this educational division both reflects and is sustained by a fundamental clash of outlook and interests between those who own, manage and control the means of production and those whose labour and lives are increasingly at the mercy of technical changes in the machinery of production. The resistance to the expansion of higher education, particularly to increasing the access of the working class, reflects the defence of the privileges of the classes who presently dominate the control of production and appropriate the largest share of its product. We have mentioned earlier in this chapter how the leaders of industry in the deepening depression of the early 1980s demanded even more savage cuts in education than those proposed by the government. But the Institute of Directors were not entirely averse to industrial change. They demanded much tougher Labour Laws. This was at least consistent since any expansion of higher education among the working class could only lead to pressure for more labour participation in setting the goals and controls of industry.

In the next two chapters we shall examine the apologia which have been invented by the more servile of the intelligentsia to justify the persistence of privilege in higher education.

CHAPTER EIGHT

The Fear of Equality

The crisis of confidence in the future expansion of higher education, described in Chapter 5 has not merely the economic aspects that we have discussed in the last two chapters. It is even more a result of a social and cultural failure. As we saw in Chapter 4, we are educationally a deeply divided society and the gap is widening. In the social and cultural life of the majority of the population, especially that 62 per cent which are occupationally classified as manual workers, higher education is an alien territory. Its subjects of study, its methods and its goals are not relevant because they are out of reach. They have little or no connection with the real problems of the world into which the child is emerging, the world of the struggle for job, family and house in an urban working class district. Escape from this environment is a relatively infrequent event, confined very largely to the highest layers of the working class hierarchy. Even for them, it is not mainly a product of their home culture, not a projection of their normal expectation, not a familiar image in their social scene but rather a visitation from another world. As we saw earlier, the very irregularity of its appearance indicates its accidental nature. It arises rather as an act of patronage from the class and the culture which they are invited to join. Its frequency has depended not so much on the number or even on the motivation of the potential aspirants from the working class, but on the number of patrons; it is a by-product of the rise of the professional classes.

The progressive intellectual often envisages social progress as limited to the extension of such patronage to increase the "opportunities" for the so-called bright children from poorer homes. The doors of every expensive public school are now ceremoniously thrown open to a tiny fraction of children of the lower classes who show themselves to have the necessary ability. The Government of the 1980s hastens to transfer scores of millions of pounds of allegedly scarce educational money to provide "assisted" places for children whose parents cannot find the full fees (though these will go mainly to children from "good families" who have fallen on hard times). It can do this the more easily from part of the savings it is making in slashing the provision of books, eliminating the school meals and reducing the teachers and staff in the deprived schools in the cultural deserts of the industrial regions. It is not difficult to understand that the example of the tiny proportion of working class children who might apparently defect in this way hardly serves as a shining example to the vast majority of their former companions who are left, but rather deepens their sense of alienation from a culture in which they know they can have no equal part. In British society these are the two cultures, not the twin worlds of the Arts and Sciences caricatured as such by C.P. Snow. In the respectable academic world the latter are never much further apart than the opposite sides of an Oxford College dining table.

The concepts of the nature of culture are complex and we do not intend here to analyse their many interwoven yet conflicting roots and meanings. However, we must examine briefly the self-images of the "high culture" of our times insofar as it claims to be the only proper subject for higher education. A critical review of the past, present and future content and subject matter appropriate for study in Universities and Colleges cannot be separated from the larger question of the relevance of higher education. Is it to be regarded as self-justifying, requiring no further reason for its existence and expense than the intellectual satisfaction of those who take part in it, or should it face the challenge of Milton "the leisure you have for your studies is by the sweat of other men's brows"? Throughout this book we have always implicitly or explicitly taken this latter position, but its full exploration must be reserved for a more detailed examination at another time.

Here we are mainly concerned to examine these questions insofar as they are held to affect the numbers of those who should be highly educated. To what degree would a further expansion of quantity be at the expense of quality? Does more inevitability mean worse? Are the essential objectives of higher education, or their proper nature so rarified and unworldly or so difficult of comprehension to common men and women that they must be restricted permanently to a few? Worse still, is there not a danger that culture itself and the pursuit of knowledge will be vulgarised and corrupted if they are exposed to the many? Such are the views of the élitists. Taken together they constitute a conspectus and an apologia of élitism as a cultural creed. They are sounded off so confidently from high places that the more modest sort of people are liable to take it for granted that they have some basis in fact.

They have none.

The onus of proof must lie with the élitists, since it is they who are attempting to restrict educational privileges which are paid for by "the sweat of other men's brows". There is no such proof. As we have seen, educational privilege, like every other kind of privilege, tends to be self-perpetuating. The slow processes of social

135

mobility have nevertheless continuously expanded the "educated classes". As we saw at the beginning of this book, the vast majority of those who have ever been highly educated are alive today. Thousands of years in which only a fraction of the population had access to the high culture of their time have given way to a period in which this proportion has multiplied by 100 times in the mere space of 200 years. Yet in every decade of this latest period, the majority opinion of the cultural élite would have been that the natural reserves of those with the essential qualification for higher education had been virtually exhausted.

We need not catalogue the changing fashions in the notion of what conventionally constituted the essential personal attributes for an aspirant to the more prestigious seats of learning whether they were birth, breeding, wealth, the right religion or simply the possession of all these qualities which was guaranteed by prior attendance at good public school. It is perhaps sufficient to summarise that they probably possessed no other continuity than they always reflected the hallmark of social prestige of the time. The intellectual emphasis of today would have been despised in the Oxford of the early 19th century when, for example, a certain professor appointed to teach chemistry had the trifling defect that he knew none, but being the respectable holder of a good church living was well able to afford to pay a young scholar to undertake his college duties in that subject. Indeed the full-time professional intellectual academic was a comparative latecomer at English Universities, which by the mid-19th century, had long become places of sinecure appointment for clergymen waiting for preferment in their dioceses.

A rather different position existed in the Scottish Universities in the late 18th and early 19th centuries where the professorial Chairs in the sciences and in the newly emerging fields of political economy were held by the greatest innovators and discoverers of their age. At that time the Chair of Chemistry at Edinburgh was held by great scientists of the calibre of William Cullen and James Black, while Newtonian physics had been taught there before it was recognised as a fit subject for Cambridge and Adam Smith had founded the science of Economics at Glasgow. It was a period when the Scottish Universities occupied a pre-eminent place in the intellectual life in Europe. From our present point of view it was simultaneously a period of extremely rapid growth in student numbers. The relatively sharp rise in enrolments in British higher education in the latter half of the 18th century culminating in the remarkable peak about 1820 shown in Fig. 2.2 of Chapter 2, was largely concentrated in the Scottish Universities where the students considerably outnumbered those in infinitely more populous

England. Far from causing a dilution of the intellectual level, this surge in growth coincided with, and was the motive force behind, an unprecedented flowering, not only in the new sciences, but in the older disciplines of medicine and philosophy.

While a significant proportion of the students, particularly in Edinburgh, came from nonconformist families in England who were not allowed entry to English Universities, the majority must have cone from the native Scottish population whose participation rates must therefore have been several times of those in England at the same period. No exact statistical data are yet available for the distribution of Scottish students among the social classes, but there are often references to their typical poverty compared with the English students of their day. It may be reasonably supposed that the same dissenting religion which enabled the ascendancy in growth of the Scottish Universities at that time also provided a powerful stimulus to the entrance to higher education from the ordinary people. Was not the heart of its teaching that each person must be able to seek the truth for himself?

The danger that it posed to the social establishment of its day, which relied on divine as well as temporal sanction to its assertion of privilege and power, meant that it must seek allies among the poor, and encourage among them a veneration of learning and a confidence in aspiring to possess it for themselves. In the century which has followed this confidence has faded as the rising middle class have taken possession of higher education and fashioned it for their purposes. But that early 19th century Scottish example of popular enthusiasm for higher education like the parallel developments of the Mechanics Institute in England, and the mass literacy led by the Wesleyans in Wales, were examples of a potential thirst for knowledge arising from common people which, far from diluting the quality of culture, was a major source of its renwal and enrichment.

Social and cultural élitism has never required other justification than natural inborn superiority of its aristocratic owners and protectors. The great artists, philosophers and scientists, though patronised by it, stood permanently above its temporary forms and fashions. The inevitable decadence of its powerful possessors is savagely satirised by Shakespeare:

They rightly do inherit heaven's graces
and harvest nature's riches from expense;
They are the lords and owners of their faces
Others but stewards of their excellence.

. . . .But. . .

sweetest things turn sourest by their deeds;
Lilies that fester smell far worse than weeds.

The meritocratic intellectual cast of modern cultural élitism is of more recent growth. Here we only have space to single out three aspects in which it seeks to justify the thesis that more means worse:

Firstly that the majority of people are too innately stupid for higher education; secondly that the diffusion of culture to the masses would cause its inevitable vulgarisation and corruption; and thirdly that to make higher education available, meaningful and useful to ordinary people would mean abandoning its source of excellence: pursuit of knowledge for its own sake.

Each of these arguments are used to excuse the abandonment of the expansion of higher education. They act as the intellectual supports for the assumptions of official policy, outlined in Chapter 5, that the natural demand for higher education is coming to an upper limit and for the financial fears examined in Chapter 7 that any further expenditure would be a waste of money. We will examine each separately, though they are frequently used interchangeably or to support each other.

The concept of a limited pool of intelligence is mainly the presumption behind the selection methods used at the school level to separate out the so-called "academic" children from the rest and to screen them for special streams or better still for better schools. Even the expensively private so-called "public schools" nowadays formally subscribe to the same policy, at any rate for their scholarship places. The tests of intelligence vary from measurement of the so-called intelligence quotient to those based on actual attainment of skills with numbers and words. It is notable that the children of the rich rarely fail to obtain entrance to one of these exclusive schools unless they are clearly among those few unfortunate enough to require special treatment for organic mental deficiency. And we have already noted how the proportion of children from the professional classes passing through all these screens, and reaching higher education is already tending towards 100 per cent. The new "scientific" justification which appeared to be provided by the invention of the intelligence test was needed in the post-war period when the previous assumptions of a natural superiority of the upper classes was apt to be challenged by the inconveniently rising tide of social democracy. The escalation of student enrolments of the period from 1955-1970 raised the fears (subsequently proved to be largely groundless) that higher education was about to be invaded by uneducated classes. In response, the defence of cultural élitism passed from the limited circle of the exclusive clubs, the senior common rooms and the more exclusive Reviews to the arena of militant propaganda and political populism.

A Professor Cox and a Mr Dyson initiated a counter attack to the evident danger of educational anarchy in a series of occasional magazines aptly titled *The Black Papers*. In an earlier period of anti-democratic reaction they would have been welcomed to the cultural wing of those parties who chose the same colour for their shirts and political programmes. The keynote articles of their first two numbers set the tone of the enterprise. The first, entitled *The egalitarian threat* was by a right-wing politician, Angus Maude, whose contributions to the creative arts or sciences we cannot at the moment recollect and need hardly detain us further.

The second issue was opened by a definitive statement of principle in the form of a paper on *The mental differences between children,* which set out to demonstrate once for all the "convincing . . . proof" that mental differences are largely inherited. The author of this and a subsequent paper illustrating the same theme was none other than Sir Cyril Burt, whose research work was universally recognised as having provided the key source of empirical evidence (indeed, virtually the only unambiguous "proof") for this theory. The theory is, of course, of vital significance for the defenders of the social apartheid in higher education (and in cultural and social privilege) since on this view the absence of the working class child from higher education is due to the regrettable but avoidable consequence of inheriting its stupidity from its unintelligent working class parents. A further inference from the theory is that the whole inequity of the social order is a consequence of a biological natural selection, so that those most fitted to lead because of their fortunate genetic inheritance, are, by and large, those who actually do lead. It follows that any interference in this divinely ordered process, or of the social and cultural hierarchy that it gives rise to, would be bad for society as a whole and even for those at the bottom of the social pile. Hence, of course, the need to repel "The Egalitarian Threat".

What a pity for such a comforting view that all is for the best in this best of possible worlds, that the evidence for this theory in Burt's work was found to be non-existent! Burt claimed to have proved this theory by the key test of examining the development of pairs of identical twins separated and brought up in different environments. In 1968 he stated that he had collected no fewer than 32 pairs of separated identical twins between 1955 and 1965. Professor L.S. Hearnshaw, who meticulously combed the private diaries of Burt after his death in 1976 finds "we can say with complete confidence that neither Burt nor any of his alleged assistants carried out any field work after 1955". Professor Hearnshaw concludes, "we are forced to conclude that the accounts given in Burt's published papers were false and that a measure of deception was certainly involved. It was the pretence of on-going research which the evidence of the diaries reveals as a complete fabrication".

Sir Cyril Burt's proof of inherited inequalities of intelligence was faked.

The whole evidence for the inheritance of intelligence has been examined minutely and methodically analysed by Professor Leon Kamin of Princeton University. He shows how all tests that have been evolved in the attempt to demonstrate this theory have consisted of either intelligence quotient tests which, in his words, are monstrously arbitrary, or of arithmetical and vocabulary materials which have been largely learned at school. Those who cannot answer are those who have not learned what in theory the teachers wished to teach them, to give the answers which are expected of them. These answers are those which come automatically to those who are steeped in the values, habits of thought, conventions, social environment and ambitions of the social groups of which the teachers form a part. Professor Kamin states' "the assumption that one who has not learned these things was prevented from doing so by his bad blood is both gratuitous and self-serving". It is not accidental that those who are so categorised as genetically deficient are always predominantly the children of the disadvantaged, the coloured, the poor. He concludes that the onus of proof of the inheritance of mental traits lies with those who assert it. There is no such proof.

The founder of behavioural psychology J.B. Watson, summed up the matter a generation ago in these words:

"Our conclusion then, is that we have no real evidence for the inheritance of traits. I would feel perfectly confident in the ultimate favourable outcome of careful upbringing of a well-formed baby born of a long line of crooks, murderers and thieves and prostitutes . . . . Give me a dozen healthy infants, well formed, and my own specified world to bring them up in and I'll guarantee to take any one at random and train him to become any kind of specialist I might select — doctor, lawyer, artist, merchant-chief and, yes, even beggar man and thief, regardless of his talents, penchants, tendencies, abilities, vocations and race of his ancestors. I am going beyond my facts, and I admit it, but so have the advocates of the contrary and they have been doing it for many thousand years . . ."

One does not have to accept unconditionally this claim of one of the most uncompromising of founders of the empirical tradition in social science (a claim which he himself admits is, of its nature, not open to complete experimental verification) to decide, nevertheless, where the balance of sense and sound judgement lies. The choice is between a vision of mankind which sees the human mind as infinitely variable, of culture which could draw its strength from a multitude of individual talents, and on the other side a narrow voyeurism which seeks to imprison human creativity within confines of response to tests of little more human significance than a crossword puzzle. As far as the latter view is concerned the final solution has already been found. The Universities should be both staffed and attended by a community of micro-computers. Even though research workers have by now shown that most children can be trained to the required facility for the tests faked by Sir Cyril Burt, much as laboratory rats can be trained to go through a maze, they are hardly ever likely to compete with well programmed electronic machines.

On its literary side, the high culture of the Universities seeks to preserve its exclusive taste and sensibility from the vulgarisation of the "word" which would result from the invasion of the mob. It assumes that those subjects which its calls the "humanities" can only be properly appreciated by a tiny élite fraction of humanity. The contradiction is not merely a play on words. It is at the heart of the conflict between two opposing views of the human condition to which correspond two different views of the nature of value. The first sees culture as essentially fragmented. Not merely the different National traditions but the different Arts, the different artists and the different aspects of their techniques as analysed by the different schools of criticisms are virtually only separated accessible to the small circle of specialists. They dread above all the dull "uniformity" which would seem to be inevitable result of the "egalitarian threat".

No one would wish to deny that the multitude of separate forms that human creativity can take, both adds to the potential richness of the quality of life and are essential means to enlarge the vision of spiritual value. But the great artists like the great spiritual visionaries have always created works which go beyond the temporary limitations of their time and place and of the audience for whom they work. The evaluation of their work is not to be measured by its conformity to the passing standards of taste, nor to the academic orthodoxies of the cultural establishments. Rather the latter are to be judged by the extent to which they are able to assist its diffusion to the majority of men and women, since its supreme relevance deserves no less an audience. This is what Beethoven proclaims in the great final movement of the D Major Symphony, or

Rembrandt in his picture of an old woman, or Shakespeare pouring contempt on the aristocratic trappings of the "culture" of the rich and powerful:

Not marble nor the gilded monuments
Of princes shall outlive this powerful rhyme.

The obsessive panic at the possible spread of culture beyond the precious circle of the few who can properly appreciate it has been expressed most forthrightly by George Steiner in his "Language and Silence":

"What, save half truths, gross simplifications or trivia, can, in fact, be communicated to that semi-literate mass audience which consumer democracy has called into the market place". Only in a diminished and corrupted language can most such communication be made effective.

Steiner has the extraordinary effrontery to go on to deplore the vulgarisation of the "wealth of dignity of speech" in the Bible in the cause of reaching out to the "semi-educated". One can only ponder which of the semi-literate apostles he would have permitted to teach the word of God and how he would have deplored the corruption of ancient Hebraic culture when Jesus preached to the illiterate mass audience from the mountain. It is perhaps most characteristic of this view of culture that it would be more concerned with accent and style of language in which the Beatitudes were delivered than with the essence of their message. One could only infer that the original text has been mistranslated since the English version contains no reference to the necessity of a literary training to appreciate them. An older authority than Steiner has it another way, "Though I speak with the tongues of men and of angels and have not charity I am become as a sounding brass or a tinkling cymbal."

Steiner is merely typical of an élitist trend in literary criticism which has come into fashion, as the poorer classes have become "mass consumers" and a culture which for centuries had been the narrow prerogative of the rich and their professional servants, has to confront the new phenomenon of "mass literacy". Its attempt to defend its previous exclusive cultural monopoly leads to a retreat to the contemplation of language as an end in itself, which is closely parallel to the "scientific" justification of "knowledge for its own sake", which we shall examine later.

Of course the defence of the privileged position of the élite as the only rightful possessors of the "word" is older than the modern period and it has always attempted to enlist the highest authority in support of its claims. T.S. Eliot, in his *Notes towards the defini-*

tion of Culture, finds it necessary to make a plea for a return to an older form of society in which "an aristocracy shall have a peculiar and essential function. A smaller group at a higher level will have equal power with a larger group at a lower level". Elsewhere he makes it clear that what he is talking about is a "really Christian society" where "the culture of its people is the incarnation of its religion". This concept of a class hierarchy as the essential form of a Christian community may seem extraordinary to those seeking some justification for it in the words of Jesus, but it is not new.

The classic example of the prejudice of a privileged class defending its interests against the invasion of its religious and cultural preserves by the ignorant representatives of the uncultured masses is still to be found in the record of the trial of John Bunyan. The whole long testimony of Bunyan and his subsequent acceptance of imprisonment rather than subserviance to the cultural and religious hierarchy of his day must be studied by anyone concerned to find the roots from which the truth of these matters must spring. Here we must suffice with one quotation:

> Mr Foster of Bedford (one of Bunyan's interrogators at his trial): "He said that I was ignorant, and did not understand the scriptures; for how, said he, can you understand them when you know not the original Greek?. . . . Bunyan: To whom I said that if that was his opinion that none could understand the scriptures but those that had the original Greek etc., then but a few of the poorer sort should be saved. This is harsh, yet the scripture saith that 'God hides these things from the wise and prudent', that is from the learned of the world 'and reveals them to babes and sucklings."

Another of the judges urged him to keep to his proper trade and social place in words which could hardly be bettered by today's defenders of the cultural hierarchy:

> Justice Keelin: ". . . . as every man hath received a trade, so let him follow it. If any man have received a gift of tinkering, as thou has done, let him follow his tinkering, and so let other men their trades, and the divine his calling . . . . "

Fortunately for the "culture" of Mr Steiner and Mr Eliot the admonitions, threats and prison sentence of the judges and the cultural, social and religious élite that they defended did not deflect Bunyan from his own view of his proper trade. In spite of 12 years imprisonment, perhaps because of it, this semi-literate tinker created a vision of a truth and a true goal of culture as a Pilgrims Progress open to all, but especially, and primarily, to the simple poor and untutored who he pictures, as much from his daily experience as by way of metaphor as "clothed with rags" and with "a great burden upon their backs".

The élitist view of the essential purity of culture which must be protected from infection by the "egalitarian threat" of mass participation, fortunately does not hold unchallenged leadership in the institutes of higher education or even among the intellectual élite itself. To some extent the spread of egalitarian ideas is understandably characteristic of the intelligentsia of the immediate post-war period. Perhaps no university system of the pre-war world was more deliberately hierarchical in its structure of supreme professorial power and more exclusive in its social and cultural apartheid than the German. It proved a relatively easy prey to corruption of Hitlerism, offering little collective resistance, first to the exclusion and dismissal of the Jews and then to its own virtual destruction. The heirs to Goethe, Kant and Humbolt had lost contact with and could not make little appeal to the common people whose great cultural heritage was being defiled.

The defences of the humanistic values can ultimately only be undertaken by humanity. A culture which isolates itself and does not seek to diffuse its values to all, must degenerate. Since the war, although the social composition of the Universities has changed little, a growing proportion of the progressive intellectual élite have seen the need for the destruction of their own élitism. This self-consciousness of the contradiction between their cultural privileges and the human values which give significance to their studies was an importance strand in the frustrations and rebellions which exploded throughout the largely middle class student world in the days of 1968. This debt that culture owes to the ordinary people was expressed nearly a hundred years ago by Matthew Arnold:

"the men of culture are the true apostles of equality. The great men of culture are those who have a passion for diffusing, for making prevail, for carrying from one end of society to the other, the best knowledge of their time; who have laboured to divest knowledge of all that was harsh, uncouth, difficult, abstract, professional, exclusive; to humanise it, to make it efficient outside the clique of the cultivated and learned."

and earlier:

"Culture . . . does not try to reach down to the level of inferior classes, it does not seek to win them for this or that sect of its own with ready-made judgements and watchwords. It seeks to do away with classes; to make the best that has been thought and known in the world current everywhere; to make all men live in an atmosphere of sweetness and light, where they may use ideas, as it uses them itself, freely — nourished, and not bound by them."

144

To which we would only add that though this is also the proper role of the men of culture of today, they can neither totally prescribe nor indefinitely control the larger scope nor limit the richness of quality of a future truly human culture to whose birth they can merely assist as best they can. The culture of the previously oppressed peoples whether in the exploited colonial or neo-colonial regions of the world or among the poor of the so-called advanced countries, or as expressed by the whole of the woman-kind whose suppression by the male has cast a universal sexist shadow over thousands of years of religious, artistic and even scientific creativity, must find its own visions, forms and goals and can only eventually be created by their struggles.

CHAPTER NINE

Retreat to the Ivory Tower

The third main strand in the apologia for the narrow exclusiveness of higher education, particularly in the more prestigious Universities, is derived from the scientific wing of the academic élite. It is embodied in the doctrine that knowledge, especially scientific knowledge, must be pursued for its own sake. Its supposedly inevitable inaccessibility to the majority is a consequence of its necessary narrow specialisation and abstractness. Nevertheless, it is assumed to be the only proper goal for University study and research. The deviation from this straight and narrow path in the interests of a popular relevance has been described by Professor Nisbet, the doyen of American sociologists, as "the degradation of the academic dogma". Although, as we shall see, this intellectual ethos is a peculiar product of the vast expansion of the positive, and especially the physical, sciences; their very success in the expansion of their vast store of factual data of the material universe has resulted in the dominance of their self-image in the modern University. Even the older and newer professional studies, the humanities and the newer social sciences ape their methods and attempt to assume the same imperviance to criteria of mere human need or even of divine sanction.

This apparent unworldliness of University studies seems to be at odds with the fact that most students, especially the majority coming from professional and managerial class backgrounds, enter with quite different motivations and ultimately find careers where the application of knowledge to material gain or social status are the goals and criteria of success. The idea that intellectual excellence is confined to the mastery of the abstract specialised disciplines and has no necessary direct relevance to the improvement of human life presents little difficulty to those from families familiar with the gamesmanship of entry to higher education. But it constitutes still another barrier of incomprehension, of mystery, to that majority of the population for whom such games are as strange as the Eton Wall game. It also provides an excellent reason for limiting entry permanently to a small fraction of the population. Only such a small fraction, it can be explained, have the motivation or aptitude to memorise the enormous collection of abstract facts and master these remote and austere disciplines.

Then again, only a limited number of experts are supposed to be needed to staff the highly specialised positions for which higher education is supposed to be a preparation. In spite of the inconsistency that the majority of students do not, and never have, aspired to this austere ideal of excellence and that most employers of graduates are quick enough to disabuse them of it, it remains a powerful feature of the self-image of the academic. If it were true, or rather to the extent that it is of some value, it would nevertheless have little relevance to the actual social limitations to entry to higher education. Rather the opposite is the case. It is the majority of students from the professional classes who enter higher education with the clearest idea of their future, predominantly non-academic careers and who dominate almost exclusively the more socially prestigious and financially rewarding professional schools such as medicine, law or management. Working class students, insofar as they are not processed into the traditionally undervalued areas of elementary school teaching, or the more familiar, but again, relatively underpaid field of engineering, are apt to find themselves in the pure sciences and arts.

Nevertheless, if we are seriously considering the possibility of higher education for all, it is a little difficult to maintain the concept that everyone, or nearly everyone in it, would be pursuing knowledge for its own sake; or that excellence should be confined by the abstractions of the specialists who know more and more about less and less, with no necessary reference to any wider cultural, social or humanistic significance. One suspects that cheerfulness would keep breaking in. Hence it is necessary to examine as briefly as we can the origin, the nature and the possible future of the highly specialised scientific studies which not only dominate the modern University, but have been the base of the dominant philosophy of knowledge of the modern age. The vast exponentially accelerating accumulation of scientific facts (parallel to the mass-production of material goods) has produced a view of the world as a mere collection of facts, all equal to each other, all equally devoid of any other human significance than their mere existence. In Chapter 2 we quoted Wittgenstein's opening sentence to his *Tractatus Logico Philosophicus* "The world is the totality of facts". The complementary doctrine of the equally positivistic philosopher Ayer was that no meaning could be assigned to any ethical statement (since, of course, it could not be statement of fact).

The concept of the pursuit of knowledge for its own sake has arisen gradually in the course of the headlong expansion of science over the past three centuries. As we have seen earlier, such exponentially accelerating processes as the growth of science, like the spread of an epidemic or the diffusion of a great new religion give the appearance of being self-propelling. Indeed, their speed of growth at any time apparently depends more on the size they have already reached than on any obvious external factor. They become their own agents of expansion. Their origin is forgotten and they seem to be autonomous and to need no other justification than themselves. This apparent isolation from the environment (which nevertheless is necessary to feed their growth) is a temporary illusion. But to understand this we have to examine their beginnings and to analyse the factors which may limit their future. And neither of these lie entirely within themselves.

The original motivation of the great adventure of scientific discovery as conceived by its founding fathers was much more closely bound to its application for human betterment. In the words of Francis Bacon in 1620 "The true and lawful end of the sciences is that human life be enriched by new discoveries and powers". Science was to be pursued, both for the clues it gave to the divine purposes and for the control it promised to give man as the master of nature. The other great prophet of the future power of knowledge, Descartes, had much the same objective that "knowing the force and action of fire, water, air, the stars, the heavens and all other bodies that surround us as distinctly as we know the different trades of our craftsmen, we could employ them in the same way to all uses for which they are appropriate and thus become the masters and possessors of Nature". But Descartes was also more responsible than any other thinker for that schism in thought which was henceforth more than ever before to separate the material and moral worlds, to create the illusion of a purely objective knowledge of the former absolved from ethical judgement or human or divine sanction; to lay the basis for the complementary dogma that moral standards were independent of factual circumstances.

The clash between these two Cartesian aspects of the relation of the advance of knowledge to the advancement of the human condition may explain the paralysis of the intellectual during the succeeding centuries in the face of ever more glaring examples of the misuse and prostitution of the enormous power of the knowledge he created. The neutrality which guaranteed his freedom for objective study also bought his silence, or rather it begat his silence, since he lacked any rational method of bringing together the ethically neutral abstractions which result from the pursuit of knowledge for its own sake and the ethical criteria which arise as soon as knowledge is applied. He had abandoned in advance any claim that his special knowledge of the former gave him any status in pronouncing on the latter. Hence, ultimately, the impotent horror of Oppenheimer who created the atom bomb, but found himself

148

without any language to convince the world of his political masters of its dreadful significance.

The notion of the pursuit of knowledge for its own sake is also linked with its fragmentation into an ever increasing number of specialist disciplines, each claiming independence in its own field. If we study some field of broad human interest such as those that constituted the original university disciplines; medicine, law and theology, it is virtually impossible to separate the purpose of study from its broader human and indeed, moral, significance. Medicine is devoted to the improvement of human health, Law to the ordering of civil society and Theology to the pursuit of God's purposes. To separate the objective, neutral, aspects of these studies from the moral questions of what constitutes health, good social order or divinely sanctified behaviour, would be to rob them of their essence.

But each of them requires the researcher from time to time to abstract certain aspects of his subject for separate specialised analysis. Thus medicine can generate a purpose for the study of biology, and hence chemistry, and ultimately find useful guidance from the abstractions of computer science or quantum mechanics.

The expansion of human knowledge has required an ever increasing proliferation of these abstract specialist fields which become more and more remote from the more direct human purposes from which they were originally derived, so that they take on the appearance of autonomous self-generating growth and generate the belief that they are to be pursued for their own sake. Indeed, there is a legitimate sense in which this apparent independence and self-justification, like that of the separate arts and humanities, like poetry, painting, music or even the multitude of sports and recreations which may be studied, practiced and refined, is to be welcomed as adding richness and variety to individual and social life. However, so long as any of them requires resources which might be devoted to other needs, or gives rise to power over nature or men, they must all be prepared to answer the challenge: "The leisure you have for your studies is by the sweat of other men's brows".

In presenting this account of the dominance of the specialist abstract disciplines in the modern University we would not attempt to deny that a significant proportion of its studies (and still more in the non-University Colleges) are of a broader character, still preserving some of the ethos of the older professions. But the essential intellectual élitism and the retreat from ethical responsibility to the amoral ethos of "knowledge for its own sake" find their justification in the academic dominance of the pure sciences and their counterparts in the rarified abstractions of pure criticism, the study of "culture for its own sake". The term "specialist" is a relatively recent invention. The Oxford English Dictionary gives the date of its appearance as 1856, which places it at the beginning of the acceleration of University expansion that we described in Chapter 2. In the intervening period it has become virtually the essential title to academic respectability.

The fragmentation of science into a multitude of apparently autonomous specialisms was a necessary consequence, and even cause, of its explosive growth. The separate sciences act as a filing system correlating and containing and explaining the vast array of observations of aspects of the material and living world which it calls facts. Of course, the so-called "facts" of science are not the "brute" facts of real experience. They are abstractions. They deal with categories like "mass", "force", "potential" or, alternatively, of "intelligence quotient", "libido", "inferiority complex"; as though they had a life of their own and could exist separately from the beings or things or processes they are attached to. In the course of constructing its scheme of interconnections each science calls into being other objects such as "atoms", "genes", "classes".

All this construction of specialised abstract models of experience is a very necessary part of the process of relating our experience of the world to our purposes and hence, of ensuring that "human life be enriched by new discoveries and powers". But the various specialised departments of knowledge rarely proceed for long by their own momentum. It is nearly always at their points of interaction where their specialised expertise is no longer self-sufficient that the major breakthrough to a new explanation of some important aspect of the universe or the vision of some new possibility of human progress takes place. This is abundantly illustrated in the giant scientific advances of our own day, such as those commonly called molecular biology, but where structural physics, biology and biochemistry, information science, and indeed almost every branch of research have combined and interacted to uncover the possibility of undreamed of power in modifying the essential nature of life as we know it. Yet the principle which brought these separate specialities together lay outside the methodology of each one of them, and the new concepts which expressed the new discoveries were not included in the original separate working rules of any.

In general, any important new principle in a specialised science will often appear to be nonsense in terms of the principles, rules, tests of validity, of the old. Even what is reckoned to be the essential nature of objective facts on which all else is built has to be reimagined and established in a new way. The ultimate test that the new science is truer than the old cannot be the old tests of validity since these are precisely what are most critically changed. How then do we establish what is objectively true? The answer is, that precisely at this point the concept of "knowledge for its own sake" fails. The new displaces the old because it serves us better, because with it we can "become the masters and possessors of nature". It is at the point of the really creative steps in knowledge that they coincide with the creative steps in human practice and human vision of the purpose and quality of life. At such points the separated Cartesian moral and material worlds must come together again. The new truth is, of course, not simply what we wish to believe, still less is it simply that which pleases the powers or the paymasters, or serves the special interests of its discoverers, or indeed of any other group of special pleading. Nor does it serve principally merely to permit mankind or its dominant sections to pursue their old ways better, or to achieve more cheaply their previous goals. The essence of an important discovery is that it gives a new vision of both ends and means; it is simultaneously to be judged on both ethical and objective grounds and indeed they act as tests of the significance of each other.

Consider the enormous changes in the moral outlook on such questions as individual criminal responsibility in relation to environment which have resulted from the discoveries of behavioural psychology, or our view of what is now called mental disorder, but was once conceived as voluntary possession by evil spirits; or on the ethical nature of homosexuality, or the moral right to property, or the relations of parents and children; and reflect how much these changes in the nature of moral conviction have depended on the discoveries of positive medical, biological, chemical and social sciences. The scientific view of the world is similarly profoundly influenced by the prevailing views of the nature of good and evil, the proper scope for human purpose. This is highlighted by the modern debate on the possibilities of genetic engineering which could change the character of human beings, and perhaps still more dramatically by research on artificial intelligence, which might conceivably create computers capable of controlling human society.

Doubtless the "brute" facts of the world may be unalterable. Unfortunately scientific research is never privileged to examine the whole brute facts. The aspects it selects for discovery and explanation are set in a framework which owes as much to the moral as to the objective view of the world. The concept of infinitely extensible absolute space, existing independently of all material objects was the essential foundation for Newton's mechanically determined world. To it was assigned the role of the ultimate cause of all material events. For Newton it was also necessary to preserve the infinitely extended existence of God who, like space, acted on all objects but was not acted on by them. Indeed, space was the "sensorium of the Godhead". In the centuries that followed, the architecture of Newton's material world became so fully accepted, self-evident, axiomatic, as to define the very nature of objective fact; and indeed, all sciences sought their ultimate objectivity within the framework of Newtonian physics. Yet Newton's world view would have been impossible without those great overall revolutions in the structure and thought of mediaeval Europe which swept away the older scholastic concepts of "substance" as they swept away the social, political, commercial, and even religious, dogma of the middle ages and replaced it by a new humanism and a new vision of the scope of human mastery of the world of nature.

Einstein ultimately demonstrated that the structural framework of Newton's world merely appeared to have an absolutely objective material existence. Space as conceived by Newton proved to be an illusion. The structure of the space of physics, and hence the whole mechanical materialism which had been based on it, is not in the last analysis anything given in nature or independent of human thought. It is a consequence of a special way of looking at the universe, of our world view of the present, and hence of the human purposes and practice that bring it into existence. These new concepts of nature which make themselves relative to the observer demand that he should become conscious of the way his purposive goals will affect what appears to him to be objective fact. They force him to be conscious of his possibility of freedom. They arise at the same time as it becomes possible for the first time in human history to free the human race from being mechanically at the mercy of the brute forces of physical nature, and as changes in the concepts of the social order, the significance of international responsibility, and of the possible destiny of human future, as revolutionary as those of the Renaissance arrive on the agenda of human discussion and decision. But the nature of these changes can no longer be discussed and decided by a small minority. They can only be brought about by the deliberate and conscious participation of the vast majority. They require the possession of the key knowledge of change by all as a universal right.

The extension of higher education beyond its present limited social basis to all, or virtually all, of the population would almost certainly require a considerable change from its present highly specialised and ethically emasculated studies which dominate the treatment of the sciences and most of the humanities. The problem of the relevance of higher education to the lives of those who study is, as we have seen, one which can be by-passed so long as they are thereby admitted to a privileged status, the preserve of a social minority. It is also true that even though the subjects studied in higher education may often have little direct relevance to life and work after graduation, their systematic pursuit can induce a confidence in the approach to new knowledge which, rather than any simple transferability of intellectual skills, enables the student to train himself in the fields he requires thereafter. And, of course, in the case of that minority of students of higher education who go on to highly specialised research or to technical employment, the training they receive is reasonably adequate, at least in the first few years of their career.

But this kind of highly specialised technical service is likely to shrink at least as a proportion of the social needs for the highly educated as a whole. The technical specialist has in the past often acted largely as a living data bank of the most important scientific facts in his field and as an agent who could collate evidence and diagnose the nature of problems and suggest optimum solutions. These functions have even invaded the older professions of law and medicine, indeed, the term "specialist" was originally mainly applied in the latter profession and the surgeon, Cutler in Shaw's *Doctor's Dilemma* became the stereotype of the expert who knew more and more about less and less.

These functions are now largely obsolscent thanks to the invention of the micro-computer, which can provide a better stocked and ordered memory and will soon be able to provide a more accurate diagnosis than the most well informed specialist. The computer is excellently fitted to take over any mental function which collates any series of factual data according to impersonal objective rules, however complex. It cannot yet undertake that kind of original research which creates an entirely new kind of knowledge, but otherwise has virtually all the attributes of an highly specialised academic and is, of course, much cheaper. Needless to say it could pass not merely the entrance examination, but the honours degree in most specialised disciplines with a 100 per cent score.

What, then, can be visualised of the form and content of higher education if it becomes as normal a human right as primary and secondary education is today. The first solution that we may dismiss is that it will be as narrowly vocational as might be desired by the current needs of employment. Relevance to work is a vital theme in education for the intermediate future, at least until the boundaries between work and leisure have disappeared. The experience and analysis of the nature of work and the schism between scientific and social theory and practice is increasingly an essential element in education. But there is even less likelihood in the future than in the past half-century that the future needs for precise skills and the future content of factual knowledge required in production and social services can be forecast in advance.

The relevance of education to work can only be solved, not merely by changing the abstract nature of education, but by changing the nature of work. No education worth the name could fit men and women for the soul destroying nature of most mass-production employment in modern society. Nor is it necessary to merely reduce the hours spent on it and increase the proportion of mere leisure. The point is to change the function of human labour and the structures which deprive most of the workers from having any function other than human robots. Insofar as production still has the nature of mass-production, and this is by no means necessary for the indefinite future, the work of robots should be done by robots. But, as we outlined in Chapter 7, this frees human labour for vital service functions, and new markets for individual craftsmanship which enormously enrich the quality of life and demand higher education for those that perform them.

The human mind returns to the human task of weighing these alternative possibilities in the light of a continually enriched sense of their good or evil consequences and an enlarged vision of the possibilities of human practice and fellowship. Of its very nature such a possible future for learning cannot be the preserve of an élite. Insofar as the present élite has a role in bringing it into existence that role might be called the destruction of élitism.

The question of how long the present institutions of higher education will remain as the most valuable form for its future development is a subject for a more technical analysis than we have time for here. We consider it an important question, but secondary to the immense widening of the franchise and the consequent changes that have been posed above. Organisational innovations such as the Open University in Britain and the vast technical possibilities of individual learning aids from micro-electronics may supersede more or less rapidly much of the ex-cathedra lecture room methodology of the past century. Incarceration of the higher education student for several years in isolation from the living society which is the true subject of his study may also have a relatively short term future. But these questions can only be settled in the hard test of practice as the doors of higher education are thrown open.

Similarly, the question of what are fit and proper constituents of courses of study is a question not to be answered by élitist prejudice. After all, engineering, which is now demanded by the politicians and industrialists to become the main point of concentration for any immediate expansion was not considered a suitable subject for our more ancient and prestigious Universities until, quite lately, the power and money attaching to it persuaded them to revise their opinions.

For a long time to come the growth of the service professions of education, health, community services, music, the arts, entertainment and recreation and the many other fields of direct human welfare which, as we indicated in Chapter 7, could become the major field of productive employment, will require an indefinitely increasing supply of highly educated generalists. They would profit enormously in quality if all, or virtually all, of their workers received an appropriate form of higher education. Their work could be designed to give them possibilities for creative judgement which would need to draw on the stores of specialised scientific and humanistic knowledge in the ways we have suggested above.

In the smaller, but nevertheless vital, future areas of material production as in agriculture the role of the worker becomes increasingly managerial in nature, both in the ultimate technical organisation of the computer controlled machinery, but much more importantly, in creating and developing new systems that both interpret and serve the needs of the consuming public. For these purposes the concept of management education as a training in the optimising of the production and delivery of goods and services becomes important, and again, there is no reason why it should not be relevant to the work of every employee.

The need for specialists in the abstract sciences and other tools of specialist scholarship will doubtless continue indefinitely. Nothing that we have argued above against their hegemony and their claim to the sole prerogative of intellectual excellence detracts from their essential importance and of their potential fascination to the human mind. Even so, it is very likely that the role of the computer in freeing their pursuers from much of the necessity for a personal memory bank of detailed facts and diagnostic methods will also free them to take possession of that wider conspectus of culture from which fundamental discovery in even the specialised fields so often springs.

In brief, we see no reason why any field of activity which is a fit and proper object of human labour, effort and invention should not be a fit and proper constituent of higher education. The point of a higher education is not to prepare for this or that particular cult of learning which is the fashion of the day, whether it be Greek grammar, dogmatic theology, production engineering or Marxist ideology. It is to enable the individual as much as society itself to become master of his future, to pass from the ranks of those who know only enough to submit to the crude demands of nature or to carry out the decisions of others in which they have had no creative part. It is the means to enable him to become one of that body of people who create goals, have the visions and take part in deciding to bring them into existence. The content of higher education, no less than its methods and institutions can only be finally decided by all those who participate in it provided that they constitute the majority of the population who also make it possible. For its proper goals can only be shaped by those who apply it to achieve the larger goals of human welfare.

The proper role of the academic élite, insofar as they remain a separate estate, is not the dominance of the goals of learning but the illumination of them and service to them. And if they shudder at the thought of physiotherapy, or even painting and decorating, taking their place beside Greek poetry, they might remember what Plato thought of poets. For the benefit of those who recoil at the thought of the loss of cultural standards, we are not recommending a relativism where all notions of value are the mere subject of individual taste. The truly creative always asserts its own standards of value and rarely measures itself in advance against the orthodox canons of taste or those dogmas of the sciences which it makes obsolete. Its touchstone is its universal significance. Its university is human society.

CHAPTER TEN

Summary: Beginning the Future

The aim of this book was to explore the idea that higher education should be for everyone. It is only about 100 years ago since the Elementary Education Act of 1870 established the principle of universal elementary education. Before that time the proportion of children in England who had any primary education after the age of 11 was probably less than those who complete full-time higher education today. In some States of modern America participation in College education up to the age of 20 or 21 is running at a higher rate than the proportion of those in Britain who stay at school beyond the age of 16. Nevertheless, in all the economically advanced countries of the world, higher education has been steadily expanding with a continuously accelerating rate over the century. We have followed the main features of that expansion to examine the question whether there is any innate reason why it should come to a stop.

In the first chapter we commenced to analyse the motive force behind the student demand for higher education. Modern society is rapidly changing. The source of change is above all, the application of new knowledge to technology and social organisation. The same changes which bring instability, unemployment and the obsolescence of their skills to manual workers enhance the importance, power and the adaptability of the highly educated.

In the second and third chapters we investigated the source of the "immediacy" of higher education, the fact that the appearance of so many college graduates seems to have all happened so suddenly. Was it the result of some over-enthusiastic policy such as the supposed implementation of the Robbins Committee Report in Britain after 1963? We found, on the contrary, that student numbers had been accelerating steadily for the whole of the previous century and that during this period they had already multiplied by nearly 20 times. This exponential expansion had proceeded at almost the same rate of annual growth in each of the main European countries after a take-off in the latter half of the 19th century. That time was one of profound change in the technology of modern industry, when the basis of the modern mass production and mass consumption society was being laid. It was also when the modern, highly specialised sciences, were taking shape and when their methods and ethos were beginning to dominate the nature of the academic world. They were beginning to be fed into application at the same accelerating rate. During this century that followed the professional and managerial classes who, as we showed in Chapter 4, came to dominate the entry into higher education, were expanding at almost the same annual percentage rate.

The almost universal international explosion in student numbers which multiplied about three times between 1955 to 1970, analysed in Chapter 3, must have arisen from causes which were much more general than the policies or provisions of individual countries. Indeed, even in Britain, the flood of enrolments rapidly exceeded the Robbins Committee estimates, based on the commencement of the acceleration in the post-1955 period. One is forced to the conclusion that the unprecedented force of expansion was in all countries powered by student demand and that government provision was continually revised and adapted to meet it. As was demonstrated in Chapter 4, it was still dominated to virtually the same extent as before by the professional and managerial classes, and those semi-professional sections of the population closest to them. Indeed, before the end of this period the participation rate for sons of senior professional families in higher education rose to about 80 per cent, whereas that for daughters of unskilled labourers remained about a hundred times lower.

It was here we analysed the social apartheid which dominates higher education in Britain (and to a similar extent the other main countries of Western Europe). It has remained virtually unchanged during the whole post-war period up to 1970. Since then it has actually widened significantly. It operates in spite of formal official adherence to the Robbins principle: that higher education should be available to everyone who has the necessary ability and attainment and wishes to pursue it. Indeed, this principle is bound to produce the pervasive social privilege which exists. This follows from the way in which the decision to attempt to enter higher education must arise.

In Chapter 4 we outlined a model of this process in terms, firstly of the perception by any individual at the age of choice of the possibility of entering a University or College, and secondly, the value he attached to entrance or to the goals to which it would lead. This valuation only becomes real to that minority of the population whose upbringing for the previous ten or more years has accustomed them to thinking of higher education as a really possible future. They come, as we have seen, from the families where education is taken for granted, and from the sections of society where the social status associated with higher education is habitually accepted as a natural right. Every step they have taken from the earliest age has carefully prepared them for this decision.

The children of the majority of manual workers on the other hand, have no such background. For them higher education is an alien world and the social roles played by the highly educated are strangers to their homes and streets. The question of their native ability hardly ever arises, since, by the time it might have been called into play, it is aready too late.

The model explains why the rate of expansion of higher education increases exponentially and does not ebb and flow with fall or rise of the total number of children aged 18 in the population. Most of these have already been ruled out long before reaching the age of choice. The age group that counts is predominantly that of children from the educated classes and the number of these, like the size of the educated classes, is continuously exponentially expanding at virtually the same rate as that of higher education itself.

Nevertheless, as we saw in Chapter 5, future fluctuations in the size of the total 18-year-old age group are used in the official projections as an excuse to back a policy of restricting the expansion of student numbers. Since this will have little effect on the entry from the still expanding educated classes, its result will be to cause a further sharp deterioration of the proportion of working class students. The failure of national confidence in the future of higher education described in this chapter marks a new stage in the British trend in which we begin to fall rapidly behind other major European countries and far behind Japan and the USA.

It marks a retreat from the idea of education as a vital form of national investment. It reflects a failure of nerve in the face of the challenge of the new age of the micro-computer and the associated rise of the new highly advanced forms of production which the knowledge revolution in bringing into existence. In Chapters 6 and 7 we examined the economic factors associated with the rise of higher education. Since 1860 world economic growth and the expansion of higher education have followed closely similar exponential paths. This cannot be merely because more higher education could be afforded by richer nations and hence was supplied, since, as we have seen, its expansion has been the result of a continuously increasing demand. Supply has followed demand, and both have often accelerated fastest, not in the richest nations, but in those struggling upwards.'

There is a dynamic relationship between the increase of knowledge and its application and the growth of the productivity of the economy. Each stimulates and is necessary for the other. But this is only completely true on a world scale. The nations which seize the lead are those which succeed in transferring their efforts and their investment to the most rapidly developing areas of production, and these are generally those which require the most significant inputs of new knowledge and hence the largest investment in higher education.

The most advanced stage is reached when the centre of gravity of economic production begins to pass from the area of material goods to the area of communication, which is, broadly speaking, the area of service industries. In these the main raw material and finished product is knowledge and the limitations to the creative application and employment of an unlimited expansion of higher education begin to disappear. Virtually all jobs become capable of improved quality and efficiency by the application of more knowledge. The need for most routine labour also largely disappears, being taken over by the micro-computer and the machines controlled by it. The border line between work and creative leisure, which has always been a hazy one for the professional and creative worker, commences to lose its significance.

Finally, in Chapters 8 and 9, we have examined the supposed cultural limitations to higher education. The onus of proof of theories that the vast majority of the population is unfitted by innate stupidity or insensitivity for access to high culture must lie with the theorists. There is no such proof. All the evidence inclines in the opposite direction. The periods of great cultural creativity have coincided with the breadth of its diffusion and the extent of creative popular participation. Besides, the humanities, like the sciences, must be relevant to humanity. All their other qualities must ultimately relate to and enrich the quality of life. Otherwise they must degenerate to the significance of the "glass bead game" pictured by Herman Hesse as the final cultural product of an élitist intelligentsia.

The predominant, highly specialised and abstract scientific nature of much of our higher education is a product of a peculiar period in intellectual history when the rapid speed of advance of the fragmented and separated sciences led to the relative isolation of their practitioners from each other and from their own origins in the problems of action and purpose. The need for such dedicated and withdrawn high priests of specialised knowledge for its own sake will doubtless always continue, and education for it be available for those whose minds incline to those lonely vistas. But they will pass from the centre of the stage. They have never been the main goal for the majority of students. Their dominance of the curriculum time of higher education will cease to be credible, perhaps even for future specialists, as the computers take over the role of storing the data, diagnosing its relevance to particular situations and displaying the possible options open for scientific interpretation. The human mind and human culture returns to human problems and judgements, the creation of new links between thought and action, the vision of new practicabilities of purpose, of new skills for mind, hand and spirit.

It has not been our aim to attempt a detailed account of the subjects, curriculum, the methods or the institutions of higher education nor of the changes that have occurred in these over the period that we have been studying, nor those that will be appropriate as higher education is extended to everyone. These are important subjects, but must be reserved for extended analysis elsewhere. Here we have only been able to deal with them insofar as they had an important bearing on the main question: the availability of higher education to all. We may note that the balance in all these matters has gone through many changes at different times and displayed a wide variation of character and emphasis in different countries and even different institutions in the same country. We may expect a similar variation to take place in the future, and though it may be possible to sketch general lines of development, the emerging goals and patterns will be formed according to the needs of the participants.

Nevertheless, throughout this study of the quantitative aspects of higher education, a central theme has emerged which links the values for which it is pursued with the forces behind its continuously accelerating expansion and enables us to give a broadly common definition embracing all, or almost all, activities normally recognised as the higher education sector in each of the advanced countries. In short, it is the level of education pursued with the aim of joining the ranks of those who make decisions in society as distinct from those who carry out other people's decisions. In the main the objectives which have propelled most students, especially those from the dominant middle class families, have been concerned with their future careers. Higher education is associated with careers in the decision making levels of society, though, of course, not all those who have reached that level have been to college, or *vice versa*. The extraordinary rapid escalation of enrolments from 1955 onwards coincided with the perception that graduation was becoming even more necessary for this purpose than before, in the coming age of the knowledge industries. It was during this period that it became virtually obligatory for the children of the most aware high professional families, instead of merely highly desirable as before. In spite of the variations in the dominant subjects, supposed standards, pure or applied emphasis, methods of teaching, procedures for entry and degree of State subsidy of students in different countries, passage through higher education served a similar social purpose in each of them as any increasingly necessary for the individual anxious to conserve, or even to improve his social status;

to remain among or to join the managers, rather than to be managed. Of course, this main theme in the motivation to enter higher education does not exclude a genuine interest in its cultural content or its scientific interest. A certain minimum attachment to the values of these for their own sake is necessary to qualify. They may also be considered as another aspect or route for the pilgrimage of the student towards independence, to becoming his own master, or joining the company of the élite group of cultural masters. In this sense, higher education may be regarded as a path to independent judgement or to achieving the professional status of a member of the opinion forming groups of autonomous experts. The jealously guarded independent status of the professional societies or the less formally defined, but equally powerful, closed circles of cognoscenti or arbiters of taste, aims to ensure the right to be the decision makers in the chosen fields (". . . others but stewards of their excellence . . ."). Even in the realm of social dissent, the intellectual frequently seeks to be the real decision maker. The left wing student of 1968 naturally aspired to leadership of the revolution.

The differences in the scope of what are recognised as fitting themes for higher education, therefore, depend more on their significance to the contemporary decision making processes; their value to the individual seeking to move from being a cog to a big wheel, than on any once and for all taxonomy of culture. Thus over the century, the sciences have moved from the periphery to dominate the ethos of the University and technology; for long sedulously excluded as mere "plumbing" from the older Universities becomes eagerly sought by them as vital to their prestige and power. Finally, in the United States Universities, management studies became the largest section before they were even recognised as suitable for the Universities of Europe. Again, we would not wish to be suspected of a complete cultural relativism. The actual historical fact that the academic dogma changes, even that it has in the course of time performed more than one complete volte-face does not imply a complete arbitrariness in standards of significance, though it does lead one to be sceptical of the arbitrary standards that hold the stage of academic fashion of the moment. Once again we must reserve the fuller exploration of the nature of value change in higher education for another occasion, since it would take us too far beyond our present theme.

But may we suggest a broad theme around which the rich variety of goals and the vast range of curricula of a future universal higher education may be given an over-arching unity of purpose. This is the theme of liberation.

This theme extends and universalises the previous role of higher education in preparing the managers and decision makers of a divided society. The pursuit of universal human liberation is a safeguard against the subjection of learning to the coteries of chance intellectual privilege, or to the changing course of corrupt political pressure.

But this theme is only possible for a universal culture. It cannot be explored within the narrow circle of a blinkered intellectual élite. Its relevance is to a truly humane society and not to the merely materialistic interests of the masters of an exploitative society.

The analogy of the independence of the professional which we have used above serves only to give some idea of the order of liberation of individual initiative which must be concurrent with, and at the same time, a consequence of, the indefinite growth of higher education. Another concept of the same type which has more overtones in the arena of organised social functions whether they be industries or social services is that of self-management. Unfortunately, although this subject has thrust itself onto the agenda of political policy because of the deepending malaise infecting and rendering increasingly unstable the traditional relationship between the master who managed and the men and women who were managed, it has lacked credibility, partly because it has not been linked with the education of the majority of the workers.

Yet it has always been a thoroughly accepted concept in organisations where the educational status is of the same order throughout. Indeed, it is an essential part of the organisational ethos of even very large Universities, though it has been traditionally confined to the academic staff. In theory anyway, and even to a large extent in practice, it has never been held to be incompatible with efficient management. As the advanced countries move into the knowledge industries, or even the service industries like hospitals, the proportion of the workforce for whom such a self-managing concept becomes, not merely credible, but essential, increases rapidly.

It follows from the above, that we do not suggest that the extension of truly significant higher education to everyone is a matter simply of educational change. It is probably truer that broad and far-reaching changes in the structures, goals and power distribution in societies have a greater influence in liberating the demand for education (which is the essential power behind its expansion) than *vice versa*. But since the latter is also an important factor in catalysing broader social changes, they cannot be considered as independently variable. The relative lack of demand from manual workers for higher education is, of course, a product, not merely of their deprived education background, but of their dependent, vulnerable position in employment and their exploited social status.

These factors conspire to render all save the most determined children from manual workers' families, or those who, by the accident of having a parent or grandparent with a much higher than average educational background, or of having been adopted for patronage by a particularly conscientious teacher, not merely apathetic, but even hostile to levels of educational aspiration which clearly have little place within the normal ambitions and work and life perspectives of their class. It is these same ambitions and perspectives which have to be changed if the latent demand for education is to come to the conscious surface.

And this means not merely restructuring education, but simultaneously restructuring the nature of work, employment, production and social organisation in such a way as both to demand and demonstrate the relevance and possibility of a much higher educational level among the people. Fortunately for the ultimate credibility of this programme, it happens to be equally necessary for the continued economic and social prosperity since, as was demonstrated in Chapter 7, it corresponds broadly to the next stage in the onwards progress of industrial change. However, once again it must be stressed that it does not happen automatically nor does each country maintain an equal position.

Projections of the future growth of higher education such as those criticised in Chapter 5 are not merely based on mistaken assumptions and a completely inadequate study of past trends, they are confused with the quite different task of formulating policy. Though we have spent much time in this book in the analysis of the past long term processes of expansion of higher education, and though we have found that for long periods they have followed exponential paths of considerable regularity, our purpose is not to make still another prophecy of the future to replace the erroneous ones which are used to bolster up present official plans. The future is to be made, not to be merely forecast, it depends much more on policies than on projections. What then, are the uses of the studies of past trends? They serve to reveal the social and political and economic factors which must be taken into account in devising policy. They show the inertias which have to be overcome.

But the future is never completely at the mercy of these past trends. What will actually happen will depend even more on the vision, the will and the determination with which we start changing them. However, we are not completely free to take any path we wish. We live in a world which is faced with sharp discontinuities in the nature of its future development. These arise from the enormous new possibilities of the application of knowledge. More inevitably than any individual country, the world economy will respond to these new possibilities. This response will set the stage within which the individual countries will have to fashion their part of the action. It is unlikely that any will be able to remain in a stationary position. The individual countries or groups will either seize the initiative and go forward or they will fall back towards the relative state of underdevelopment. Whether we take the former path or the latter will undoubtedly depend on whether we are able to increase indefinitely both the demand for higher education and its utilisation in the economy, the social services and in raising the quality of life.

Where does the responsibility lie in the mounting of a comprehensive policy, both for education and for its use in the economy? As we have seen, it would also require a restructuring of large areas of industry and the economy, as well as the even more difficult tasks of retraining and of humane and liberating social transition. The ultimate responsibility for orchestrating all the necessary responses from education, industry, the social and public services, and the organisations and institutions of workers and professionals of all kinds must lie with governments. In the past, when the interconnection and problems of balance between these various factors was less apparent and when the hectic processes of spontaneous growth of each could proceed far without much regard for that in the others, it may have been possible to disregard the need for such a comprehensive policy, though, as we have seen, such spontaneity was always at the mercy of the sharp changes in the leading edge of development, which in turn occasioned the sharp changes in the relative position of different nations. But now the interconnections between knowledge and application became ever closer. The time lag between discovery and application becomes ever shorter. The hazards of losing momentum become greater. The social strains and confrontations become more intense.

Yet though the responsibility for policy must lie with government, it does not follow that the necessary initiative will come from that source. Indeed, the policy itself must ultimately derive, not merely from the variety and complexity of the various factors of production, public service and education, which must be co-ordinated. Though their actual present states and possibilities of growth both constrain and set the scene for a policy of what we might now call human resource investment and development, they do not determine its goals. These must arise from the participants themselves. Only goals which embody the aspirations of the majority of the people can fire their desire for knowledge. A culture truly representative of the majority will not be the caricature feared by Steiner or Eliot, or by Pasternak, who moaned that Mayakovsky had suffered a second death when he became posthumously the popular poet of the common Russian people. But neither will it be simply a diluted version of the high culture of today, though doubtless the great creative artists will retain their universality as they always have. Nor will the relevance of knowledge to social needs be a simple projection of the needs of today's ethically emasculated market economy. The pressure for change must increasingly come from below. The main question is not how to change the policy of government, but how to generate the popular demand for change. The former will almost inevitably be restricted to the narrow short term perspectives and penny pinching policies that have been outlined in Chapter 5, unless they are shaken from their complacency by a rising tide of informed demand.

The responsibility for generating this demand lies firstly on those who are already highly educated, and who are also conscious of the unnecessarily exclusive nature of their privilege; the teachers at all levels, the research workers and the creative writers. They are the cultural élite whose proper moral role is the destruction of élitism as an exclusive creed. But equally it lies with the real activists, by which we mean the dedicated workers in the trade unions, the community organisations, the parent/teacher groups, the multitude of organisations concerned with human welfare, those who give their energies because their primary concern is with the quality of the lives of those among whom they work, rather than the grinding of the axes of personal ambition or particular political sectarianism. The aim of this book is to suggest to them that their efforts cannot be successful unless all their other goals include and imply the extension of higher education to almost everyone. Education is not by itself a solution to, nor perhaps the principal weapon in, the struggle of the deprived majority of human beings to achieve freedom and full participation in deciding their own destinies. But it is a marker of the extent of travel towards success, an essential test of whether the progress achieved is merely temporary or records a permanent advance in the human condition. We have endeavoured to demonstrate that there is no known reason why the vast majority of the people should not make that advance. The will is all.

CHAPTER ELEVEN

Towards a Policy for Universal Higher Education

This book was originally planned to end with the previous chapter summing up the case for extending higher education to everyone. It implied the need for a deliberate political strategy to realise this objective. But the validity of the argument and the importance, even the urgency, of moving decisively towards the objective, does not depend on a prior solution of all the policy problems involved.

Indeed, the movement towards universal higher education is bound to be a complex process hardly predictable in detail. We have aimed to show that it is unlikely to be achieved by education policy alone. Educational liberation, like all great advances in the extension of freedom, can only follow from a broader struggle for economic social and political liberation. In this struggle the content, the forms and the institutions of education, are bound to be changed as they reflect the aspirations and experience of vastly greater numbers of the people. It is important to realise this dynamic nature of the future course of development of higher education, since otherwise its expansion will be viewed as a mere extension of its present models to full mass-production scale.

This mechanical projection of the arid orthodoxies and emasculated professional specialisms of late 20th century high culture into the indefinite future underlies the scepticism of some intellectuals of the extreme left, as well as the extreme right. The former sometimes see all institutionalised education as a means of stabilising the capitalist social *status quo*. The extension of access to higher education to a proportion of working class children is then viewed as a strategy of defusing the struggle of the class for liberation. The views of the latter have been examined in Chapters 8 and 9. It may only be added here that their opposition to the "dilution" of their meritocratic society became so extreme in the early 1980s that some of them welcomed and supported savage cuts in the budgets of their own institutions, even though they cut into their own intellectual privileges for the sake of the greater good of combating the democratisation of higher education.

The view of many "progressive" educationalists lies somewhere between these two extreme positions. They tend to see the practicable future as a very gradual widening of social access by the simple expansion of higher education, conceived mainly in its present forms and content. However, the dilemma remains that the spontaneous vast expansion of access over the whole post-war period has only slightly reduced the relatively much greater participation of the professional and managerial (or so-called "service") classes and has in fact increased their absolute numerical superiority, particularly in the Universities. Hence the most optimistic forecast of this group is that expansion must lead to more inequality before it eventually might lead to more equality. The expansion of access to higher education is still seen as an extension of patronage, enabling a proportion of the more intelligent children of the working class to climb to an higher cultural and social position than their parents and effectively to become associate members of the professional and managerial classes.

The apparent apathy of many working class parents to the prolongation of the education of their children appears merely as an irritating and somewhat incomprehensible "conservatism" to "progressive" intellectuals who favour this kind of scenario. They have no concept of the struggle for education arising from the struggle of the working class for wider economic and social liberation.

We have given reasons in the foregoing chapters for holding the view that the higher education is far too important to be left to policies based on any of these defeatist or half-hearted projections. It is necessary to develop still further the reasons why we believe this to be the case. They rest on the demonstration that we made at the outset, that all the means of production and reproduction of our material and social and cultural life are in the process of being ever more rapidly transformed by the impact of new knowledge. At the same time the enormous problems of poverty, deprivation and conflict throughout the world are such that it is inconceivable that this continuous revolution in our ways of work and social organisation can be halted before they are solved. Increasingly only those with higher education will be able to take part in deciding the outcome. In the meantime, it is possible that its expansion could lead to an increase rather than a decrease in inequality, not only in education, but in every other form of social and material privilege, and above all, in the privilege of skilled and creative employment. Hence the present and immediate future situations are socially and culturally unstable. It is necessary for any viable education policy to be so interwoven with social and economic policy, to be designed to overcome just those inertias which we have described in the preceding chapters, whose mechanical acceptance leads to one or other of such scenarios of rejection or muted acceptance, as the three which we have mentioned above.

It is not our objective here to attempt to put forward a comprehensive policy to this end. Indeed, we would hold that the social and economic changes that are necessary may be more important than changes in the forms and formalities of education in releasing the latent demand for higher education among the majority of the people. We have defined higher education as that level of education associated with participating in the decision making levels of production and social organisation. It is probable that only as a democratisation of the management of society comes to be seen as practicable by the majority of the people that they or their children will fully visualise the need for higher education for themselves. And as they begin to conceive of its necessity they will have to participate in changing its very nature and its forms.

Hence any programme or policy for educational change must be flexible and open to continuous transformation in the light, not only of educational experience, but experience in the wider deomocratisation of industry and public service. The fact that we can be certain about the need and the practicability for a continuous extension of higher education to everyone does not depend on certainty about the precise sequence of steps required to bring it about. These will have to be learned by the experience, not only of the policy makers and managers of educational institutions, or even by the teachers, but also by the experience of the participants. As we suggested in the last chapter, the actual extension of higher education to ever wider sections of the working people must be the actual diagnostic test that that policy is progressing in the right direction, provided always that its extension is accompanied by its proper application; the ever widening participation of the people in the management and design of their own futures; the liberation of their own creative lives.

The mechanical projections of future higher education rest on a misconception of the dynamic of its past development. We have shown in the first chapters that the rate of student enrolments has been continuously accelerating since the middle of the 19th century. Its growth has been concurrent and closely parallel to that of the professional and managerial classes in modern society. This is not surprising since over the major part of this period the children of these classes have dominated the entrance to Universities and Colleges. Modern institutions of higher education differ more or less sharply in character from those of the previous several centuries, mainly because they reflect the intellectual needs of these professional sections who now execute the functional management of the major industries and State services. During this century of unprecedented expansion, although the Universities have remained the main institutional form of higher education, their inner content, the self images of their members and their concepts of the nature of learning have been more or less completely transformed.

The illusion of the immutability of high culture probably persists because the nature of culture and hence the nature and content of higher education has always been given its form and definition by the intellectual sections of the professional classes. Indeed, this has always been their main social role and the *raison d'etre* for their patronage by the real rulers of each succeeding period. It is this continuity of social function which underlies the concept of a continuous intellectual tradition, and indeed does give a certain continuity to certain of the forms, and especially of the rituals embodied in the cultural and educational institutions. But the objectives towards which the pursuit of knowledge is directed and the purposes expressed in those objectives have always been shaped by the interests and values of the dominant ruling classes.

But in the capitalist State, the general interests of the ruling capitalist class and their classic form of distributing profit and power among themselves by the operation of the "free" market, can only be served by a high culture which accepts the task of providing an intellectual apologia of the *status quo* aimed at acceptability to the whole population. To carry out this function the intellectual classes, and to an increasing extent the whole of the professional classes, have to invent an ethos which is at least formally separated, even from the values and objectives of their own patrons. Objectivity, intellectual integrity, puts on its modern amoral, neutral, positivistic face. The concepts of knowledge for its own sake and its professional counterpart of efficiency for its own sake assume their over-arching cultural significance.

Of course, none of these features of the role of intellectuals in society are entirely new. Prototypes of the modern "dispassionate", purely objective, quasi-scientific culture have always existed, as have individual professional servants of the ruling class, with the prescience to conceive of their role as the wider one of impartially serving the whole of society. But in neither case would they have been able to escape from the fact that the intellectual world in which they speculated, or the practical action open to them, was basically defined and constrained by the dominant purposes of the dominant rulers of their societies.

But it is only in the past 100 years or so that higher education has become completely impregnated with the values of the professional classes themselves. The character that these have imposed on the Universities and other institutions was briefly outlined in Chapter 9. Even ancient Universities to which entry had for centuries been the prerogative of birth or social status (with only a tiny proportion admitted on intellectual performance) were forced to adopt the meritocratic principles of selection which legitimise the new status of the professional classes.

As we have seen in Chapters 6 and 7 this corresponded to the new stage of development of capitalist economy in which new knowledge moves from the periphery of the forces of production to a central position, where "cultural" capital overtakes material capital in its dynamic effect on industry and State services and where the professionally qualified become increasingly the actual functional controllers and the managers of both State and private enterprise. And as we have seen in Chapters 8 and 9, this was inevitably accompanied by a more or less fundamental change in the character of the culture of higher education.

Even as late as the mid-19 century, the self-image of the leading Universities would have still been as centres of an integrated and essentially holistic culture, expressing values still essentially based on orthodox (State) religious foundations. They would have hardly conceived the possibility of embracing a large part (perhaps the majority) of their modern curriculum. The secular, highly specialised, fragmented and amoral life of the majority of their modern academic counterparts would have been almost unimaginable.

It was not merely that science, and later technology, were to become increasingly dominant and eventually indeed, to take the largest share, both of University studies and also of their resources. It was rather that the positivistic philosophy which reflects the enormous proliferation and separation of modern sciences and sub-sciences was to cast its methodological shadow over almost the whole of University studies. The word "specialist" with its implication of hegemony over fields of discovery absolutely closed (indeed incomprehensible) to the outsider, had not been invented in 1850. By 1950 it had become for all practical purposes the only recognised badge of academic respectability.

Again, we would stress that this essentially modern elevation of ignorance of any learning, except one's own narrow field, to a principle of cultural orthodoxy reflects the new social function of the professional classes who were now asserting their own proliferation and reproduction as the main aim of higher education. The professional classes, as we have stressed, have grown with exponential acceleration in the century from 1850. They have moved into the centre of the management of the economy and the State. But they have not yet changed the essential relationships on which the division of the production of society is based. While they may compete for control with the capitalist class itself, they have not replaced that class, at least in Western capitalist society. Their influence is based, not on the ownership of the means of production, nor of formal power in the State, but on their function as necessary experts in the increasingly complex business of running the institutions of modern society. But they were drawn into these functions precisely because of their specialised knowledge. Their strength depended on their autonomy as specialists. It is this autonomy which also expresses their weakness. They are indispensable in their own relatively narrow areas of control. But this very indispensability of specialised knowledge may render them incapable of more general responsibility. The amorality and neutrality also reveals its limitations, its relative impotence in the main issues which confront society as a whole. Their cultural archetype is an Oppenheimer, supreme in his master of the science necessary to create the Atom Bomb, but unable even to imagine the language in which to argue the necessity for its social control.

The nature of higher education has changed. It can change again. The principle agent of change has been precisely those classes in society who have penetrated it and virtually taken it over. We may expect that the future transformation of higher education to serve the needs of the whole people will similarly be accomplished only in the course of their penetration of it and in the concurrent democratisation of the application of knowledge to social praxis. Thus we may also reject the pessimism of those left wing intellectuals who are sceptical about the extension of access to the existing institutions of higher education. The democratisation of higher education cannot wait until its present content, social functions and institutional forms are transformed. While the struggle to widen the access to the existing institutions and the existing professional social functions for which they prepare cannot be a final goal, it must be a major instrument for the changes in both, which will ultimately emerge as necessary.

It does not follow from this, as some of their spokesmen would claim, that the present professional (or intellectual) class is the new universal class, nor that present high culture is the ultimate universal model for culture. Its limitations, which we have only briefly sketched above, are only too apparent. In those States where its bureaucratic and technocratic wings have taken over the main control of society entirely from the older propertied classes, it has even become the main conservative force, holding back the economic, political and social liberation of the majority of the people through its own limited vision and narrow range of self interests.

Hence a programme for higher education for everyone can only mature as part of the struggle of the majority for their liberation from all the constraints and social and economic barriers which hold them in an alienated and subordinate position. It will take shape as the organisations of the community and particularly of the working class assert their demands, but also as they incorporate into those demands their experience, their needs, their own growing concepts of the relevance of knowledge to human welfare, to the liberation of their class, and indeed of the liberation of society as a whole. The task of refashioning a universal culture cannot be undertaken by any group less than the majority of the people. The only universal class is everyone.

A strategy of demands for the development and reform of Higher Education must include the following areas, all of which are interdependent:

the expansion of student enrolments, both absolutely and by the ever-widening participation of the working class;

institutional change directed towards a comprehensive system of higher education of real equality of status;

the reform of the curricula of higher education to make it relevant to the cultural and social potential and the economic and political interests of the majority of the people;

the application of education throughout all areas of employment and social life to raise the dignity as well as the productivity and creativity of work and to give vitality to the quality of life and culture of the common people. Each of these aims stands in sharp contrast to the present policy, indeed, they each demand a complete reversal of present trends.

In contrast with the escalation of the 60s and the reversion to steady expansion of the early 70s, the last decade has witnessed, for the first time in post war period, indeed, probably for the first time for at least 50 years, policies deliberately planned to reduced the entry to higher education below the effective demand. The net effect has been almost wholly at the expense of working class participation. There is no evidence that the momentum of expansion of entry from the professional and managerial classes has been in any way inhibited.

The first attack came by the decimation of entry to the teacher training colleges as described in Chapter 5. The students so eliminated were essentially those with the lower entry qualifications previously acceptable for teacher training for primary and secondary modern schools. This was one of the most significant channels of entry of working class children, since it enabled even those late developers who were able to rise to the necessary minimum level after the inhibiting effects of early cultural deprivation, to get a foothold in higher education. It can have hardly affected the position of the children of the professional and managerial classes. In fact, the fairly sharply rising proportion of those classes in the University entry of this decade (as compared with a relatively constant percentage during the previous decade), is probably to be explained in part by their transfer from Teacher Training College to University studies. By contrast, the proportion of working class students in the Universities also fell steadily from 1970 to 1980 (from 30 per cent to 23 per cent) which is consistent with the almost complete absence of any transfer from the shrinking area of teacher training. The same picture is probably broadly true for the entry to Polytechnics.

The fact that the decimation of the teacher training colleges was largely carried out under a Labour Government may account in part for the fact that this heavy blow at the participation of working class children in higher education met with relatively little organised opposition from the working class movement. The official excuse for it was the supposedly declining numbers of school children to be expected from the demographic forecasts. Yet, throughout the whole period concerned, the same output of teachers could have been used to introduce urgently necessary staffing increases in the primary and secondary schools in the deprived areas. These are almost the only external factors which can help to offset the cultural disadvantages of working class children. Unfortunately, education, which could be the major investment in future cultural capital and eventually in economic productivity, was regarded solely as a consumption item in the National budget.

Alternatively, a part of the effort and capital resources of the Colleges could have been used to supplement the gravely inadequate provision for further education, particularly of those who leave school at the minimum age. As it was, new College buildings were in some cases abandoned before the last bricks were laid, and many decades before the loan charges for their construction, which had been incurred by the local authorities, would be paid off. Worse still, the large numbers of highly skilled staff who were displaced, were to be the first of a growing tide of redundancies and premature retirements throughout the higher education system in the following decade as the resources of all higher education were to be squeezed. This waste of assets of the highest importance to future material, as well as social progress, was the main sign of the failure of National confidence that we have described in Chapter 5.

A cessation of expansion to the Universities and Polytechnics, still more, a planned fall in enrolments, will be bound to cause an even sharper decline in the proportion of working class entrants than that of the decade of the 70s (shown in Fig. 4.1b). The reasons for this will now be obvious. There is no indication at all of any lessening of the expansion of demand for places from the children of the middle class, particularly those from professional and managerial families. The continuous expansion of the age group of University entry from these classes is almost independent of overall demographic factors, since the classes themselves have been expanding exponentially for many decades as a proportion of the population, because of economic and social changes in the structure of employment (as shown in Fig. 2.6). Indeed, their future rate of increase is almost bound to escalate from the previous figure of about 2.5 per cent per annum to nearer 5 per cent per annum partly as a result of the student explosion of the period from 1955 to 1970. But an examination of the entering qualifications to Universities shows, as would be expected, that those from the working class have markedly lower formal ('A' level) standards than the entrants from professional families. As we have demonstrated in Chapter 8 this has little to do with differences of innate ability, but like all differential social class performance is to be expected from the infinitely more favourable early cultural and motivational environment of children from educated families.

However, faced with a stationary or declining enrolment, it is almost inevitable that admission tutors to Universities and Polytechnics will use formal entrance qualifications as the main test of whom to eliminate. It will not be the children of the educated classes. We may forecast that with a stationary total annual enrolment the proportion of working class entrants will decline steadily from this factor alone.

Furthermore, this will be supplemented by an absolute decline in the number of working class children who, though minimally qualified, do not apply for admission, and even more by those who, though qualified to stay on at school to prepare for admission, leave at the minimum age of 16. Already in the first years of the 80s the enormous rise of unemployment among the working class is having this direct effect, as the social security payment available to the unemployed 16 year old (but not available if he or she stays at school) becomes necessary to supplement the family budget.

A continuous expansion of enrolments to higher education is a necessary (though not sufficient) condition even to maintain the present proportion of working class students. Although the age participation rate for the children of the most senior professional class has now reached a logistic limit and expansion of entry from this source will be limited to the (nevertheless relatively fast) rate of expansion of the class itself; this is by no means yet the case for other large sections of the higher income groups, particularly the children from the managerial and executive classes. In fact, the continued expansion of the age participation rate from these groups is most probably a major factor in the continued buoyancy of demand for University places, despite the decline from the children of the working class. It may be presumed that this continued pressure from the middle class will be satisfied since the strategies of preparation open to the parents of children from these privileged income groups can almost guarantee successful placement in higher education.

Hence, it would not be difficult to estimate a minimum rate of overall expansion of enrolment into higher education which would be necessary to leave vacancies for an expanded intake from the working class. By this method it would be possible to establish annual targets for enrolment which would then require to be monitored, both for actual overall numerical achievement and in terms of progress towards a more equal social participation. The establishment of such a process of setting annual targets for the expansion of higher education, instead of the largely irrelevant projections based on erroneous use of demographic data must be demanded as a main base for future planning policy. Nevertheless, however necessary targets may be for planning processes, the actual entry policy must aim to take every qualified applicant each year. The continuance of the Robbins principle though, as we have seen, not sufficient to extend the social franchise of higher education, is a minimum condition to avoid its more or less rapid decline.

To give an indication of the overall quantitative expansion that is necessary we may estimate that unless total enrolments increase by at least 5-6 per cent per annum, i.e. between the average rate for the first half of the century and the escalated rate of the 60s, then there will be little possibility for a long period of increasing the participation of the working class in higher education. It may be noted in passing that even with this rate of annual expansion, it would take Britain over 25 years to catch up with the overall age participation rates already achieved in Japan and the USA.

Given a commitment to provide places for every qualified applicant, the main long term problem is to increase the effective demand from the underprivileged sections of society, from the children of manual workers and especially those from the deprived areas, particularly from girls, who are under-represented throughout the social strata, but above all, from the daughters of unskilled workers whose present chance of entering higher education is almost negligible. The factors which depress the demand from these sectors of the people are well enough known in broad outline, though there is little understanding of their relative weight. In Chapter 4 we summed their total effect as resulting in a low perception of the chances of success in gaining entrance to higher education, so that the value attached to it lacks reality.

Our competitive education system is like a ladder in which a large proportion of the children fall behind at each stage. In such a system, survival depends crucially on the family and class environment which must provide by example and support, both the motivation and method of adaptation to the existing educational cultural patterns. It reflects the values, aspirations and outlook of the lives of the professional classes, from which most students naturally emerge. The sheer unreality of the idea of higher education as a possible future, must be the major long term factor retarding the growth of a spontaneous demand for it among working class children until, in most cases, it is too late. For those who do survive, the cost in lost wages or social security benefit, particularly in the crucial years from 16-19, may take them out of the race. Finally, the absence of educational opportunities and economic help to bridge the educational gap between school leaving and University or College entrance takes over as main impediment to those who might win through to a late appreciation of the value of more education.

Any programme of action designed to increase the effective demand for higher education from working class children must involve a simultaneous attack on all these questions, since they are closely interrelated. The most immediate effect could probably be obtained by eliminating the economic disincentive to leave school at the minimum age by providing grants (at least at the level of the corresponding social security payments) to those staying on at school or at Sixth Form Colleges, or taking bridging courses in further educational institutes. At present the State spends about six times the amount of public money on the post-school education of the child of a senior professional family as on the child of a labourer. The poor are truly being taxed to educate the children of the rich. This measure would only slightly redress the balance, particularly since for some years to come it would be largely recouped from a reduction in unemployment pay. On the other hand the proposal to provide merely a token grant of a few pounds a week for this purpose, as was proposed previously by a liberally minded politician, would probably have the opposite effect, since it would have little effect on the bulk of working class children and merely further subsidise those from better off families or from the most skilled sections of manual workers.

More generally, it is necessary to secure that virtually all school leavers continue their education in some form of full-time or part-time further education and training. For many years to come the accessibility and apparent relevance of these courses to a major proportion of children from working class families must appear to be much greater than the more remote possibility of entrance to higher education as presently conceived. Nevertheless, they can, and should, be conceived as bridging courses leading to the possibity of later entry to full higher education. In our view it is a profound mistake to consider that this aim must be in conflict with either their short term relevance or their suitability for students with little previous formal qualifications. Most of the technological studies which, with their scientific counterparts, consume the major part of the resources of present-day higher education had their origin in the Mechanics Institutes of the 19th century, long before the Universities had the vision to see their future importance. Even until recently there was a continuous ladder, almost unique to this country, of technical education from the craft to the professional level. It is vitally urgent that ladder be restored, but in such a way that a much larger proportion of those starting on it are given the opportunity of spending the educational effort and time necessary to ascend it.

But even more in the non-technical fields, and especially in the expanding service areas, is it now necessary that all young workers (especially those not able to obtain employment) should be provided with relevant education courses capable of reaching professional level. This is already becoming an evident necessity in all employment connected with the health services and indeed, in community care occupations of every kind. But in the growing areas of the service industries in general, ranging from entertainment of all kinds to every form of consumer needs, the scope for a higher level of human interest and personal skill could be based on a relatively unlimited continuation of educational opportunity. One need only mention the recent transition of many areas of work in the medical field (nursing, physiotherapy, chiropody etc.) from the status of relatively unskilled (and poorly paid) labour to full professional and graduate status, or the even more recent burgeoning of the relevance of further and higher educational studies to the communications industries, to entertainment, sport and leisure provision of all kinds.

This country, which had perhaps the oldest tradition of some form of continuity from elementary craft training to full professional status has for many decades lagged behind its major competitors in the profession of universal post school education and training of this intermediate kind. We stress again that this should be regarded as an end in itself only from the short term point of view, but conceived in the longer term as a bridge to a more comprehensive system of universal higher education. As we showed in Chapter 1, it is only the latter which can give that general capacity for self-management and equal participation in decision making which is ultimately necessary in a democratic society. But nevertheless, the areas of intermediate further education must probably play a vital part, both in the period of transition, and indeed in providing the experience which will widen the concept and enrich the curriculum and content of future higher education.

The vital importance of the further education system in this transition period lies, above all, in its tradition and experience in providing continuing education and training, which is nearest to universal in its breadth and scope. It has never insisted on any prior qualifications and is practised in devising courses to suit every possible kind and level of demand. It has flexibility to provide both the motivation and the cultural bridge for the late developer, however late. At the same time it has always suffered from the vulnerability consequent on its own flexibility. As we pointed out in Chapter 3 it has always been used by education authorities both National and Local as a surge tank which could be expanded to take a temporary bulge in demand, but cut severely as the effective demand receded. Precisely this casual and irresponsible attitude of successive administrations has been mainly responsible for the fact that its work has never been accorded the cultural status and importance that it deserves, nor have its students, coming as most of them do, from the more deprived social sectors, been given the financial underpinning accorded to the middle class youth entering formal higher education.

The most glaring example of this is that whereas maintenance grants for all students entering full-time higher education are mandatory, only a small proportion of those wishing to enter full-time courses in further education or even in the Polytechnics on intermediate level courses can obtain grants (which are at the discretion of the education authorities). It would be difficult to find a more flagrant example of the principle of robbing the cultural have-nots to pay for the increased culture of those who already have it. Hence, a vital immediate goal in the struggle for the access of the working class to education is the abolition of this discrimination in grants. Even more anomalous is the system which decrees that virtually no full-time student in higher education pays any fees, whereas part-time students who come, on the whole, from the poorer sections of the population, are charged an increasingly large proportion of the cost. The complete abolition of fees throughout our educational system is therefore a vitally needed reform if the economic barriers to educational equality of opportunity are to be removed.

Before moving on to consider the interrelation of all parts of the further and higher education system, it is necessary to mention, however briefly, that the major institutional contribution to the objective of increasing the effective demand for higher education from the children of the working class cannot be made by the institutions of post-school education alone, though they can do much to cultivate it as it does emerge and to revive it when it has been interrupted. But the main instrument of the education system itself in stimulating the demand for education must inevitably be the primary and secondary schools. The idea that schools and post-school education can be fundamentally in competition with each other for the major share of a limited pool of resources can only be fostered by those politicians and professionals who have no interest in extending the social franchise of education.

If, as we assert, school education must have as a major objective, the preparation of children from working class families for an equal opportunity of progressing to higher education, then the expansion of resources that they must require for this purpose must lead to an increased demand for further and higher education. Conversely, the current policies of actually reducing the effective demand for higher education will inevitably be used to justify further restrictions on the schools since they are designed to lead to earlier school leaving and a smaller demand for the provision of upper school staff. But above all, a serious strategy of development of educational motivation among children coming from deprived backgrounds requires more school resources, particularly of highly qualified staff than the rather easier task of monitoring the learning of those already motivated.

This book, which is essentially about higher education cannot attempt to deal with these problems of primary and secondary schools, but can only recognise that the educational main effort must lie in these areas. However, we must recall one theme which, though a matter for the schools, is essential to the concept of higher education for everyone, that we have developed in the earlier chapters. This is simply that secondary education should aim to prepare virtually all children for the continuance of their education in further, and eventually higher, education. We stress this because of the apparent conflict that may arise between this aim (when it is conceived as only relevant to the most "academic" minority) and the aim of a more practical preparation for life (and for their appropriate station in it) for the majority.

The detailed problems of curriculum and teaching methods in secondary education cannot be treated here. But we have been concerned to dispel the illusion that those who pass on to higher education have inherited some special "academic" cast of mind which alone qualifies them for it. We have dealt with the breakdown of the supposed evidence for this concept in Chapter 8. The complementary illusion is that the remaining majority of children (who happen to come from working class families) are more "practically" minded and hence, would not find it possible to take advantage of higher education. Of course there appears to be a great deal of pragmatic reality in this division of children into "academic" and "practical" types. But it arises mainly from the self-perpetuating nature of the socio-cultural division of labour which we have discussed earlier, and partly from the narrowness and sterility of much in the present conspectus of higher education which both reflects and sustains these social divisions. Inevitably, therefore, the struggle to raise the motivation of the children of manual workers for continued education poses complex problems at school level which can only find an ultimate solution as the nature of higher education itself, and hence the shadow it casts before it on the schools is changed. But nevertheless, the division of children into those suitable and those unsuitable for higher education must be combated at every stage of the primary and secondary schools.

Reform of the system of higher education will not in itself be sufficient to create the effective demand for it, especially among the children of the under-represented social strata. But the present chaotic mix of unconnected further and higher educational institutions present a major barrier to the emergence and satisfaction of that potential demand. It is sometimes justified as presenting opportunities for the widest range of abilities and of fulfilling so-called vocational and non-vocational needs. But even in its entirety, and apart from the enormous difference of status and resource allocation of its various parts, it fails to draw into systematic post-school education the majority of school leavers.

Its main weakness is the relatively complete absence of effective inter-relationship of its various parts. Transfer from one part of the system to another is rare. It freezes the social apartheid in education which has been formed at the school level. It helps to freeze the division between two cultures of the professional classes on the one hand and the working class on the other. Hence, it also reflects the political, economic and social divisions between the masters of society and the masses. It also gives a form and institutional credibility to the illusion that there are two kinds of knowledge, pure knowledge pursued for its own sake by the intellectual élite in the Universities and practical knowledge which is the business of the other (public) part of the system and the only kind necessary to provide for the majority of the people. If higher education is ever to be realised for the majority of the people, there must be a comprehensive system. To emphasise the ultimate aim the appropriate institutional form and title should be the Comprehensive University.

The credibility of this as an educational institution has already been established in several parts of the world, but principally in the United States, where in several States the majority of school leavers proceed to some section or other of the State University. These Comprehensive Universities comprise a considerable number of largely self-governing Colleges of varying kinds, falling mainly within a regular pattern of community colleges, liberal arts and other undergraduate colleges and graduate schools. Our aim is not to suggest that all these components of a comprehensive system of higher education, yet have equal intellectual status, still less a uniformity of curricula. But they have a broad parity of social status and resource allocation and they are integrated into common educational aim to provide the maximum flexibility of movement from one part to another.

They cannot and should not attempt that peculiar concentration of specialist undergraduate training which we have described as the prevailing characteristic of many departments of our own Universities, yet they educate a much larger proportion of their population to research doctorate level than their British counterparts. They demonstrate that even if such narrow criteria of excellence were regarded as the critique of quality, there is no need to sacrifice quality to quantity. Of course, there are American academics who look with nostalgic envy at the open élitism of the British system. It is perhaps a more rewarding system for the privileged few who enjoy it and for the academics who enjoy the privileged position of ministering to them. The basically comprehensive system of higher education in America, largely within the University network, provides higher education, mainly full time, which now takes in about 50 per cent of the total age group, about four times the proportion in Britain.

However, we mention the American scene simply to show the feasibility of the concept of a comprehensive university, not to suggest that it should be copied by this country. Japan has also reached almost American levels of popular participation in university level education, using a much more classical form of university institution, both private and public, but taking advantage of the unprecedented demand from its extremely rapidly developing economy for graduates, to stimulate the effective demand for higher education from all sections of the population.

In many countries the surge of student unrest and consequent public criticism which followed the escalation of student enrolments in the 60s, led to more or less drastic reforms in both the institutional form and internal government of the universities and colleges. In most European countries the rigid previous structure of professional authoritarian government of the universities was changed by Government decree to admit the representation of other staff, including non-teaching employees and of students. This was followed in some cases by formal moves to set up comprehensive universities such as the Gesamthochschulen in several States of Germany which brought together the equivalent of our universities, colleges of education and technical colleges into one institution. In other countries, such as France, the non-university colleges were upgraded in importance and given priority over the universities in the allocation of resources. In Scandinavian countries a very rapid widening of the entry of the working class children to universities was set under way. These changes in their various ways are further indications that the old division between high culture enshrined above all in the European universities and the more mundane business of so-called vocational training, is breaking down.

Again, we are not suggesting an imitation of the practices of the other European countries. Indeed, from the point of view of social apartheid in higher education, they have previously been even more rigidly upper and middle class oriented than the British, largely because their industrial development, coming later, owed less to the ingenuity and invention of the skilled worker. Hence, their development of technological education did not arise, as in Britain, from the Mechanics Institutes, but coincided with the emergence of the professional class of engineers and scientists. However, as in so many other fields of social development, Britain is tending to remain frozen in the institutional pattern of the beginning of the century and falling far behind in areas such as the provision of further education in which it formerly led the world.

Much of the rather sterile controversy about the structure of further and higher education in Britain in the post-war period has centred around the division of political control, status and objectives of the two sides of the so-called binary system.

Britain is now the only major country where all the universities are formally private, legally autonomous, self-governing, chartered bodies. On the other hand, virtually all further education and non-university colleges have been formally and legally under the control of public authority (for the most part the Local Authorities) during the whole of the century of their development. Yet today, well over 90 per cent of the income of both sides of the binary system comes from public funds, including student fees of British full-time higher education students, which are nearly all mandatorily payable by local education authorities. This means that the broad objectives of universities are as subject to public control as those of the colleges in the so-called public sector.

Indeed, the universities generally respond relatively faithfully to the Government-set targets, such as the overall student entry and the proportions admitted to the various main areas of study such as the Science-based, the technological, the Arts-based and the Medical schools. The public control over these main parameters of university planning has been somewhat more precise than in the public sector itself, a consequence of the fact noted in earlier chapters that the latter has acted as a flexible (and hence less planned) provision for the overflow from the universities in times of rapid expansion. Examination of the post-war history of resource allocation would show that the unit costs of the universities have also been rather more susceptible to deliberately planned trends approved by government departments. The reason for this is similar. It is easy to forecast the costs of the relatively narrow range of studies in universities compared with the very much more complex and sometimes chaotic range provided in further education in the public sector.

The proper general areas for public planning are precisely these: student intake in the various main areas of study and the control of costs. To which we would add the monitoring of the necessary progress towards the elimination of the social apartheid in higher education. The question of division of responsibility for such overall public planning and target fixing in post-school education between National and Local Authorities is a matter of pragmatic administrative sense rather than a matter of principle. The more important point is that the admission targets and the admission conditions in each sector and indeed (though less precisely) in each institution, should be keyed in with each other in order to eliminate borderline barriers to the continuity of educational advance of students.

The concept of the "comprehensive university" must imply an equivalence of status and complementary functions in each of its constituent parts. The word "university" also implies that within the overall targets properly set by the public bodies, and subject to proper accountability for the resources provided by public funds, each comprehensive institution should be self-governing. It need only be added here, that this means that all sections of members of the institution, students and non-academic staff, as well as academic staff, should play an appropriate part in the overall government of its objectives and in the decisions about the internal allocation of its resources. Indeed, the word "university" has never quite lost the meaning of the whole corporate body of teachers and scholars and it is a natural extension of that meaning to include in its community of learning all the other workers who now are vitally necessary for its function. The concept of a university also implies a universality of fields of interest and an integrated development of knowledge in its relation to society. This is more consonant with the comprehensive university that we have in mind than the fragmented assemblies of unconnected specialist departments who have been held together in uneasy and arbitrary balance in universities in the recent past.

It is not necessary to have a blueprint for the organisation of a comprehensive university to commence the process of linking all post-school education together in a comprehensive system. Within overall National rolling targets for the progressive extension of further and, ultimately, higher education to everyone, appropriate regional and local co-ordinating bodies can be set up. Much previous experience of co-operation at these levels can be utilised. There is no sound reason why the universities should not be included. The fact that, for the present, the intake of full-time students of most universities is National and indeed, international, is no barrier. In fact, the universities have always conducted a great deal of much more localised education, especially in adult education, but also in their special relation with colleges of education. On the other hand, the public sector colleges which previously were the only ones subject to local or regional co-ordination have always undertaken a proportion of higher education with a national, and even international, entry.

The question of academic freedom which is sometimes posed as requiring special treatment for universities is equally relevant to all forms of education. It is not necessarily less protected in countries where the universities are entirely subject to the formal planning of national or regional authorities. It requires constitutional safeguards of the rights of all members (not merely the senior academic staff) of educational institutions to pursue the truth and to publish it freely. It requires above all, a National as well as institutional recognition of the essentially international source of discovery and knowledge and hence, of the main substance of education. In recent years it is unfortunately precisely on this cardinal point that universities, who should be the main guardians of internationalism, have failed to resist Government intervention, particularly the enormous (and internationally almost unique) fee discrimination against foreign students. In fact, it is doubtful whether the private constitutional structure of universities has shown any special value as a protection against attacks on matters supposed to be cardinal to the defence of academic freedom. Among these, the tenured position of academic staff, supposed essential protection against political or other discrimination has recently been shown to be no less vulnerable than that in the public sector against the remorseless economic pressure from the Government. The protection of academic freedom cannot and should not be considered to be in conflict with the planning and co-ordination of educational entry targets and resource allocations with the broad objectives we have discussed above.

The curriculum, the range of subjects considered appropriate for higher education has changed out of recognition over the last century. Yet it may be the even wider range comprehended in the further education system as a whole, which appears to the academic mind a main obstacle to integration into a comprehensive university. It is still widely supposed that there is a distinction of principle between vocational and academic subjects, between profound and the superficial areas of study. Yet insofar as these distinctions have any significance, they can be found co-existing in most subjects within higher education itself. How much so-called research at the post-graduate level is often trivial, a mere tidying up of odd corners of conventional doctrine or the accumulation of a few more of the millions of pieces of factual data which swell out of the bloated research journals? And how much apparently abstract scholarship among the academics is motivated and shaped by no other than the most vocational of purposes, that of promotion in the academic profession itself.

No further or higher education programme of any but the shortest length should be merely vocational in the sense of being tied and restricted in its relevance to a specific job. As a general rule the future viability of such narrow training will be too vulnerable to the onward march of technological change to be of more than temporary value. On the other hand, it is desirable that the majority of educational courses at all stages of life should be more clearly understood in their relevance to practical life than they are now. It is its lack of apparent applicability to the life and the environment of the educationally deprived child which constitutes the most impenetrable barrier to her appreciation of the value of learning. The son of the professional worker is not necessarily more sensitive to the intrinsic interest of abstract thought. He can merely see its applicbility to interests as material as his own standard of living exemplified in the importance of academic qualifications to the professional licences of his parents.

There is no subject of study from theology to theoretical physics which is intrinsically so non-vocational or abstract that it does not gain immeasurably in significance from an appreciation of its impact on human practice. And conversely there is no so-called practical subject from carpentry to chiropody which cannot with advantage be made the subject of more and more profound science and human creative concern. Above all, education or training worthy of the name, of anything more than the shortest duration must link together knowledge, practice and value. The fact that we can consider these aspects of education as intrinsically separable or separately attached to some areas of study rather than others, merely reflects the fragmented charcter of a social order and social division of labour which, for the time being, alienates the majority of workers from the product of their labour and from the control of their own lives.

Since the nature of employment is still the most important factor affecting the quality of life of the majority of people, it is natural that the relevance of education should continue to be grasped most directly in its application to work. But the role of education is always properly directed towards the enlargement of freedom. Education for liberation must always seek to raise the awareness of the student, not only of his own latent talents and interests, but simultaneously of the welfare of the larger human society in which he acts and in which his own creativity can find expression. This essential progression from education to application to human welfare was well expressed by the Scottish philosopher and theologian, John MacMurray, in the precept: "Knowledge is for action and action is for friendship".

Two final comments on the problem of the curriculum of the comprehensive university are necessary in this context. The first is cautionary and repeats the warning we made in Chapter 1 about the confusion of relevance, even vocational relevance, with the merely technical. The notion that even a narrowly conceived economic growth is being held up because of an insufficient emphasis on the technological in further and higher education is an illusion. In actual fact, although Britain has been declining steadily in economic terms, compared with its competitors for a century and even more rapidly in the past decades, it has probably had a larger proportion of its students in the areas of engineering and the hard sciences than almost any other advanced country (see Table 11.1).

The real reasons for decline have been explored in Chapters 6 and 7. They lie in the failure to apply the talents developed in the whole spectrum of education and in the failure to develop the education and to deploy the creative ability of the whole of the workforce. The main weakness has always lain in the structures, especially the management structures of productive industry which have always reflected the continued predominance of the older, capitalist, class in Britain, compared with the more rapid growth of the influence of the professional classes among competing States.

However, the second comment must emphasise that in the new post-industrial world of the future the "relevant" curriculum cannot be achieved by merely correcting the deficiencies of the past. The content of higher education must grow out of the struggle to make it universal and the simultaneous struggle to change the nature of work and social life to give knowledge a new significance to everyone. A vital role in this movement must be played in the development of studies which are relevant to the struggles for liberation themselves. This country lags behind many in the provision of trade union education. The Trade Union movement itself, of course provides an increasing network of courses for its members, mainly on trade union practice, and these need to be extended further. But this is not a substitute for the development of trade union studies as an important area within all further and higher education.

TABLE 11.1

Proportions of Higher Education Entrants in Main Field of Study

New Entrants per cent

Subject	Britain 1973	Germany 1974	Japan 1972	Sweden 1972	USA (graduates) 1974
Pure Science	28.1	21.2	24.2*	11.9	8.6
Technology	15.3	9.6		10.9	5.3
Agriculture	1.7	2.3	3.6	0.7	1.4
Total Science and Technology	45.1	33.1	27.8	23.5	15.3
Social Science inc. Law	19.5	20.2	43.9	46.7	36.5
Humanities	18.8	23.7	14.2	25.6	15.8
Others, inc. Education, Medicine, Fine Arts	16.6	23	14.1	4.2	32.4

*Note: In Japan most science students are enrolled in technical colleges and classified as technology students; it is therefore not possible to separate the science and technology figures.

Source: I. Hecquet, C. Verniers and L. Cerych, Recent Student Flows in Higher Education, International Council for Educational Development. Paris 1976.

At this moment almost every university and polytechnic in Britain has developed special institutes for Management studies. The annual expenditure of public money in each of many of these, far exceeds the total amount of public money spent on trade union education throughout all levels of education in the country. A large part of this public money is devoted to teaching managers the tactics and strategy of countering the demands of Trade Unions. Yet there is not a single university or polytechnic institute of trade union studies performing a task of similar scope for the education of trade unionists. The contribution of the universities to this equally important field of vocational studies is confined to a relatively insignificant sprinkling of evening extra-mural classes in the field of adult education.

In the various military training schools large sums of public money are spent on training young men to make war, with some evidence of an increasing emphasis on special preparation for dealing with civil disturbances. Up to the time of writing only one university had established a school of peace studies, and this was only initiated as a result of voluntary subscriptions from supporters of the peace movement. Yet the struggle for peace is not only one of the most vital aspects of all future human progress, but one which has engaged, more than any other, the disinterested and active support of a large and continually increasing proportion of the people.

The area of community studies is another vast field where the struggle which arises spontaneously in a multitude of voluntary organisations from Tenants' Associations to societies for the protection of ethnic minorities, should find educational expression. To some extent and in some aspects these fields of concern are dealt with in professional and semi-professional courses for various kinds of social workers. But it is inevitable that the orientation of these studies should be largely determined by the role of their graduates in the management side of social service departments of Local Authorities. This is not to deny their importance (or indeed, the significance of all management education), nor to suggest that they cannot promote a concern for the welfare of those who are managed. But in a divided society the struggle of the people themselves for their own liberation must find its own educational weapons and its own areas of special relevance, sometimes complementary to the expertise of management, but directed in the first place to the defence and advancement of the interests of the people at the bottom, if necessary, in opposition to those in authority.

We may properly consider the three fields of studies just mentioned as exemplifying a new dimension in higher education which may be termed the "applied humanities". Others that are beginning to develop include environmental studies of all kinds, studies concerned with the development of recreational activity and entertainment and the domestic arts and the rediscovery of popular culture. They offer new opportunities for discovering the relevance of the Arts, Humanities and Human Sciences to the practical tasks of creating a human society. Unlike so many of the abstracted and specialised ways of approaching these fields of study which, in the recent past, have aped the positivistic methodology of the hard sciences, the applied humanities would return in a new way to an older tradition.

They are essentially normative; like the oldest disciplines of medicine, theology and law, they are openly directed towards the creation of a good society. They are interdisciplinary and lend themselves to that mix of learning and practical experience developed (in the first place in the technological fields) in the so-called sandwich courses, or in the more extended part-time courses. But in cases such as we have mentioned above, periods of practical experience can often be within organisations and institutions which arise from the association of the people in pursuit of their liberation; trade unions, peace organisations, community organisations, educational institutions and service institutions in poor countries overseas, workers' co-operatives, famine relief organisations and organisation for the legal and social defence of the poor or of the ethnic minorities. They help to bring into the content and curriculum of higher education, experience which can serve to illuminate its relevance to the children of underprivileged sectors of society and to act as a bridge to the much wider participation of the working class.

We have sketched above the main landmarks along the route to a programme of universal higher education. We have not attempted to set out a detailed map of a future system of comprehensive universities because this cannot emerge as a result of educational reform alone. The speed of advance, the actual balance of institutional composition and curriculum content at each stage must be integrated to the maximum extent with the creation of opportunities for the imaginative use of learning in social life; especially work, but also in all aspects of recreational and community activity. There is no intrinsic lack of the necessary economic resources or the cultural reserves required by such a programme. Given the necessary social purpose and will behind it, it would become self-fulfilling, powered by the enormous new fund of human capability and productivity released. The basic new asset exploited in all human progress, whether of material, cultural or moral nature, has always been vision and discovery and dissemination of knowledge and its application in social praxis.

Only a government which is dedicated to the democratisation of the application of knowledge will wholeheartedly develop its dissemination among the whole people. This is, above all, self-evident at the level of higher education which is knowledge at the level of decision making in the productive economy as well as in the State. In modern advanced societies the converse is also true. In general only those classes of the population who participate in higher education can have full access to the management and control of affairs. Again, we are not concerned here with the details of political programmes or doctrines. But if socialism connotes in general the democratisation and equalisation, among all classes of the people, of the control of the means of production, the economy and the social organisation, then only a government dedicated to democratic socialism can pursue the cultural and educational aims we have outlined. The reason is that these are the main areas of practice which increasingly require higher education for their planning, control and management and hence, are the main justification of its relevance.

Since this book is essentially about the British scene, it would take us too far away to attempt to analyse in detail why, in the United States, an apparently major progress towards universal higher education has taken place under governments mainly dedicated to anti-socialist programmes. Although this numerical attainment of majority participation in America is evidence of the credibility of an institutional organisation of mass higher education, its political establishment does not provide a model for the rest of the world. It rests on a basis of material wealth, and a concommitant relative hegemony over world material resources which can hardly be envisaged for more than a small minority of powerful States at any one time. The disadvantaged majority balancing the favoured minority in the case of the United States, are in reality the poor of the world, whose lives are increasingly dominated by American based multi-national companies.

It is natural that it is in the United States, where the growth and power of the professional classes has proceeded fastest among Western nations, that some of their spokesmen see themselves as the source of the momentum for the extension of higher education to ever-wider sections of the population. The exponentially accelerated expansion of these classes, as we have stressed in Chapter 4, has indeed been the mainspring of the concurrent growth of student enrolments. It has taken place mainly through the next process of upward social mobility from immediately lower socio-economic groups and, particularly in the United States from the upper layers of the manual working class.

We have stressed in many sections above the reasons why this process of gradual upward mobility is revealing its limitations elsewhere in the world, and particularly in Britain. Ultimately, it is the self-interest and the self-image of the professional classes; and particularly of their intellectual wing, their essential meritocracy and élitism, the corresponding amoral, competitive, and hence isolated and fragmented nature of their cultural models, which prevents them becoming the future universal class. They cannot generate from their ranks the necessary social force to sustain either the economic and social transformations, nor the cultural and moral conviction which must underpin the completion of the democratic process.

Nor do the self-styled socialist republics of the East necessarily provide a better scenario for the creation of a truly democratic culture and higher education. Indeed, the whole cast of their emphasis on the narrow and even more technically dominated culture is demonstrated by the fact that all the highly educated are now described and conceived of as "specialists". In these countries, the élitism of the professional bureaucracy bears a strong resemblance to its counterpart in the capitalist West. Of course, there are major differences in the formal ideology of education. In the early years, the numerical expansion of educational opportunity in these States rose considerably above that of European States, and began to match that in the United States. The main difference was probably that, whereas the expansion of opportunity was based in the latter case on the emphasis of "freedom", in the former it was supposed to exemplify the advance to "equality". But in neither system has education to the highest levels ceased to be dominated by the motive of conserving privilege, nor has its role as an agent for social control in the interests of the continuance of privilege been fundamentally transformed. Both demonstrate the limitations of cultural patronage by a dominant and managerial class as the agent for the indefinite expansion of culture to the whole people. It has played a part in lifting a section of the underprivileged to a consciousness of their latent powers, though only within the context of joining the system of privilege into which they emerge.

Individual intellectuals and progressive groups can still play an essential role in assisting the underprivileged in their societies and through the world to find a language for their aspirations and a form for their struggle. But in the realm of education, and especially higher education, the full participation of the ordinary people will only be achieved to the extent that they become conscious of its necessity and struggle for it themselves. Their main instruments for emancipation in this field, as in every other field of economic, political and social liberation, are their own organisations, their trade unions, their community organisations, their political parties. Indeed, the educational, the economic and the social, are all aspects of the same campaign. They cannot be achieved separately; they are essentially interdependent. Ultimately they are all aspects of a new culture, a new vision of the purpose of knowledge and its incorporation in action. The only basis for a truly human culture is that it should express the common humanity, the basic equality of status and the liberation of the free creative genius of all the people. The only universal class is the human race.

CHAPTER TWELVE

Postscript:
The 1981-82 Cuts in Higher
Education

In the summer of 1981, the government announced a programme of cuts in public expenditure in the universities, which, together with the rapid fall in overseas students occasioned by the policy of imposing full-cost fees, was calculated to reduce their income by £180,000,000 by 1983-4, about 20 per cent in real terms. A similar policy of financial squeeze was imposed on the polytechnics and other public sector colleges. While it is not possible to make an exact calculation of the financial loss to these latter institutiuons, since the local education authorities still have some small discretion in providing supplementary sums, the officially expected redundancy of staff was of the same numerical order as that from the universities, indicating an even greater degree of cutback.

At the same time the Secretary of State, Sir Keith Joseph, let it be known that the major objective of the squeeze was to reduce the numbers of students entering higher education. The tuition fee for British students was halved, not with the intention of making it easier for the very small proportion of those who pay their own fees, but with the stated objective of eliminating any financial incentive to increase productivity by taking more students at much less than average cost. Indeed, it was made clear that if higher educational institutions failed to make the target reductions in student entrants they would suffer still further financial penalties by withdrawal of treasury grant. Thus for the first time in a century the expansion of demand from qualified British applicants was set in reverse. The Robbins principle was openly abandoned and a deliberate policy calculated to exclude the majority of qualified applicants coming from the manual working class was initiated.

The ceiling for British entrants to universities was set at 70,000 per year, about 10,000 less than the number entering in 1980. The social impact of this will be readily appreciated from a brief examination of the social trends analysed in Chapter 4 and illustrated in Fig. 4.1b. The demand from qualified applicants from the professional and managerial classes has been rising steadily for the past 8 years by more than 6 per cent per annum. This has, we have seen in Chapter 4, is a consequence of the long term exponential of those classes significantly accelerated in the past decade by the recruitment to them of the flood of graduates in the 1960s. These factors, together with the higher than average birth rates in these socio-economic classes, are certain to maintain, if not to increase, the annual rate of expansion of their demand for higher education for several decades. On the other hand the demand for higher education from children of manual workers has become almost stationary. Moreover, the proportion of university applicants with the top examination grades ('A' levels) has become consistently twice as high among children from the professional and managerial classes as that of children of manual workers.

Assuming that the universities continue to select mainly on past examination performance we may readily calculate that the majority of working class candidates will have been squeezed out within a decade.

By 1990 their entering numbers will have been reduced from the 1979 peak of 18,000 to less than 9,000. On the other hand the entering children from the professional and managerial families will have actualy increased from 43,000 to 46,000 per annum. However, the surplus demand, mainly from the children of the same upper classes, will by then have more than equalled the total restricted entry to the polytechnics and colleges. Even in 1980 over half of the entering students to these public sector higher education places were provided from those who had failed to obtain university entrance. By 1990 they will have been glutted by the surge of qualified applicants overflowing from the universities. As we have seen already in Chapter 4 (Table 4.5) the composition of the polytechnics probably hardly differs socially from that of the universities. By the end of the decade they may have even fewer working class students than the universities.

We are now set on a political course which must, if unchecked, return us to a degree of social elitism in higher education, not of the pre-Robbins, but of the Victorian period.

It may be noted that the estimated cost of compensation for the many thousand of university and college staff who will be made redundant in this programme will more than offset the savings in university and college running costs during the whole remainder of the life of the present parliament. The average cost per student during this period will, in consequence, rise sharply by about the same proportion as the cuts.

It follow that if, as well as may be expected, the programme is reversed by a changed government in 1984, there will have been no saving at all in net public expenditure. Moreover the extra cost of recovering lost momentum will have escalated even further because of the enormous disorganisation caused by this unprecedented attack on higher education.

But the most significant loss will be the destruction of the chances of higher education for upwards of 40,000 students, mainly from the working class within the record space of just over two years and the wanton waste of the expensive training and high talents of up to 10,000 academic staff and a corresponding number of other higher education workers. The fact that the present government cannot hope to save any real money within their own parliamentary lifetime by such devastating cuts, shows their determination to re-introduce a corrosive degree of social elitism into higher education at all costs.

Nevertheless, it is vitally necessary that any political party aiming at alternative government, and particularly the Labour Party as the parliamentary representative of the working class, should pledge itself to reverse these cuts. The minimum immediate programme must be to restore Robbins principle and as we have shown, in Chapter 11, this must entail a preparation for regular annual increases of the order of 5-6 per cent per annum, even to maintain the present numbers of students from manual workers' families. To begin the change the social balance of higher education to reflect more truly the real distribution of potential talents throughout the people will entail the additional measures we have outlined in Chapter 11.

Naturally there will be some scope for real economies in the cost of higher education per student in a greatly expanded programme. They could become much more evident in a more completely integrated system leading to a comprehensive university. They require careful planning over a long period to avoid the wasteful disorganisation created by the present measures and the preceding decimation of teacher training. But they will only be obtained if education, including higher education, is no longer regarded as a mere consumption of public resources, to be ruthlessly pruned by the demands of monetarist dogma, but as a vital part of public investment. Unless the rate of investment in education is revived and accelerated, all other forms of capital investment will suffer the fate which falls to them within those economies that fall into the obsolescence we have described in Chapters 6 and 7.

8 February 1982

FURTHER READING

Sources

Unless otherwise stated in the text of the book, the source for the data in all the tables and figures will be found in the following paper by the author, E.G. Edwards and I.J. Roberts: British Higher Education. Long Term Trends in Student Enrolment, *Higher Education Review*. London, Spring 1980.

The same article contains a detailed review of recent publications and research papers in the fields of Chapters 2, 3 and 4.

The following additional short bibliography is not intended to be comprehensive or impartial, but to enable the reader who wishes to explore further some of the sources considered most useful by the author.

Educational Documents and History

An excellent review of the main official documents since 1816 is by:
J. Stuart Maclure. *Educational Documents. England and Wales 1816-1967*. Methuen, London 1968.

Other official government documents on higher education are detailed in:
E.G. Edwards and I.J. Roberts. loc. cit.

Histories of higher education are generally lacking in reference to the numbers and distribution of students. The following are cited for general background studies.

L. Stone. *The University and Society*. Vol.1 and Vol.2. Oxford University Press. London 1975.

F. Ringer. *Education and Society in Modern Europe*. Indiana University Press, Bloomington and London 1979.

A.D.C. Peterson. *A Hundred Years of Education*. Duckworth and Co. London 1960.

S.J. Curtis and M.E.A. Boultwood. *An Introductory History of English Education since 1800*. University Tutorial Press. London 1960.

D.B. Horn. *A Short History of the University of Edinburgh*. The University Press. Edinburgh 1967.

General Background, the Impact of Science on Society, the Knowledge Revolution

D. de Solla Price. *Little Science, Big Science*. Columbia University Press. 1963.

H.W. Menard. *Science Growth and Change*. Harvard University Press 1971.

I. Spiegel-Rösing and D. de Solla Price. *Science Technology and Society*. Sage Publications. London 1977.

W.H.G. Armytage. *The Rise of the Technocrats*. Routledge and Kegan Paul. London 1965.

Christopher Evans. *The Mighty Micro*. Victor Gollancz. London 1979.
(An excellent account of the impact of the micro computer).

D.A. Schon, *Beyond the Stable State*. Temple, Smith. London 1971.

A Toffler. *Future Shock*. Pan Books. London 1970.

P.F. Drucker. *The Age of Discontinuity*. Heinemann. London 1969.

E. Semper and P. Coggin (Editors). *Hidden Factors in Technological Change*. Pergamon Press. London 1976.

F.F. Darling. *Wilderness and Plenty*. BBC. London 1970.

E. Leach. *A Runaway World*. BBC. London 1967.

G.R. Taylor. *The Doomsday Book*. Panther. London 1972.

H.A. Simon. *The Shape of Automation for Men and Management*. Harper and Row. New York. 1965.

Sir Leon Bagrit. *The Age of Automation*. Weidenfeld and Nicolson. London 1965.

The Social Apartheid

B. Jackson and D. Marsden. *Education and the Working Class*. Penguin. London 1966.

K. Kelsall, A. Poole, A. Kuhn. *Graduates, The Sociology of an Élite*. Methuen. London 1972.

G.C. Homans. *The Nature of Social Science*. Harcourt, Bruce and World Inc. New York. 1967.

G. Neave. *Patterns of Inequality*. N.F.E.R. Publishing Co. Windsor 1976.

A.H. Halsey. *Changes in British Society*. Oxford University Press. Oxford 1978.

A.H. Halsey, A.F. Heath, A.J.M. Ridge. *Origins and Destinations*. Clarendon Press. Oxford 1980.

I. Reid. *Social Class Differences in Britain*. Open Books. London 1977.

O. Banks. *The Sociology of Education*. Batsford. London 1976.

E.P. Thompson. *The Making of the English Working Class*. Pelican. London 1968.

O.E.C.D. *Education, Inequality and Life Chances*. O.E.C.D. Paris 1975.

J.H. Goldthorpe. *Social Mobility and Class Structure in Modern Britain*. Clarendon Press. Oxford 1980.

J. Illich. *Deschooling Society*. Calder and Boyars. London 1971.

The Impact of Knowledge and Higher Education on the Economy Costs and Benefits

W.W. Rostow. *The World Economy*. Macmillan. London 1978.

D.H. Meadows, D.L. Meadows, J. Randers, W.W. Behrens III. *The Limits to Growth*. Potomac Associates. London 1972.

J.K. Galbraith. *The New Industrial Estate*. Hamish Hamilton. London 1967.

J.K. Galbraith. *The Affluent Society*. Hamish Hamilton. London 1969.

J.K. Galbraith and N. Salinger. *Almost Everyone's Guide to Economics*. Andrew Deutsch. London 1979.

O.E.C.D. *Occupational and Educational Structures of the Labour Force and the Levels of Economic Development*. O.E.C.D. Paris 1970.

J. Sheehan. *The Economics of Education*. G. Allen and Unwin. London 1973.

G. Psacharopoulos. *Returns to Education*. Elsevier. Amsterdan. 1973.

O.E.C.D. *Residual Factor and Economic Growth*. O.E.C.D. Paris 1977.

B. Ahamad and M. Blaug (Editors). *The Practice of Manpower Forecasting*. Jossey Bass Inc. San Francisco 1973.

See also most of the books listed under General Background.

The Problem of Cultural Equality

L.J. Kamin. *The Science and Politics of I.Q.* John Wiley. New York 1974. This book contains an extensive review of the literature of Intelligence Testing.

R. Williams. *Keywords. A Vocabulary of Culture and Society*. Fontana 1976.

R. Williams. *Culture and Society*. Penguin. London 1971.

Richard Hoggart. *The Uses of Literacy*. Chatto and Windus. London 1957.

Richard Hoggart. *Speaking to Each Other*. 2 Vols. Chatto and Windus. London 1970.

R. Fox. *The Novel and the People. 1937*. Lawrence and Wishart. 1979.

L. Goldmann. *The Human Sciences and Philosophy*. Jonathan Cape. London 1969.

F.R. Leavis. *The Common Pursuit*. Penguin. London 1952.

G. Steiner. *Language and Silence*. Penguin. London 1966.

T.S. Eliot. *Notes Towards the Definition of Culture*. Faber and Faber. London 1948.

J. Harrison. *The Reactionaries*. Gollancz. London 1966.

G. Lukacs.*History and Class consciousness*. Merlin Press. London 1971.

H. Marcuse. *The Aesthetic Dimension*. Papermac. Macmillan. London 1979.

H. Marcuse. *One Dimensional Man*. Sphere. London 1964.

M. Arnold. *Culture and Anarchy*. Smith and Elder. London 1891.

J. Bunyan. *The Pilgrims Progress.*

Shakespeare. *The Sonnets.*

Sciences and The Ivory Tower

J.D. Bernal. *The Social Function of Science*. Routledge. London 1939.

J.D. Bernal. *Science in History*. Watts. London. 1954.

M. Jammer. *Concepts of Space*. Harvard University Press. 1970.

D.A. Schon. *Invention and the Evolution of Ideas*. Tavistock. London 1963.

T.A. Kuhn. *The Structure of Scientific Revolutions*. University of Chicago Press. Chicago 1970.

Ernst Cassirer. *The Problem of Knowledge*. Yale University Press. New Haven 1950.

Ernst Cassirer. *An Essay on Man*. Yale University Press 1944.

H. Rose and S. Rose (Editors). *The Radicalisation of Science*. Macmillan. London 1976.

H. Rose and S. Rose (Editors). *The Political Economy of Science*. Macmillan. London 1976.

See also most books listed under General Background.

VIETNAM WEAPONS HANDBOOK

DAVID ROSSER-OWEN

Patrick Stephens, Wellingborough

First published in 1986

British Library Cataloguing in Publication Data

Rosser-Owen, David
Vietnam weapons handbook
1. Vietnamese Conflict, 1961–1975—Equipment
and supplies   2. Arms and armor—History—
20th century
I. Title
959.704'3   DS559.8.E7

ISBN 0-85059-838-9

*Patrick Stephens Limited is part of the
Thorsons Publishing Group*

Photoset in 10 on 11pt Helvetica Light
by Avocet Marketing Services, Bicester, Oxon.
Printed and bound in Great Britain on 115 gsm
Fineblade cartridge for the publishers,
Patrick Stephens Limited,
Denington Estate, Wellingborough, Northants,
NN8 2QD, England.

CONTENTS

INTRODUCTION

This is not a book about the Vietnam War as such, but looks at the weapons that were used by those fighting it on the ground. Greater considerations about the war, therefore, will not be found here. The war itself did not produce any major changes in the design of ground weapons and the weapons that did appear during it — the American M16 Armalite rifle, for example — were largely the result of thinking and development independent of the conflict. New weapons did appear, it is true, but these were air-delivered like the Maverick television-guided anti-armour missile or the Pave Way family of laser-guided 'smart' bombs. Great strides were made in electronic counter-measures (ECM), electronic counter-counter-measures (ECCM) and in techniques for rescuing downed aircrew. The conflict also had an effect on tactics and the use of ground weapons. Helicopters came into their own both as transports and as gunships, and tactics of helicopter ambushes developed using machine-guns and shoulder-launched missiles. Directional anti-personnel mines, such as the American M18 Claymore, became a feature of vehicle and troop ambushes. However, the weapons in use were the same as those which were on issue in other parts of the world.

The book is primarily concerned with the 'American phases' of the war — what has often been called the 'Second Indo-China War' — and largely covers the period after March 1965 when US personnel were changed over from an advisory role to a ground-combat role (the build-up of US troops began with the arrival at Da Nang of the US Marine Corps' 3rd Marine Expeditionary Force (3MEF USMC)). However, some geographical and historical background might be in order to place the conflict into context. Also, because a number of the weapons used by those fighting against the Americans and their allies came from earlier phases of the war, a brief background will hopefully explain how and why this came about.

The war in Vietnam was the longest lasting conflict this century. In its several phases it involved British, Indian, Gurkha, Japanese, French, North and West African, Australian, New Zealand, Filipino, South Korean, Thai, Taiwanese (Republic of China), Spanish, American and, of course, Vietnamese troops of various ethnic origins and political persuasions. It ended spectacularly on 30 April 1975, when Russian-built T-55 main battle tanks of the North Vietnamese regular army entered the grounds of the Presidential

List of Tables

7

Acknowledgements

The author expresses his grateful appreciation to the Leverhulme Trust for the award of an Emeritus Fellowship and to the University of Bradford for the provision of additional research assistance, both of which contributed considerably to the research underlying the present book. Most of the statistical data presented in the first four chapters was collated by my research assistant Mr I.J. Roberts, who also contributed very significantly to the theoretical analysis and to several papers which have appeared in research journals. Claudette Wild typed and checked most of the manuscript with patience and precision.

The errors and infelicities which remain are the sole responsibility of the author.

Foreword

The positive educational forces which produced the revolution against a divided secondary system in post-war Britain are still well at work. The comprehensive reform which resulted from that earlier revolution is nothing like complete, for selection and privilege still hang on. But the extended common educational experience has gone far enough to have added considerable fuel to the demand for continuing education in life as a new universal right.

Demand is being passed up the line. The 16 to 19 age group is experiencing dramatic changes of which most people, even in education, are as yet unaware. Even fewer are aware of the demands which lie beyond, including the right to higher education for all.

Ted Edwards is particularly suited to articulate the higher education demand, for he alone of all the United Kingdom's university vice-chancellors was willing to stand up and be counted among the growing band of reformers arguing for comprehensive education in the 1960s. At a time when so many of his colleagues were denouncing this now popular change as a threat to educational civilisation, he saw how clearly necessary it was in order to raise society's standards.

In this book he looks ahead again, and sees that for the sake of those same standards, higher education, like secondary education before it, cannot remain the privilege of a largely middle class minority. It must be transformed into an experience all can share.

Higher education's nature, methods, content and structures will have to change dramatically before they can meet the majority's needs or match their lives, particularly in the case of women. But once the process really begins, the experience of making continuing education a reality in all parts of the post-education, will itself produce the new ways and means, and a withering away of unacceptable divisions. For this is what is happening at secondary level now, if only slowly.

First, however, myths have to be demolished about adults as they once had to be about children. The main one is that most adults do not have the capacity for rigorous, extended education. As one who had worked in extra mural university teaching and Open University preparation during the last fifteen years, I have n o doubt that what is missing is not people's ambition, interests or capacity, but society's agreement to encourage that ambition, cater for that interest, and provide for that capacity to be realised through a new radical development of our education service.

Before this, however, there must be a new consensus on universal educational rights. As this book documents so well, the extension of higher education which the Robbins era produced was impressive. But higher education was only available still to those who could 'qualify' or who were thought 'able to benefit'. Decisions about both these crucial matters were delegated to the same small elite who had already qualified and already benefited. Not until there is a new agreement that these decisions be taken by society as a whole — by people themselves — will the gates be open and the resources found.

This book argues the case for opening the gates and finding the resources, not merely to extend social justice to individuals, but, equally important, to meet society's own real needs. If post-industrial Britain is to 'grow on' harmoniously and productively, the struggle for social change, including a higher education revolution, becomes a practical necessity.

What must begin now is the long slow process that has characterised the struggle for all the educational advances of the past, starting with the extension of simple literacy to all. The very same argument that started it must be brought into higher education: that which was once a privilege for the few shall in future be agreed as a right for everyone who wants it.

Caroline Benn

was an ally of Germany, and Germany was an ally of Japan, the Japanese had allowed the Vichy Governor-General of Indo-China, Admiral Jean Decoux, nominal freedom to rule the country. The Vichy government in metropolitan France fell with the Allied Invasion in June 1944 and General de Gaulle's Free French took over. Some nine months later, on 9 March 1945, at 21:30 hours the Japanese attacked the French garrisons which fought back bravely but were eventually overwhelmed. By this time the French forces in Indo-China were commanded by the Free French generals Mordant, Alessandri and Sabattier and were thus part of the Allied forces in Asia. The Free French appealed to the Americans in nearby Yunnan Province of China for help, but were ignored on orders from the very highest level of US government.

By mid-July 1945, the collapse of Japan was imminent and the Emperor had been making discreet overtures to the Allies for terms of surrender, which were ignored. The atomic bombs were dropped on Hiroshima and Nagasaki on 6 and 9 August and Japanese Imperial forces largely stopped fighting. The Vietminh put into action the Indochinese Communist Party's Tan Trao plan (decided at a 'national conference' held in that village in Tuyen-Quang Province north-west of Hanoi on 13 August 1945) to seize control of the centres of power from the Japanese before the arrival of the Chinese and British, and thus present them with a *fait accompli* so that post-war government would be in the hands of the ICP. On 19 August the Vietminh seized power in Hanoi and on 23 August the People's Committee for the South was established in Saigon Town Hall with six of the nine members belonging to the ICP.

A Declaration of Independence of the Vietminh-controlled 'Democratic Republic of Vietnam' was made on 2 September, the date of the official Japanese surrender, and was followed by rioting in Saigon and Cholon. On 13 September Major General Gracey and the advance elements of 20th (Indian) Infantry Division, some 750 men, arrived in Saigon and promptly acted to restore order. SEAC refused to recognize the Vietminh's seizure of power and restored the French administration. Eventually, after some months of fighting, French authority was re-established south of the 16th Parallel.

In the North, the Chinese Nationalists made no attempt either to restore lawful authority or to secure their own or the Japanese stocks of weapons and ammunition. As a result considerable quantities of both found their way into Vietminh hands. The excesses of the centuries-old Chinese enemy of the Vietnamese led to the

Vietminh eventually renegotiating the return of French authority to the North. An opportunity for a peaceful transition to post-colonial independence of a democratic kind was badly handled by the French after their return to the North, leading to the war which broke out on 19 December 1946, just over a year after their return. Thus the beginning of this tragic conflict can be taken as starting either in December 1946, when the Vietminh attacked the French, or in September 1945, when the British restored French rule in the South. The Vietnamese Communists consider the entire conflict, that ended in 1975, to be one war. Truong Chinh, a Central Committee member, wrote that the start of their 'heroic resistance' was on the night of the 24–25 September 1945. So it is clear when the Communists date the beginning of the Vietnam War.

The Americans and their allies found themselves facing an enemy which was well organized and experienced in fighting a modern western army, but which had not been so successful against a CRW-trained force. The Vietnamese Communists had at their disposal a variety of weapons from Japanese, French and American manufacturers, and were able to make their own modifications to many of them. An example of this is the addition of a longer barrel to the French MAT49 sub-machine-gun and the rechambering of the weapon from 9 mm to take the Soviet 7.62 mm × 25 pistol cartridge.

THE TWO SIDES AND THEIR SOURCES OF SUPPLY

During the 'American phases' of the war in Vietnam, the two sides were effectively the Free World forces of the South Vietnamese (Republic of Vietnam — RVN), the Americans, the Australians and New Zealanders, the South Koreans and the smaller contingents from certain other countries, against the Communist forces of the North Vietnamese (NVN) and the Viet Cong (an abbreviation for *Viet-Nam Cong San* — Vietnamese Communist), supposedly made up of 'freedom fighters' from the South. Not all of these were, in fact, Communists. Many members of the VC were conscripted from villages under Communist control, or were simply 'press-ganged' into joining. Others joined for adventure, prestige, and similar motives. A few were actually Marxist-Leninist 'believers', and if the Malayan experience were true also of Vietnam, they were looked upon by their fellows as being somewhat cranky. None of this affected their fighting abilities, which were considerable, and all cadres underwent constant political indoctrination.

In January 1949 the Chinese Communists captured Peking (Beijing) and by the end of the year they had extended their control over the whole country. It was when Communist China had reached the Vietnamese border that considerable quantities of weapons and ammunition of both Chinese and Soviet manufacture were able to reach the Vietminh overland, and these were available for the fighting against the ARVN and its US advisers in the mid-1950s. Chinese artillerymen also took part in the final battle of Dien Bien Phu. After the break between Moscow and Peking happened in the late 1950s, the Vietnamese moved into the USSR's orbit, being historically distrustful of China. The USSR continued to supply military material, both of its own and east European manufacture.

As the American effort escalated in the South, so did Soviet backing for the Vietnamese Communist forces and the port of Haiphong (to the south-east of Hanoi) became extremely busy with shipping carrying supplies to the North. The Americans did little to stop this traffic even when they were bombing North Vietnam during Operation Rolling Thunder in 1968. It was only during Operation Linebacker in 1972, that President Nixon ordered the mining of Haiphong harbour, and Soviet supply tailed off dramatically as a result. However, although the People's Republic of China

(PRC) and the USSR were the major suppliers they did not send their latest and best equipment for use on the ground. It was only in the air-defence war in the North that the USSR contributed modern ground-control intercept (GCI) radars, anti-aircraft guided missiles, MiG-21 interceptor/air superiority aircraft, and such equipment. This was partly in self-interest, to see how they would fare against American aircraft with an eye to the western European front.

Some weapons, mostly copies and modifications, were made in North Vietnam. The output of NVN factories was seriously impeded by US air strikes, and facilities were dispersed and broken down into smaller units. This also limited their effective output. Operation Linebacker I destroyed nearly all targets of any military value in North Vietnam, and the Communist forces soon began to run out of everything. By the time the last US combat troops left the country the war was containable by the South Vietnamese forces on their own (with continued American supplies) and possibly also winnable. US Congressional failure to fulfil its treaty obligations to supply military *matériel* to South Vietnam gave the Communists the incentive to bring forward their planned 1976 offensive. During the fighting in 1975 the South Vietnamese found that they were unable to resupply themselves with ammunition and other *matériel* which was supposed to come from the USA, and their resistance was overwhelmed.

Most American equipment was of their own manufacture; however certain specialist units used small quantities of other countries' weapons, such as the West German Heckler and Koch HK MP5 sub-machine-gun. With the exception of Australia and New Zealand, all the major Free World contingents used American weapons and equipment, although some of it was made under licence in their own countries. The Philippines' troops also used the West German Heckler and Koch G3 rifle as well as the American M16.

Australian and New Zealand weapons were mostly of British make, although frequently built at the Commonwealth Small Arms Factory, Canberra, Australia. They also used weapons produced at *Fabrique Nationale*, Herstal, Belgium, and FFV Ordnance Division, Eskilstuna, Sweden. They adopted certain American weapons (such as the M16 rifle, the M60 general-purpose machine-gun, and the 105 mm M101 towed howitzer) in Vietnam, but continued also to use their familiar British equipment. There are photographs of Australian infantry patrols carrying both M16s and L1A1 self-loading rifles (SLRs).

PISTOLS AND
SUB-MACHINE-GUNS

Both pistols and sub-machine-guns (SMGs) are essentially close-quarter weapons whose accuracy beyond 100 m (109 yd) is considerably diminished. In close country, such as jungle, or in fighting in built-up areas (FIBUA), they have a useful function, but in other military situations their value is questionable particularly after the introduction of assault rifles with an automatic-fire capability such as the Soviet AK47 or the American M16. Nevertheless, they are often issued to those personnel who need their hands free for other tasks but need also a weapon for personal protection, such as medical orderlies, doctors and radio operators. Pistols are also found as a 'back-up' weapon carried by troops on the ground and are the principal 'survival' weapon of aircrew. They are frequently worn by officers and military policemen for personal protection when there is some risk, or as a part of parade uniform.

Many soldiers in Vietnam, particularly in the Special Forces, used privately owned hand guns. Here is an example of a modified .22 target pistol with plastic moulded butt and hand-machined muzzle brake (US Army via MARS).

They are also worn for prestige reasons by some officers. Pistols or sub-machine-guns are issued to the crews of vehicles, both 'soft-skinned' and armoured fighting vehicles (AFVs), where space and manoeuvrability are problems, although the introduction of the M16 rifle in Vietnam meant that the crews of soft-skinned vehicles and armoured personnel carriers (APCs) could be issued with this more useful weapon.

With its automatic-fire capability, small size and light weight, the M16 tended to take over many of the roles previously performed by SMGs. Before the introduction of the M16 in the early 1960s, SMGs were commonly used on jungle and close-country patrols where a rapid wall of fire over short ranges was required. In such circumstances scouts and trackers were often issued with SMGs or even shotguns. SMGs are also useful weapons for use in covert operations, as are pistols, and both sorts of weapon were used in this way by US Special Forces in Vietnam.

In Communist countries the pistol is a particular status symbol of the officers. Apart from ones that were captured, or stolen from South Vietnamese armouries, the most common pistols in use with the NVA and VC were the Soviet Tokarev TT33 7.62 mm and the Chinese copies of this, the Types 51 and 54. There were also some Makarov PMs and the Chinese copies, Types 59 and 68. Pistols made in eastern European countries tended to be copies of the Tokarev and Makarov, and some of these may have been acquired. The most widely available pistol in Vietnam was the American Colt M1911A1 .45 in which, apart from being the standard issue to US personnel, was provided in considerable quantities to the South Vietnamese, South Koreans, Filipinos and Thais. Many of these were captured, or taken off downed US aircrewmen, and found their way into favoured Communist hands.

COMMUNIST FORCES

Tokarev TT33 7.62 mm pistol (USSR) and Types 51 and 54 (PRC)

The Tokarev TT33 was first introduced in the 1930s, using the basic Colt self-cocking design. It was used extensively by Soviet forces during World War 2, and was produced — sometimes with modifications — in nearly all Warsaw Pact countries and the People's Republic of China (PRC). The Chinese Type 54 variant could be distinguished from the Soviet TT33 by the serrations on the slide and by the Chinese ideograms on the pistol grip. The Soviet TT33 had alternate narrow and wide vertical cuts, whereas the Types 51 and 54 had uniform narrow markings, to aid gripping the slide when manually cocking the weapon. There was no safety mechanism but the hammer could be locked at half-cock and the weapon was normally carried with a round in the chamber. There was a distinct possibility of an accidental discharge if the pistol was dropped or sharply jolted. Production of the weapon in the USSR stopped in 1954, but continued in other Communist countries, notably the PRC. The pistol fired the Soviet 7.62 mm × 25 Type P pistol cartridge, although the Hungarians produced a 9 mm variant for the Egyptians which was not a success. It operated on a recoil single action, feeding ammunition from an 8-round box magazine. The pistol was quite heavy, weighing about 1 kg (2.2 lb) when loaded, and was 196 mm (7.72 in) in length.

Makarov PM (USSR) and Type 59 (PRC) 9 mm pistol

The Pistolet Makarov (PM) replaced the Tokarev in the early 1950s in the Warsaw Pact countries, and was produced in the PRC as the Type 59. It was copied from the West German Walther PP (police pistol) of the 1930s, but was chambered for the 9 mm round rather than the 7.65 mm cartridge of the original pistol, using the Soviet's 9 mm × 18 ammunition rather than the NATO 9 mm × 19. It became the standard pistol in most Euro-Asian Communist forces. The pistol grip was slightly bulky, making firing it a little uncomfortable. Soviet-manufactured weapons had a star in the centre of the pistol grip. The pistol was operated by a blowback, self-loading double action, and loaded from an 8-round box magazine. It measured 160 mm (6.3 in) in length and weighed 800 g (1.8 lb) when loaded. There was a simple safety catch at the rear of the slide, and a slide stop on the outside of the receiver, both of which could be operated by the firer's thumb (if he was right handed).

PPSh41 (USSR), Type 50 (PRC) and K50M (NVN) 7.62 mm sub-machine-gun

The PPSh41 SMG was designed by the Soviet design bureau of

George Shpagin in 1940 and was adopted for issue in 1941, meeting the Red Army's need for an easily-mass-produced, rugged weapon. It became quite popular with German soldiers fighting on the Russian Front, and some PPSh41s were converted by German armourers to fire 9 mm Parabellum rounds. The weapon had a fire-rate selector lever positioned just in front of the trigger, allowing the rate of fire to be changed rapidly without the weapon moving off the point of aim. The two-piece bolt handle allows the bolt to be locked in either the forward or the rear position. The original weapon had two different magazines; a 71-round drum or a 35-round box. The drum magazine seems to have fallen out of favour, and most of this type of weapon seen in Vietnam used the box. This may have been a result of the Chinese connection. The PRC Type 50 SMG differed only slightly from the PPSh41, mainly in that it only fitted the 35 round box magazine. The most interesting variant of the weapon was the K50M, which was a Vietnamese modification of the Type 50. The Vietnamese removed the wooden butt stock and replaced it with a wooden pistol grip and a French-style sliding wire butt stock similar to that on the MAT49. At the front end of the weapon, they shortened the perforated barrel jacket, left off the muzzle brake, and attached the foresight to the barrel, giving the gun a shape strongly reminiscent of the MAT49. The K50M ended up being about 500 g (1.1 lb) lighter than the PPSh41 at 3.4 kg (7.5 lb) as opposed to 3.9 kg (8.6 lb). The weapons were all blowback operated and had an effective range of about 150 m (164 yd).

MAT49 modified 7.62 mm sub-machine-gun (NVN)

The design for a new sub-machine-gun produced by the *Manufacture d'Armes de Tulle* (MAT) in 1946, using the 9 mm Parabellum cartridge, was adopted by the French Army in 1949, hence the designation MAT49. The weapon was widely used by French forces in Indo-China, and many found their way into the hands of the Vietminh and thus were inherited by the Viet Cong during the American phases of the war in Vietnam. The Vietnamese modified the weapon to fire the Soviet 7.62 mm × 25P ammunition and its PRC equivalent by fitting a longer 7.62 mm barrel, but kept all the essential features of the MAT49 although they replaced the 32-round box with a 35-round magazine. The remarkable features of the French weapon, and its Vietnamese variant, were the sliding wire butt stock which could be pushed forward out of the way for carrying and pulled to the rear if it was to be used in firing. The magazine housing on the receiver could also be rotated forward through 90° (even with the magazine fitted) to lie along the barrel. In this position, if the butt stock was pushed in, it was held between two raised ribs on each side of the magazine housing giving the whole thing a certain security. These features of the weapon made it particularly suitable for parachute troops and others who needed compactness in carriage. At the back part of the pistol grip was a grip safety, which was operated by the action of squeezing the pistol grip when firing a round. This released the safety catch. When the grip safety was not squeezed, it locked the bolt in the forward position, and locked the trigger when the weapon was cocked. The lock was released by the pressure of the palm of the hand. The weapon thus could not be accidentally discharged. The Vietnamese modification increased the cyclic rate of fire from the 600 rounds per minute of the French weapon to 900 rpm.

The earlier French sub-machine-gun, the MAS *(Manufacture d'Armes de St Etienne)* Model 1938 — or MAS38, was also used in Indo-China and a number of these found their way into the hands of the Viet Cong. The original 7.65 mm-long cartridge lacked penetration, but it seems that only a proportion of the captured MAS38s were converted to take the Soviet 7.62 mm × 25P round. This was probably because the MAT49 was a better and more available weapon, and as the American phases of the war progressed other equipment appeared both from Communist sources (such as the Type 50/ PPSh41 SMGs) or from Free World forces (such as captured M3A1 'grease gun', M1A1 Thompson, or the Swedish FFV Model 45 'Carl Gustav' SMGs). The ubiquitous AK47 and M16 assault rifles tended to supersede SMGs in all the forces in the conflict.

FREE WORLD FORCES

The most common pistols used by the FW forces in Vietnam were the standard issues in the American and NATO armies, namely the Colt .45 in and the 9 mm Browning. A certain amount of individuality seems to have been shown by Americans and their allies, other than the Australians and New Zealanders, in their choice of pistols and so a wide range of commercially-available hand guns was used. Practically any pistol on sale in the USA turned up in Vietnam, but the most important were the issued weapons.

Colt M1911A1 .45 in automatic pistol (USA)

In 1896, Colt purchased four pistol designs from John Moses Browning. In 1900 they produced the .38 in Military Model using .38 ACP (automatic cartridge, Colt pistol) ammunition. At later US Army pistol trials it was decided to use the larger calibre .45 in ammunition as it had been found in the Philippines to have more stopping power. Modifications to the Colt 1900 Military Model incorporated some of the features of Browning's 1905 design, and thus that pistol became the joint ancestor of both the Colt M1911 (which was the outcome of the modifications) and the Browning High Power 9 mm pistol. Developments at the Springfield Armory, begun in April 1923, resulted in several improvements to the M1911 and this improved weapon was adopted by the US Army in 1926 as the M1911A1 and has remained almost unchanged ever since. It saw widespread service in World War 2 and Korea, and was in use by the South Vietnamese, Filipinos and South Koreans as well as the Americans in the Vietnam War. It weighed just over 1 kg (2.2 lb) and was 218 mm (8.6 in) in length. It was recoil operated and loaded from a 7-round box magazine, having an effective range of about 50 m (54.7 yd). There were two safety

Cleaning and checking a Colt M1911A1 .45 automatic pistol (US Army via MARS).

devices; a safety catch, mounted just forward of the spur on the frame, and a grip safety at the upper rear part of the pistol grip which fitted into the web of the palm between the thumb and index finger. The pressure exerted by the palm when firing released the grip device and unlocked the safety. The weapon fired .45 in M1911 ACP (automatic cartridge, Colt pistol) ammunition, the considerable stopping power of which made the M1911A1 a useful back-up arm.

Pistol Automatic 9 mm FN Browning High Power L9A1 (Belgium)

The American automatic pistol designer John Moses Browning worked for a while at the Belgian arms company *Fabrique Nationale* at Herstal, and this connection was maintained in the design and designation of this pistol. It was based on Browning's 1935 design and during World War 2 it was produced for Australian, British, Canadian and Nationalist Chinese troops by the John Inglis Company of Toronto in Canada, while the FN factory was making them for German SS troops. After the war, FN-made pistols tended to be used by the British, Australian and New Zealand forces, although Canadian-manufactured weapons were also on issue. Thus some of these pistols in service with the Australians in Vietnam were of the Inglis variant, although most — and all the New Zealand ones — came from the original Belgian manufacturer. The L9A1 Browning was also used by the Taiwanese contingent in the war. The weapon weighed 800 g (1.8 lb) and was 203 mm (8 in) long. It was recoil operated and loaded from a 13-round box magazine — a useful feature on a military hand gun. It had an effective range of 70 m (76.6 yd). There was a simple safety catch at the rear of the frame, which held the slide in place and prevented it from moving. Removal of the magazine disconnected the trigger.

Although the North Vietnamese and the Viet Cong used some captured M1911A1 Colts, it is not known of any instances when L9A1s were used by the Communist forces.

M1A1 Thompson .45 in sub-machine-gun (USA)

The introduction of the M16 rifle, with its automatic-fire capability, in the early 1960s tended to remove many of the sub-machine-

A crewman of the Vietnamese Junk Force searching a suspected Viet Cong fishing boat for arms and contraband. He is carrying an M1A1 Thompson .45 sub-machine-gun (US Navy via MARS).

guns from the FW forces' scene. Nevertheless, SMGs continued to be used and were certainly in evidence before the M16's arrival.

The Thompson SMG was first manufactured in series production in 1928 and was designed to take a variety of box magazines or a 100-round drum. It became a popular weapon with American gangsters during the years of Prohibition, earning it the nicknames of the 'Chicago typewriter' and 'Chicago violin' (from the violin cases that were often used to carry it in to avoid detection). A cheaper version was made for the Army as the M1 SMG and a further version, cheaper still and with certain modifications, was produced during World War 2 as the M1A1 which dispensed with the drum and only used a 20- or 30-round box magazine. Several were taken out of mothballs for the war in Vietnam, having been put into reserve after the Korean War. The gun was blowback operated and loaded from a vertical-feed box magazine. It fired the same .45 in ACP cartridge that the M1911A1 pistol did. It had a wooden butt stock, pistol grip and fore stock, and measured 810 mm (31.9 in) in length. It was quite a heavy weapon, weighing 5.37 kg (11.8 lb) when loaded with a 20-round magazine, but was very reliable and had good stopping power.

Several of these weapons were captured by the Communist forces and copies of them were made in VC and NVN factories. Few modifications to the original gun were made, perhaps the most significant was the use of a fixed firing pin, and often the wooden butt stock was dispensed with.

M3A1 .45 in/9 mm SMG ('grease gun') (USA)

The M3 SMG was nicknamed the 'grease gun' because of its shape, which looked remarkably like the tool used for injecting axle grease into the nipples of vehicles. It entered service with the US forces in 1942 and was produced in response to the need for a cheap, easily-mass-produced sub-machine-gun as the Thompson

Members of the South Vietnamese Civil Defense Guard being instructed in the use of the M3A1 'grease gun' (US Army via MARS).

A Viet Cong prisoner carrying a captured M3A1 (via MARS).

was quite an expensive weapon even in its M1A1 variant and quite complicated to make. The M3 used die-stamping where possible. Part of the design specification was for a gun that could be easily converted to take 9 mm ammunition, and this could be done by changing the barrel, bolt, magazine housing and magazine. The normal variant was for firing .45 in ACP ammunition. The M3 had an unusual, but fairly foolproof safety device. The ejection port cover was fitted with a projecting lug which, when the cover was closed, locked the bolt in either the cocked or battery position. To fire the weapon, the cover was opened. On the M3A1 variant the complicated cocking mechanism was simplified by the addition of a hole in the bolt, into which the firer's finger was placed to draw the bolt to the rear, thereby cocking the weapon. It was a blowback-operated, automatic-setting gun loading from a 30-round box magazine. However, the cyclic rate of fire was quite slow (450 rounds per minute) and this allowed the firer to control the movement of the gun when firing bursts and even to squeeze off single shots. It was a lighter weapon than the Thompson, weighing around 4.5 kg (9.9 lb) (depending on the variant) when fitted with full magazine, oil bottle and sling. It featured a retractable wire butt stock, similar to the MAT49, and measured 757 mm (29.8 in) with the stock extended and 579 mm (22.8 in) when it was retracted. The weapon was also made in the PRC, and the Type 64 SMG incorporated many of its features.

F1 9 mm sub-machine-gun (Australia)

The F1 SMG was produced at the Small Arms Factory, Lithgow, New South Wales as replacement for the Owen SMG of World War 2 fame. It retained the particularly noticeable feature of the Owen Gun, the forward-sloping box magazine mounted vertically on the top of the receiver. However, the F1 was designed to accept the 9 mm 34-round magazines of Canadian and UK manufacture for interoperability. The F1 had a cylindrical body which extended forward over the barrel (and was perforated for cooling) and rearwards to form the butt (the butt stock was a wooden insert into this). This meant that there was no torque or turning movement to lift the weapon away from the point of aim when it was firing on fully

The Australian F1 9mm sub-machine-gun (Lithgow Small Arms Factory via MARS).

automatic. As the magazine was mounted on top of the gun, the sights were offset to compensate for this, nevertheless there was a blind area to the left front. The gun was a blowback-operated, selective-fire weapon and had an effective range of 200 m (219 yd). It measured 714 mm (28.1 in) in length and weighed about 4 kg (8.8 lb) when loaded. It was designed to fit the L1A2 bayonet, which was common to the L1A1 self-loading rifle. It had a cyclic rate of fire of between 600 and 640 rounds per minute and used the standard 9 mm × 19 NATO Parabellum cartridge.

L2A3 9 mm Sterling sub-machine-gun (New Zealand)

The standard issue SMG of the New Zealand armed forces was the British L2A3 Sterling, which came into service in 1956. It used the standard 9 mm × 19 NATO Parabellum ammunition, and could fit the magazines of the Australian F1 and the Canadian C1 SMGs. The body of the weapon was made up of a cylindrical receiver, perforated at the front end for cooling, which extended over the barrel, a cylindrical bolt with return spring and a folding butt stock. The magazine housing was on the left side of the weapon, and when the magazine was fitted it curved slightly to the front. When held in the firing position, the magazine lay along the left wrist — quite a comfortable position for the firer. The gun could fire single shots or automatic. There was no burst-fire setting, and the normal automatic use was to fire short bursts of three to four rounds anyway, which was a matter of training and familiarity with the weapon. The gun used a 34-round box magazine, but there was also a 10-round magazine available. It weighed 3.47 kg (7.6 lb) when loaded, and measured 690 mm (27.2 in) in length when the metal butt stock was extended. When this was folded forward, the gun was 483 mm (19 in) in length. It had a cyclic rate of fire of 550 rounds per minute.

Model 45 9 mm sub-machine-gun (Sweden)

This gun was the standard SMG of the Swedish armed forces, and was known generally as the 'Carl Gustav' (not to be confused with the medium anti-armour weapon with the same nickname). There was a silenced variant, and this weapon was used by some of the

The Swedish Model 45 'Carl Gustav' sub-machine-gun (MARS).

US Army Special Forces in Vietnam. Some must have fallen into the hands of the Communist forces, as there are photographs of Viet Cong carrying what is clearly a Model 45. The gun was a blowback-operated, automatic-fire weapon loading from a 36-round, two-column, wedge-shaped box magazine. The magazine housing was situated underneath the gun about half-way along the receiver and acted as a forward hand grip. A perforated cowling covered the front end of the barrel for cooling and for protection of the firer's hand. It weighed 4.2 kg (9.2 lb) and was 808 mm (31.8 in) long. The butt stock was a rectangular wire device which was hinged at the top at the end of the receiver and at the bottom, at the base of the pistol grip. It could be swivelled forward for compactness in carriage. The gun fired the Swedish 9 mm × 19 M39B Parabellum round. It has been copied in Indonesia and the Egyptians manufactured the Model 45 for a time as the 'Port Said' under licence from the Swedish maker, FFV Ordnance Division at Eskilstuna. It is possible that the Viet Cong weapons came from Indonesia or Egypt, but capture from Americans or South Vietnamese Special Forces personnel seems more likely. The VC and the NVA would retrieve weapons from the bodies of servicemen killed or wounded and add them to their armouries.

RIFLES AND CARBINES

The soldier's principal weapon is the rifle, sometimes fitted with a sword (also known as a bayonet) for close quarter fighting. It gives him great accuracy over considerable ranges, enabling him to fulfil his principal task which is to kill the enemy. The design and operation of the rifle did not alter much from the French Chassepot of the 1870s until John C. Garand of the Springfield Armory produced his gas-operated, self-loading rifle in 1929. This weapon was adopted by the USA in 1939 and it featured in increasing numbers throughout World War 2, the Korean War and the earlier part of the Americans' involvement in Vietnam. It was eventually replaced in 1957 by the M14, which was a development of the M1 Garand and used the NATO standard 7.62 mm × 51 ammunition. During World War 2, the Germans identified a need for an assault rifle (*Sturmgewehr*) A machine carbine had been developed by Haenel in 1941 and modified by Schmeisser in the light of combat experience on the Russian Front. In 1943, this weapon was designated the MP43 (MP standing for *Maschinenpistole*) although it was not in fact an SMG (the equivalent of the 'machine pistol'). The rifle was redesignated a year later to MP44, and later that year was more accurately renamed by Hitler himself as the Sturmgewehr 44 (StGw44). The concept of use of this German weapon was to make it a universal arm at section (squad) level, so doing away with rifles, sub-machine-guns, and even light machine-guns. Many of these weapons were captured by the Russians and closely studied.

The StGw44 and the M1 Garand have given rise to many derived weapons, the principal ones of which played prominent roles in the Vietnam War. The Belgian armaments manufacturer *Fabrique Nationale* at Herstal produced a new weapon in 1948 called the Fusil Automatique Léger (FAL). This rifle, using the idea of a gas-operated self-loading weapon with an automatic capability of Garand, was adopted by many armies. The British used some FALs, produced under licence at the Royal Small Arms Factory, Enfield, but removed the automatic fire setting. With further modi-fications this became the L1A1 self-loading rifle (SLR), and was adopted by the Australians and New Zealanders. The weapon was used extensively by British, Malaysian, Gurkha, Australian and New Zealand troops in the Borneo Confrontation Campaign (1962–65). It was also used by the Commonwealth contingent in Vietnam. The USSR produced a simplified version of the StGw44, which made great use of die-stamped steel parts, in 1947. Claim-

ARVN soldiers in 1963 still using the M1 Garand (US Army via MARS).

ing that it was an original design by Mikhail Kalashnikov, the new weapon was called the Avtomat Kalashnikova 47 (AK47) and has become the standard small arm of all Communist armies. It is the most widely used rifle in the world.

The Soviets also produced a rifle during World War 2 which had features strongly reminiscent of the Garand design. Sergei Gavrilovich Simonov designed an anti-tank rifle (the PTRS) during the war, and after that conflict he produced a scaled down version to fire the 7.62 mm × 39 M43 cartridge. This weapon — the SKS — was a light, gas-operated, self-loading carbine which had the unusual feature of a permanently-attached, folding-blade bayonet. The AK47 and the SKS were made in the PRC and issued as the Type 56 (both of them, confusingly). The Chinese also produced a rifle which incorporated the best (for their purposes) features of the SKS and AK47 and was designated the Type 68. All of these were in use with the North Vietnamese Army and the Viet Cong.

It has been known for some time, certainly since World War 1, that most firefights take place at ranges less than 300 m (328 yd). This fact was taken into account in the design of the StGw44, the SKS and the AK47 although the SKS is said to have an effective range of 400 m (437 yd). As such great ranges as the 914 m (1,000 yd) at which British regular infantrymen classified on the SMLE (short-magazine Lee Enfield) before World War 1 were not needed, a lower-powered cartridge could be used. The StGw44

29

and AK47 used the German 7.62 mm Kurz (short). Lower-powered ammunition means lighter weight, and this in turn means that more of them can be carried. Ammunition expenditure in firefights has been increasing steadily since the introduction of the Chassepot rifle in the Franco-Prussian War (1870–71) and enough of it has to be carried or brought forward in some other way for the soldiers to conduct the battle successfully. This means that in the first instance at least the fight takes place with what the infantryman is carrying on his person. Various designs for weapons that can fire smaller-calibre ammunition, and also take account of other improvements in design to aid effective fire (such as the in-line recoil), have been around in the West since the end of World War 2. In the mid-1950s in America, Eugene Stoner of Armalite Inc produced a design for such a weapon. A modified version was submitted to the US Army Infantry Board, Fort Benning, which had laid down a requirement for a lighter, shorter range rifle (but having ranges at least comparable to the M1 Carbine). The result was the 5.56 mm AR15 Armalite, which was taken into service as the M16, and which came to be the most commonly used rifle among the Free World forces in Vietnam.

Until the advent of the AK47 and M16 rifles, soldiers other than the infantry used a variety of smaller weapons (such as pistols and SMGs) for personal protection. The two assault rifles altered that, and these weapons can now be found with soldiers of all arms and services, as they answered the need for compactness, light weight and high rate of fire. The role of the infantry is to close with the enemy and kill him, and to take, hold and dominate ground. Only the infantry man can do this, and in close country this means marching for long distances to and from a firefight carrying everything that he needs with him. Warfare in South-East Asia is on ground ideally suited to the infantryman's skills, and over which other arms and services (including air forces) operate at a disadvantage. Often, non-infantry find themselves employed in an infantry role in such a conflict. This is either because of the need for more and more foot soldiers to take on the burden of patrolling or 'search and destroy' missions, or to defend facilities (such as artillery firebases). Infantry skills are, after all, basic to all servicemen and are the foundation on which 'special-to-arm' training is built. In this role, the rifle (or carbine) and the various support weapons play a major part.

Carbines were originally shorter rifles supplied for use by cavalry and mounted infantry. The weapon was shortened either by reducing the length of the barrel or the butt stock or both. Although the compactness of rifles after the M16 has improved, many manufacturers produce carbine versions of these weapons making them even handier. Even the AR15 (the Armalite Inc original designation of the M16) had a carbine variant with a shorter barrel. Of course, shortening the barrel reduces the accuracy and effective range of the weapon. However, if it can still manage combat ranges of up to 300 m (312 yd) reasonably well this need not matter too much. Some manufacturers gave their product a carbine-style feature by providing a telescopic butt stock. This was an option with certain variants of the West German Heckler and Koch G3 (the G3A4), HK33 (the HK33KA1 and HK33A3), and was a permanent feature of the Colt Commando Assault Rifle. The Colt weapon was a response to a call from the Vietnam War for a shorter, handier version of the M16 (manufactured by Colt's Industries) specifically intended for use in the close quarter battle (CQB). Originally designated a survival weapon, it performed so well in the sub-machine-gun role that the US Army Special Forces were issued with it. The barrel was reduced in length and the butt was a telescopic straight tube with the length controlled by a large catch underneath near the shoulder piece. The shorter weapons tended to find favour with specialist troops, airborne soldiers, vehicle crews and the like. As these carbines had a selective fire capability, allowing them to fire bursts or fully automatic, they tended to replace the pure sub-machine-gun not least because they used the same ammunition as the rifles which made logistics and resupply much easier matters.

Prior to the introduction into Vietnam of the M16 rifle, the standard issued weapon with US forces was the M14 (firing the NATO standard 7.62 mm round) and the Commonwealth contingent used the L1A1 SLR. The M16 tended to displace the M14 completely from US use, but the Australians and New Zealanders — fresh from the experiences of the Borneo Campaign — kept the SLR while also adopting the M16. The power of the SLR had been amply demonstrated in Borneo. In the reduced combat ranges of close country fighting, it had been discovered that even if an enemy took cover behind trees of smaller girth a well-aimed round fired at the tree would pass through it and kill or injure him. Although the M16 could put down a lot of fire in a short time it was felt that it lacked 'stopping power', a complaint that was made again in 1982 by Royal Marines after the Falklands War. Some M14s, and the heavy-barrelled light support variant (the M14E2), found their way into the hands of the Viet Cong.

The M14 was kept on by the Americans as the sniper rifle. Called, until recent years, the US Rifle 7.62 mm M14 National Match (Accurised) it also had a target shooting-sniper variant known as the M1A. The rifle, with certain modifications, was recently redesignated the M21. The Australians adopted the British Parker-Hale Model 82 7.62 mm sniper rifle, and the New Zealanders used this rifle and the British L42A1 7.62 mm sniper rifle (which was a rebarrelled modification of the old No 4 .303 in, itself an improved version of the SMLE). The Soviet sniper rifle, used by the NVA and the VC, was the Dragunov SVD 7.62 mm, a well-designed and well-built precision arm which some Western users consider to be the best sniper rifle in the world to the present day. Communist forces in Vietnam did, however, use any rifle for sniping, often firing over iron sights. Both the Dragunov and the M14 (M21) were gas-operated, self-loading weapons. Only the M21, however, had a colectivo firo capability, allowing it to fire on automatic. Both the Model 82 and the L42A1 are bolt-action, single-shot rifles. All the rifles fed from magazines, although the British weapons could also use a manual single-round feed which some snipers prefer.

COMMUNIST FORCES

AK47 (USSR), Type 56 and 56-1 (PRC) 7.62 mm assault rifles

The Kalashnikov and its copies became the universal hallmark of Communist and Communist-supplied forces around the world. It was a simple, almost crude, weapon made largely from steel die pressings. It was very easy to operate, and has been described as a 'peasant's weapon'. The safety and fire selector were the same lever, located on the right side of the rifle. When this lever was lifted fully upwards, it jammed the bolt in the forward position thereby preventing its operation. To fire the weapon this lever had to be pushed downwards to one of two fire selections, and the rifle cocked. The first setting was automatic and the lower one was single shot, which reflects the underlying philosophy that it is preferable to fire fully automatic. It was, after all, an assault rifle

Right *A member of a US Navy SEAL (Sea-Air-Land) team finds the mud deep as he makes his way ashore from a boat. He is carrying a Stoner Mark 23 Commando 5.56mm machine-gun, a weapon unique to the SEALS* (US Navy via MARS).

Above *A US Navy SEAL team prior to a mission in April 1970. They carry a wide variety of weapons including Stoner machine-guns with both box and drum magazines, M16s and M26 and M61 grenades (US Navy via MARS).*
Below *An M29 81 mm mortar team in action (MARS).*

Above *Marines of the 1st Battalion, 26th Regiment, firing an M19 60mm mortar in South Vietnam, 1967* (USMC via MARS).

Below *Under the camouflage is an M113 armoured personnel carrier crewed by ARVN personnel* (MARS).

Above *A US Marine Corporal training an ARVN recruit to fire the M60 machine-gun* (USMC via MARS).

Below *A Marine Corporal using a flame thrower during operations at Khe Sanh in February 1968* (USMC via MARS).

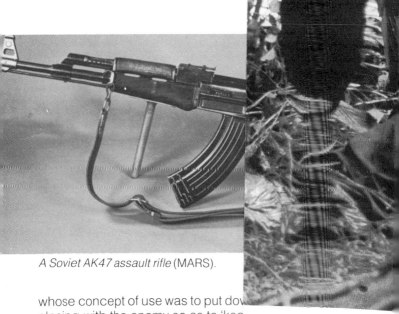

A Soviet AK47 assault rifle (MARS).

*A capture
along the*

whose concept of use was to put dow
closing with the enemy so as to 'kee
shoot the rifle like a sub-machine-g
Although the weapon was gas operat
unlike on most Western rifles. It fed
box magazine and had an effectiv
measured 868 mm (34.2 in) in len
(11 lb) with a loaded magazine. The
one had a fixed wooden butt stock ar
folding metal butt stock which was
release above the pistol grip. The f
699 mm (27.5 in) when the butt was f

butt) or /
from 195
Vietnam.

The Chinese Type 56 did not have
models were fitted with a permanentl
that folded back underneath the b
estimated that a single VC or NV
reliable weapon could hold a well-s
company. The Chinese folding-butt
as the Type 56-1, but did not featur
Type 56s. By 1968 most NVA ar
equipped with Type 56-1s.

The SKS
self-load
remarkab
the tip of
The Chi
This cop
bayonet.
which ha
single ro
magazine
was the

Although the Soviet Union gradu
the principal supplier of the Vietna
slightly modified variant of the AK4

Soviet AK47 assault rifle being used by a US Ranger on patrol ong Nai River in 1970 (US Army via MARS).

KMS (folding butt) t hat were issued to the Soviet Army
onwards found their way to the Communist forces in

SKS 7.62 mm S monov (USSR) and Type 56SKS (PR C) self-loading rifles

and the Type 56SKS) was a conventional gas-operated,
g rifle of a similar g eneration to the American M14. Its
e feature was the pe r manently-attached folding bayonet,
vhich lay in a recess in the forestock when not required.
se actually called the weapon the Type 56SA carbine.
of the SKS feature a longer barrel and had a needle
he rifle fed from an attached 10-round box magazine,
to be loaded throu gh the breech opening using either
nds or a 10-round magazine charger. Although the
was non-detachabl e, a unique feature of the weapon
elease catch whic h allowed the magazine to swing

North Vietnamese troops training with Type 56SKS self-loading rifles (MARS).

downwards so that rounds could be spilled out for unloading purposes. The rifle had an effective range of 450 m (492 yd). It weighed nearly 4 kg (8.8 lb), and measured well over 1 m (1.1 yd) in length. It was not particularly widespread among the Vietnamese Communist forces, probably for the same reason that the bigger Western rifles were not used by other South-East Asians. The smaller rifles such as the AK47 or M16 better suited the small stature of the inhabitants. Also in close country, and where concealment of the weapon was desired, such a large rifle as the SKS (or Type 56SKS) was a disadvantage.

MAS 49 7.5 mm self-loading rifle (France)

After World War 2 the French Army used a gas-operated, self-loading design produced by the *Manufacture d'Armes de St Etienne* as the rifle for re-equipping their soldiers. Many of these came to be used by the Vietnamese on both sides of the DMZ, both during the war against the French and afterwards against the

Americans and their allies, but their use declined with the availability of other weapons. The 7.5 mm ammunition became a problem for the Vietnamese as stocks diminished, although some weapons were recalibrated to fire 7.62 mm cartridges. The length of the weapon — over 1 m (1.1 yd) — was a disadvantage to both South Vietnamese and the NVA and VC. As larger numbers of AK47s and Type 56s became available, the MAS 49s tended to be relegated to lower echelon troops or to disappear altogether. The rifle had a wooden butt and fore stock, and had the interesting feature of an integral grenade launcher at the end of the barrel It had an effective range of 600 m (656 yd), and fired only on semi-automatic feeding from a detachable 10-round box magazine. The weapon weighed nearly 5 kg (11 lb). A luminous night sight could be fitted to the rifle.

Dragunov SVD 7.62 mm sniper rifle (USSR)

Some of these sniper rifles appeared towards the end of the conflict in Vietnam. It was a semi-automatic, gas-operated sniping rifle which had been purpose built for that task. It used the well-proved basic Kalashnikov action, but had been strengthened to take the M1908 rimmed 7.62 mm cartridge of the old Mosin-Nagant rifle. The butt stock was an unusual cut-away design which developed from the rear of the pistol grip. A cheek piece was attached to the butt for a more comfortable firing position. The weapon had an effective range of 900 m (987 yd), and used the Soviet PSO-1 telescopic sight. The rifle was, however, also fitted with ordinary iron tangent sights. It was long — 1,224 mm (48.6 in) but weighed only 4.4 kg (9.7 lb). Although it was a gas-operated self-loading weapon it only fired single shots, lacking an automatic setting. It fed from a 10-round detachable box magazine.

Its appearance in the latter stages of the Vietnam War can be viewed really as a form of 'field trials', for its widespread adoption by the Soviet and Warsaw Pact armies took place in the late 1960s, replacing the M1891/30 sniping rifle. Some of the older rifles were seen in the Vietnam theatre, as was the Mosin-Nagant upon which the Dragunov SVD 7.62 mm sniper rifle was modelled, but the length, lack of rapid firepower and the unusual cartridges which they used made their value less desirable. This was particularly so when there were other rifles that could perform the type of sniping tasks required of them by the Vietnamese.

FREE WORLD FORCES

M16 (AR15), M16A1, and Colt Commando 5.56 mm rifles (USA)

Eugene Stoner of Armalite Inc produced a design for a 5.56 mm rifle during the 1950s, and after trials by the US Army Infantry Board at Fort Benning and certain modifications a version was produced for the US Air Force in 1961 with the designation AR15. The Army took a number of the rifles for evaluation in Vietnam, and followed this up with a large order. Increasing numbers were required over the years — 85,000 were taken in 1963, 100,000 in 1965 and a further 100,000 in 1966. By 1969, the US Army had accepted the M16 as the standard rifle and by 1980 over four million had been produced. Colt took over the manufacturing in 1962, and although some were produced by other firms under an agreement with the US government, most M16s have been made by Colt. The M16A1 was a later variant whose chief modifications

The leading man of this US Marines patrol is carrying the Colt Commando whose shorter barrel length can easily be seen compared with that of the M16 held by the second man. Note M26 grenades attached to the leading man's belt (USMC via MARS).

Above *Carrying M16s and festooned with ammunition for an M60 machine-gun, US Rangers board a UH-1D helicopter after a reconnaissance mission* (US Army via MARS).

Below *An artillery forward observation officer 'spots' a target for a US Marine firing an M16 during Operation Prairie II* (USMC via MARS).

were a burst-fire selection and a plunger-type 'bolt assist' for forcing the bolt home if the return spring fails to do this for any reason. It was also produced in a shorter-barrelled carbine version.

The Colt Commando was a shorter, handier weapon based on the M16 but specifically intended for the close quarter battle. The barrel had been reduced to 254 mm (10 in) and, to compensate for the greater muzzle flash produced as a result of the shorter barrel, a large flash suppressor was fitted. The butt was a telescopic tube whose length was controlled by a large catch underneath at the shoulder end. The M16 family were gas-operated, selective-fire, self-loading rifles feeding from detachable 20- or 30-round box magazines. A typical rifle weighed just over 3 kg (6.6 lb) and measured 990 mm (36.6 in) in length. The Colt Commando was 787 mm (30.9 in) long with the butt extended and 711 mm (28 in) when telescoped. The flip aperture rear sight of the rifles was contained between flanges (for protection) on the fixed carrying device located on the receiver above the pistol-grip trigger mechanism. This carrying handle gave the M16 some of its characteristic outline. The design of the weapon incorporated the 'in-line recoil' feature that had been known about for some years before. This meant that the recoil from firing drove the weapon in a straight line along the line of sight, so that the tendency for the rifle to move off the point of aim was considerably reduced. It also tended to limit the climbing effect when firing on automatic or bursts. The handiness of the M16 meant that it became the standard weapon of all arms and services of the US forces in Vietnam, and was widely adopted by the Americans' allies too.

L1A1 7.62 mm self-loading rifle (UK and Australia)

The Australians and New Zealanders in Vietnam adopted the M16 as a replacement weapon for their sub-machine-guns. The standard personal weapon remained the SLR, which was manufactured in Britain at the Royal Small Arms Factory, Enfield, and in Australia at the Small Arms Factory, Lithgow, New South Wales. It was a gas-operated self-loading rifle adapted from the Belgian FN FAL to suit the requirements and philosophy of the British and Commonwealth soldier. The FAL was used in the last moments of the Malayan Emergency (which ended in 1960), and its SLR descendant performed sterling service in the Borneo Campaign (1962–65). Experience in Borneo with the weapon was repeated in Vietnam,

A British L1A1 SLR as used by the Australians and New Zealanders in Vietnam (G. Cornish Collection via MARS).

and the rifle has been retained with the sole modification require-ment for a shorter version for close country use. This variant the Australians designated the L1A1-F1. The SLR weighed 5.4 kg (11.9 lb), and was 1,136 mm (44.7 in) long. It had an effective range of over 600 m (656 yd), and fed from a 20-round detachable box magazine. The 30-round magazines of the L4A4 Bren light machine-gun (LMG) and the L2A1 heavy-barrelled light support weapon (heavy-barrelled FN) were interchangeable with the 20-round ones of the L1A1. The power of the rifle was such that the firer could engage a target sheltering behind small trees and still inflict fatal wounds.

M14 7.62 mm NATO calibre rifle and M14 National Match (Accurised) sniper rifle (USA)

Until the introduction of the M16, the M14 was the standard rifle of the US forces and saw service in Vietnam from 1957 onwards until its replacement. The M14 National Match (Accurised) was the sniper rifle variant, which has been renamed the M21 in recent years. Production of the M14 ceased in 1964. A further variant was the M14A1 which came close to being a light machine-gun, leading one authority to call it a 'machine rifle'. The A1 had a pistol grip, a folding fore-hand grip about half-way down the forestock, a folding bipod, a shoulder strap, and a sleeve was fitted over the muzzle to act as a compensator when firing fully automatic. This helps to keep the barrel down and prevent 'climb'. The M14 was

Above *On patrol in 1966 carrying M14 7.62 mm rifles* (USMC via MARS).

Below *Men of the US 1st Infantry Division armed with M14s survey a Viet Cong sniper position, October 1965* (US Army via MARS).

adopted in 1957 as the successor to the World War 2 M1 Garand, and was basically an evolution of that rifle.

The main and more obvious improvements on the M1 Garand were the gas system and magazines. On the M1 the magazine was fixed and had to be loaded using a charger. On the M14, detachable 20-round box magazines were used. The normal M14 fired semi-automatic only. A slide-on bipod could be provided, and the rifle fitted the M76 grenade launcher which was slipped on to the flash suppressor and secured to the bayonet lug. The M14 weighed 5.1 kg (11.2 lb), with a full magazine and cleaning kit carried, and measured 1,120 mm (44 in) in length. It had a maximum effective range on automatic with the M2 bipod fitted, and on semi-automatic without the bipod, of 460 m (503 yd). When the bipod was added, the semi-automatic range increased to 700 m (766 yd). A special suppressor was fitted to the muzzle of the sniper rifle which did not affect the performance of the bullet, but reduced the velocity of the emerging gases to below that of sound. This made location very difficult as the target heard only the 'crack' of the passing bullet and no 'thump' from the rifle.

L42A1 7.62 mm sniper rifle (UK)

The New Zealand Army adopted the L42A1 and the Australians the Parker-Hale Model 82 as their sniper rifles. During the Vietnam War the current rifle was the L42, which was a conversion of the .303 in Number 4 bolt action rifle. It used a heavier barrel, calibrated to 7.62 mm, and the fore stock was cut back to about half-way along the barrel length. A wooden cheek piece had been fitted to the butt stock. The magazine held ten rounds and the cartridges were bolt-fed into the breech. Individual single rounds could be laid on the breech, when the bolt was back, and fed into the chamber. This allowed the firer to wipe the cartridge clean of any dust, dirt, and oil which might affect its performance. This was a practice favoured by many snipers and match competition shooters. The rifle weighed 4.4 kg (9.7 lb) and was 1,181 mm (46.5 in) long. The range was limited by the sights and the abilities of the firer, but was not less than the 800 m (875 yd) required of a good sniper rifle. Such ranges were rare in many parts of Vietnam, and most sniping opportunities could be handled by the normal-issue rifles.

GRENADES AND RIFLE GRENADES

Explosions and metal shrapnel are useful ways of breaking up concentrations of the enemy, for demoralizing him, stunning him long enough to close with him and attacking him in his hides and dug-outs. For many years from the fifteenth to early nineteenth century soldiers used a spherical bomb with a length of fuze hanging out to set it off. The shape looked very like a pomegranate fruit, which is called *granata* in Spanish after the name of the Andalusian city of Granada. From this came the word grenade.

These weapons went out of fashion during the later nineteenth century, partly because they were heavy (up to 1.8 kg (4 lb)), dangerous to the handler and needed specialist soldiers — grenadiers — to use them, and partly because the older-style siege warfare had been made obsolete by artillery. However, during the Russo-Japanese War (1904–5) a need for hand-thrown bombs was found and both sides took to improvizing hand grenades. World War 1 gave the development of grenades several boosts, as it proved to be an extremely useful weapon in trench warfare.

Two principle types of hand-grenade emerged. Offensive grenades were designed to be used by an assaulting infantryman who could throw it and not be a victim of his own bomb. This was produced by having a high-explosive filling in very thin metal walls. The metal fragments did not have enough kinetic energy to harm the thrower but the considerable flash and blast would daze and demoralize the enemy long enough to close with him. This effect has recently been refined into 'stun grenades' using cardboard walls and an explosive mixture that maximizes flash and blast pressure. Defensive grenades used thick metal walls and often further metal fragments in the filling, to increase the size and number of shrapnel pieces. By the use of special fitments and a gas cartridge it became possible to fire defensive grenades from a rifle and hurl them at an attacking enemy.

With the coming of the tank, a new threat arose to the infantry-man. Part of the counter to the tank that was used by some armies was the anti-tank grenade. This became possible by develop-ments in fuze mechanisms which allowed an impact detonation, coupled with the use of a shaped charge of explosive. It had been found that a hollow or shaped charge would concentrate and direct the explosion into a small area, thereby considerably increasing its effect well above what might have been expected from the amount of explosive used. Anti-armour hand-grenades were not very popular in Western armies, as the user has to be almost suicidally close to the tank, but they have been used to great effect by soldiers equipped by the USSR in which army they are still employed. In the 1973 October War in the Middle East, Egyptian soldiers found that the Soviet RKG3M anti-tank hand-grenade could penetrate 165 mm (6.5 in) of armour plating, enough to defeat the front armour on the US-made M60 Patton main battle tank. RKG3s were used by the Communist forces in Vietnam, along with other types of grenades supplied by the USSR and the PRC, as well as many captured ones. They are ideal in the close quarter battle, for attacking bunkers and strongpoints, and neutralizing machine-guns.

Most hand-grenades cannot be thrown beyond 35 m (38.2 yd), and have a maximum casualty radius of about 15 m (16.4 yd). Thus there is a gap in the high-explosive cover given to defenders between 50 m (54.7 yd) out to the lowest range of the supporting mortars — about 300 m (328 yd). To cover this gap, many armies have reintroduced rifle grenades, or adopted special grenade launchers. The Americans in Vietnam used two such launchers — the M79 40 mm (which looks like a large shotgun and is used by the British Army for firing 'rubber bullets') and the M203 40 mm which is fitted to an M16 rifle. Both these weapons have a maximum effective range of about 400 m (437 yd).

Apart from high-explosive hand-grenades, there are also gas-grenades of various sorts and smoke-grenades. Smoke is an essential part of the soldier's battle, enabling him to move without being observed by the enemy — something that is vital when cover is sparse or when he is in actual contact. The type of gas-grenades that were used in Vietnam were of the riot control type — mostly CS gas — which were used particularly in the Viet Cong tunnel complex of Cu Chi (north-west of Saigon) to flush the VC out. The main smoke used tactically by the infantry is white phosphorus, principally because it gives an instant dense white cloud. It is also a very effective anti-personnel weapon. Smoke, especially coloured smoke, is also used for ground-to-air signalling. This indicates the position on the ground to the aircraft and gives an idea of wind speed and direction if the aircraft is going to land.

COMMUNIST FORCES

F1 anti-personnel defensive hand-grenade (USSR), Type 1/M33 (PRC)

This grenade was introduced into the Soviet Army during World War 2 and had a notched cast-iron body similar to the British Mills 36 or the US Mark II. As with those two, a number of fragments from the base plug and filler could be lethal out to some 200 m (219 yd) depending on the sort of ground on which the grenade went off. This could be as dangerous to the thrower as it was intended to be to the enemy, and so he was well advised to throw the grenade from cover. It weighed 600 g (1.3 lb) and was filled with TNT. It had a delay fuze, giving 3–4 seconds before detonation. The effective fragment radius was about 15 or 20 m (16.4 or 21.9 yd) (not forgetting the base plug), and the grenade could be thrown to a distance of 30 or 45 m (32.8 or 49.2 yd) according to the skill of the user.

RG42 anti-personnel defensive hand-grenade (USSR), Type 42 (PRC)

This was another World War 2 grenade of the Soviet Army. It was a fragmentation concussion grenade, which was shaped like a tin

A selection of NVA hand grenades displayed by the US Navy's Explosive Ordnance Disposal Team No 33 in Saigon — from left to right an RGD5, two F1-type 'pineapple' grenades and an RG42 (US Navy via MARS).

can. It contained a separate fragmentation sheet inside, which was formed into a grooved diamond pattern. The filler was TNT and the delay fuze gave 3–4 seconds. It was thrown in the same way as the 'egg-shaped' grenades and needed to be used from behind cover. It weighed 436 g (15.4 oz) and had an effective fragment radius of 25 m (27.3 yd). The grenade could be thrown about 40 m (43.7 yd).

RDG33 anti-personnel hand-grenade (USSR)

Although obsolete in the Soviet Army, this grenade was used by the Communist forces in Vietnam. It was a stick-grenade that could be used in either offensive or defensive roles. Offensively it was a seamed tin-plate cylinder with a screw thread to allow the attachment of a metal throwing handle, and had a lethality radius of some 5 m (5.5 yd). To convert it into a defensive grenade, a pre-grooved diamond-pattern metal sleeve was fitted over the outside of the cylinder. It was held in place by a stud on the cylinder engaging with a notch on the sleeve. In this role it had a lethal fragmentation radius of 25 m (27.3 yd). In the defensive role it weighed 722 g (1.6 lb) and in the offensive form 508 g (1.1 lb). It had a delay fuze of 3–4 seconds and was filled with 85 g (3 oz) of TNT.

Captured RDG33 stick grenades, RKG3 anti-tank grenades and a 7.62 mm DPM light machine-gun (US Navy via MARS).

RGD5 anti-personnel defensive hand-grenade (USSR), Type 59/M32 (PRC)

At the time of the later years of the Vietnam War this was the latest Soviet hand-grenade and was designed to replace the F1. It was an 'egg-shaped' grenade with a smooth sheet-steel body joined horizontally. Inside the body was the fragmentation liner, which was serrated in the Soviet models and smooth in the Chinese ones. It was just over half the weight of the F1, being 310 g (10.9 oz). It was filled with 110 g (3.9 oz) of TNT, and used the standard UZRG fuze giving a delay of 3–4 seconds. Being lighter, it could be thrown farther than the F1, and had an effective fragment radius of 15 to 20 m (16.4 to 21.9 yd).

RKG3 and 3M anti-tank hand-grenade (USSR), RKG3T (PRC)

This was another grenade which appeared in the later years of the Vietnam War. It was introduced into the Soviet Army to replace the older RPG40, RPG43 and RPG6 anti-armour hand-grenades and to supplement the RPG7V anti-armour grenade launcher. It had a stick-grenade appearance. In the throwing handle was a four-panelled fabric drogue which was pulled out when the grenade was thrown. This completed the arming of the weapon and stabilized it in flight. It also ensured that the weapon could be dropped on to the top of an armoured vehicle from a height. The RKG3 was capable of penetrating 125 mm (4.9 in) of armour, and the RKG3M was proved in the 1973 October War in the Middle East (where it was used by the Egyptian Army) to penetrate 165 mm (6.5 in). It contained a shaped HEAT (high-explosive anti-tank) charge of 565 g (1.2 lb) of mixed TNT and RDX in a steel (RKG3) or copper (RKG3M) cone. The fuze was an instantaneous impact type, and there was an effective fragment radius of 20 m (21.9 yd). The whole grenade weighed 1.07 kg (2.35 lb) and so a thrower had to keep under cover to avoid the fragments (as well as the tank's guns) as it was difficult to hurl the grenade far beyond the fragment radius. Although earlier grenades, and with lesser penetration, the RPG6, RPG40 and RPG43 were also used in Vietnam. Their methods of operation were almost identical to that of the RKG3, but they were stabilized in flight by strips of fabric instead of the drogue of the later weapon. The weights and shape of the grenades were very similar, as was the fragmentation radius. The filling used was TNT and the penetrations were 100 mm (3.9 in) for the RPG6 and 75 mm (3 in) for the RPG43.

Home-made grenades (VC)

The Viet Cong proved to be adept at manufacturing grenades in the field. The collecting of the materials required great courage, not least because the main source of the explosive was from unexploded American shells and bombs. The casing would be cut open with hacksaws and the explosive extracted. Not a few VC were killed when the bomb or shell detonated. Fragmentation particles were made imaginatively from all sorts of materials, including the gravel used for surfacing roads. The grenades were contained in tins, mostly American in origin, gleaned from the debris that the US forces left behind on a battlefield. Thus beer cans, C-ration (American 'compo') tins and other suitable containers would be used. The Australians quickly learned the value of the 'burn-bash-bury' drill they were taught at jungle warfare school, but American rubbish continued to be a rich source of material for the VC throughout the war. Captured or looted American grenades were also employed.

FREE WORLD FORCES

Mk2 anti-personnel defensive hand-/rifle-grenade (USA)

The Mark 2 grenade was later replaced by the M26 and M61 grenades. It had the classic 'pineapple' shape of World War 2 hand-grenades and consisted of a serrated cast-iron body filled with 57 g (1.9 oz) of flaked TNT. Although it had a stated fragmentation radius of about 10 m (10.9 yd), there was the same problem of base plug and other fragments reaching as far as 200 m (219 yd) from the point of impact that the Soviet F1 and the British 36 grenade had. It weighed 595 g (1.3 lb), and a fit thrower should have been able to reach at least 30 m (32.8 yd) with it. It could be fired out to 140 m (153 yd) with a service rifle fitted with an adaptor and a blank charge. It had a 4–5 second delay fuze.

M26 and M61 anti-personnel defensive hand-grenades (USA)

This was a two-part, smooth-bodied grenade which was joined horizontally at the middle. It weighed 425 g (15 oz) and was made of a thin sheet-steel wall with a notched fragmentation coil inside. The detonation effect was to send 1,000 fragments out to 10 m (10.9 yd) with a 50 per cent hit probability against standing men in the open. The filler was 156 g (5.5 oz) of Composition B with 8 g (0.28 oz) of tetryl pellets. It had a 4–5 second delay fuze and could be thrown to about 40 m (43.7 yd). The M61 was the same grenade with a slightly different actuation block. In the A2 variant, the M26 had an M217 electrical impact (with overriding delay function) fuze making it into an impact-detonated hand-grenade.

M79 40 mm grenade launcher (USA)

There was a great variety of 40 mm grenade cartridges which could be fired from both the M79 and the M203 grenade launchers. They were fixed munitions, consisting of a cartridge case and projectile. Among the options were a number of high-explosive grenades,

US Rangers equipped with M79 grenade launchers and M16s move in on Viet Cong positions near Saigon during January 1968 (US Army via MARS).

Men of the 503rd Infantry (Airborne) Regiment dug-in and under fire, November 1967. They are equipped with M79s, M16s and a variety of grenades (US Army via MARS).

including an airburst projectile, buckshot (multiple projectile), smoke, parachute smoke, flares and riot control CS gas-grenades. The M79 was a single-shot, shoulder-fired weapon which broke open like a shot-gun for loading and the cartridge was inserted in the breech. A rubber pad was fitted to the shoulder piece of the butt stock to absorb some of the shock. The grenades were fin stabilized in flight. A trained man could shoot grenades into nominated windows in a house at 150 m (164 yd) range. At further ranges it was necessary to know exactly how far away the target was, as the round had a very high trajectory. A large flip-up sight was fitted about half-way down the barrel, and a simple leaf foresight was attached to the end of the barrel. The rear sight was calibrated to 375 m (410 yd) in 25 m (27.3 yd) intervals. The tactical use of the weapon required the gunner to be dedicated to the M79, so he could carry no other weapon apart from a pistol. The overall length of the weapon was 737 mm (29 in) and its loaded weight was nearly 3 kg (6.6 lb). It had an approximate maximum range of 400 m (437 yd).

M203 40 mm grenade launcher (USA)

The M203 was developed to fulfil a requirement for a rifle-grenade launcher package to replace the M79, which was only a grenade launcher. It was fitted to the M16 rifle so the gunner could take a normal part in the firefight using the rifle until he was needed to fire his grenades. It appeared during the final years of the war. It was a lightweight, single-shot, breech-loaded, pump-action weapon which was attached to the M16 rifle and fired from the shoulder. The safety catch was housed inside the trigger guard just forward of the trigger. To fire the weapon the catch had to be pushed forward. The M203 had its own trigger assembly which, when fitted to the rifle, lay in front of the magazine, which served as a pistol grip for the launcher. A special perforated receiver fitted on to the rifle. On top of this was the sight assembly of the launcher, which was graduated in 25 m (27.3 in) increments from 40 to 400 m (43.7 to 437 yd) (for the quadrant sight fitted to the rifle's carrying handle) and in 50 m (54.6 yd) intervals for the leaf sight fitted to the receiver from 50 to 250 m (54.6 to 273 yd). The weight of the rifle and launcher together was approximately 5 kg (11 lb). The M203 had a maximum range of 400 m (437 yd) approximately, a maximum effective range for area targets of 350 m (383 yd) and for point targets of 150 m (164 yd).

MACHINE-GUNS

Although machine-guns of various sorts (especially the Gatling and Maxim Guns) existed before World War 1, it was only in that conflict that their importance on the modern battlefield came to be realized. They dominated no man's land between the lines of trenches, and it became almost impossible to move in the open without attracting their fire. The design of Hiram Maxim came to be adopted by nearly all armies, the main exception being the Hotchkiss favoured by the French, as their medium machine-gun. It was during this conflict also that the light machine-gun was born.

The water-cooled, tripod-mounted, belt-fed medium machine-gun (MMG) and its higher-calibre derivative the heavy machine gun (HMG) tended to be absent from the Vietnam War except in an anti-aircraft role, although they were on occasion used otherwise. The Free World forces used an air-cooled MMG in either .30 in or .50 in calibre — the Browning 'thirty cal' or 'fifty cal'. The HMGs of the Soviet 14.5 mm KPV type tend towards the cannon classification (20 mm). The KPV actually fires a round that was originally developed for use by an anti-tank rifle.

The Germans developed a machine-gun after World War 1 which could function in a bipod-mounted light role, or in a tripod-mounted (with a heavier barrel) sustained-fire role. Thus was born the general-purpose machine-gun (GPMG). The German MG34 and MG42 were used boldly and imaginatively, and after World War 2 the idea was preserved and developed. Most NATO armies adopted the GPMG principle, and for a while this type of gun ousted the light machine-gun (LMG) as the section (squad) support weapon. The Soviet Army also adopted a GPMG — the PK — but kept LMGs in its sections as well. The US Army GPMG is the M60, and this was accepted as the GPMG for the Australian Army also when it went to Vietnam. The British LMG during World War 2 and afterwards was the .303 in Bren Gun in various marks. When the country standardized on NATO 7.62 mm ammunition, the Mark II and Mark III Brens were converted, using a Canadian breech block, to become the L4 series Bren LMG. This weapon was favoured over the GPMG by the Royal Marines for naval use, and the gun was used extensively as the main light support weapon during the Borneo Campaign (1962–65). This experience was shared by the Australian and New Zealand Army serving with the Commonwealth Brigade, and the L4 Bren was kept and used in Vietnam.

The portable light support weapon gives a section (squad) commander much-needed automatic firepower to win a firefight and support his attack. It also provides weight of fire when in the defence, enabling large bodies of troops to be engaged and defeated. In defensive positions, the number of machine-guns tended to be increased and often heavier calibre weapons were provided to 'beef up' the firepower. Thus, in many of the Fire Bases set up by the US Army and ARVN Special Forces sandbag sangars or fire trenches were equipped with .30 in or .50 in Browning MMGs and HMGs, as well as having as many M60s as could be provided. Machine-guns, however, use a lot of ammunition and belt-fed ones use more than box-magazine types. Resupply is therefore a major headache for the force commander. The amount of ammunition of all types expended in a 'siege' such as at Plei Me in October 1965 is staggering. Plei Me, defended by 400 Montagnards, together with US and ARVN Special Forces and Rangers, commanded by Colonel (then Major) Charles Beckwith USASF, successfully held off attacks from two North Vietnamese regiments (each equivalent to a small British Army brigade) until relieved by the 1st Air Cavalry. The NVA had ringed the Fire Base with 12.7 mm (.51 in) HMGs.

During the Vietnam War, an older type of machine-gun principle was revived. The Gatling Gun, first made in 1862, used a method in which a number of barrels were arranged in a circle which was rotated. As a loaded barrel reached the 12 o'clock position, the round in its chamber was fired and the barrel rotated away to reload and cool down, and allow another loaded barrel to be fired. This method was taken up, and the hand-cranking of the old Gatling was replaced by an electric motor to turn the barrels. The Gatling Gun could produce a cyclic rate of 1,000 rounds per minute for brief periods, but reloading slowed this down in practice. Using the electric motor and belt feeding, the General Electric M134 Minigun could produce between 4,000 and 6,000 rounds per minute at a top rate. The gun was, however, used on aircraft and helicopters and was not a ground weapon although it could have been used to good effect fired from sangars or APCs. The AC-47 gunship used a Douglas C-47 Dakota aeroplane fitted with three Miniguns on its left (port) side. When the gunship opened fire at ground targets, the smoke seemed to puff out of the side of the aircraft giving rise to its nickname of 'Puff the Magic Dragon'.

Most of the machine-guns used by the Communist forces were, of course, of Soviet or Chinese origin. These were supplemented by those they captured or otherwise acquired from the Americans and their allies. In common with other equipment supplied to the Vietnamese, North and South, by the USSR and the PRC the machine-guns they received were not always the latest. However, they were well tried and tested and extremely robust, being quite forgiving of rough handling. They were also very effective. The heavier calibres were used often in anti-aircraft roles, both north and south of the DMZ, and also featured in the helicopter ambushes that the NVA and VC laid on for US 'search and destroy' missions, often inflicting heavy casualties to men and machines.

COMMUNIST FORCES

DP range 7.62 mm light machine-guns (USSR & PRC)

The Degtyarev Pekhotniy (DP) was designed by Vasily Alexeyevich Degtyarev and first appeared in 1926. In 1944 it was modernized by Shilin to become the DPM — DP modernized. These two weapons have given rise to a number of derivatives. The DPM was manufactured by the Chinese as the Type 53 LMG. A World War 2 development of the DPM eventually came into service in 1946 as the RP46 and the Chinese version was known as the Type 58. A wholly belt-fed derivative of the basic Degtyarev design was the RPD and RPDM, which the Chinese made as the Type 56 and 56-1 LMGs. These were all section (squad) support weapons, and although they were no longer in service with the Soviet and Warsaw Pact armies, they were used in Vietnam. All were gas operated. The DP and DPM (Type 53) fed from a 47-round pan magazine. The DPM had improvements over the DP in having a pistol grip and a stronger bipod. The RP46 (Type 58) was intended as a company support weapon, and so was fitted to use a 250-round belt as well as the 47-round pan, and a carrying handle was fitted to the forward end of the body (about half-way along the length of the whole gun). The RPD (Type 56 and 56-1) was the final version of the range. It was a purely belt-fed gun, with the belt contained in a drum attached below the gun allowing for easier carriage and for one-man operation. There was a wooden carrying grip over the barrel and gas cylinder, forward of the ammunition feed tray. All the members of the series were over 1 m (1.1 yd) long and weighed in excess of 7 kg (15.4 lb). The RP46 actually weighed

13 kg (28.6 lb). They all had an effective range of 800 m (875 yd), and had only the automatic setting for the rate of fire.

RPK 7.62 mm light machine-gun (USSR) and TUL-1 7.62 mm light machine-gun (NVN)

Soviet policy has been to replace older weapons with designs by Kalashnikov since the adoption of the AK47 rifle. The RPD Degtyarev-designed section machine-gun has thus been replaced by the Kalashnikov-designed RPK — the Ruchnoi Pulemet Kalashnikov. It was first seen publicly at the 1966 May Day Parade in Moscow. Some of these weapons were sent to the Vietnamese. The Vietnamese also produced their own LMG based on the Chinese Type 56 assault rifle and the RPK, called the TUL1. The Vietnamese gun lacked the rate controller which was a feature of the RPK. Using the basic AK47 design, both guns were gas operated and could feed from any of a 40-round box, the AK47 or AKM 30-round box, or a 75-round drum magazine.

The gun had a heavier barrel than the assault rifle upon which it was based, and measured 1,030 mm (40.5 in) overall. It weighed 5 kg (11 lb) and had the normal LMG effective range of 800 m (875 yd). Sighting was by a post foresight and a leaf rearsight graduated in hundreds of metres from one to ten. There was also a windage scale. A U-shaped battle-sight notch on the leaf rearsight gave coverage over the ranges 100 to 300 m (109 to 328 yd) — the standard combat setting. A bipod was fitted well forward on the barrel and could be folded underneath and clipped in place for carriage.

DSh K38 and K38/46 12.7 mm heavy machine-gun (USSR) and Type 54 (PRC)

The 12.7 mm Degtyarev-Shpagin heavy machine-gun, and the Chinese Type 54 version of it, have been used extensively by many guerrilla movements and had considerable use in Vietnam both in a support role and as an anti-aircraft machine-gun. The original design was produced in limited numbers in 1934. In 1946 the cartridge feed mechanism was replaced by the shuttle system of the RP46, and this weapon was named the K38/46. The parts were not interchangeable. The K38 had an instantly recognizable large

Above *DSh K38 12.7mm heavy machine-gun on its tripod mounting after being discovered in an arms cache by ARVN troops* (MARS).
Below *Souvenirs for the Marines — captured DSh K38s* (USMC via MARS).

circular drum-like feed mechanism, whereas the K38/46 had a flat rectangular feed cover. The K38 fed from the left side of the gun, and the K38/46 could be easily adapted to feed from either side by changing some parts in the feed mechanism. There was a quick change barrel. That of the K38/46 had a unique muzzle brake which was absent from the K38 barrels.

The ground-role mount was the Sokolov-designed wheeled carriage, which had a seat for the firer reminiscent of the World War 1 Hotchkiss. Some versions also had a small protective shield for the firers. The wheeled mount allowed the gun (which was very heavy at 36 kg (79.2 lb) to be moved easily by man, animal or vehicle. The AA mount was effected by removing the wheels, gun, shield and axle. The three legs which formed the trail of the wheeled mount were then opened out, and the gun replaced on what was the saddle seat. The special AA ring sight was inserted into a dovetail fitting on the left side of the receiver. This Model 1943 AA sight needed two men to operate it but proved very effective nevertheless. The normal ground sights were orthodox. The foresight was a screw-up pillar, the rearsight a two-pillar leaf with an elevating screw at the top to move the cursor up or down. There was a U-shaped combat setting on the cursor for use when the leaf was down. The sight radius was 1,111 mm (43.7 in). The effective range of the gun was 2,000 m (2,187 yd). The gun was gas operated, automatic fire only, and fed from a continuous metallic-link belt holding 50 rounds.

SG43, SGM (USSR), Types 53, 57 (PRC) 7.62 mm Goryunov medium machine-gun

The Goryunov was originally produced by the designer Peter Maximovich Goryunov to supplement the fire of DP and DPM LMGs. It was a simple, robust and reliable gun, which was gas operated and fed from the standard Soviet closed-pocket-type belt of 250 rounds used on the RP46. It could be mounted on a wheeled carriage, and even adapted to fit the older Sokolov wheeled mount, or on a Sidorenko-Malinovsky tripod. Both wheeled carriages could be inverted and used as AA mounts. All models of the Goryunov had a quick-change barrel which had a chrome-lined bore and a carrying handle. The gun fired automatic only and with the easily-changed very heavy barrel 5 kg (11 lb) it was simple

Viet Cong SG43 7.62mm machine-guns on anti-aircraft mountings (MARS).

to keep up a good rate of fire. The foresight was a cylinder positioned between two protectors and the rearsight was a U-notch mounted on a tangent leaf. The gun fired from the open breech position. Because it used a closed-pocket belt, the cartridge had to be withdrawn from the belt by the loading mechanism, lowered to the level of the barrel and rammed into the chamber by the bolt. The cartridge feed slide could be quickly removed without stripping the weapon, and many captured guns in Vietnam were found to be inoperable because the VC had taken off this vital component and thrown it away before abandoning the gun. The empty gun was heavy, weighing nearly 14 kg (30.8 lb), and measured well over 1 m (1.1 yd) in length. The sight radius was 850 mm (33.5 in), and the gun had an effective range of 1,000 m (1,094 yd). The PRC version of the SG43 was called the Type 53 heavy machine-gun, and the SGMB variant was known as the Type 57 HMG.

M08 7.62 mm Maxim (USSR), Type 24 (PRC) medium machine-gun

This World War 1 MMG was used by the VC both in ground-support and anti-air roles. The models used were the M1910 steel-jacketed version. It was a water-cooled, belt-fed, automatic-only machine-gun. The effective ranges were in excess of 1,000 m (1,094 yd). The Russian and Chinese variants of the original German 08 model used the Sokolov wheeled mount, allowing the gun to be easily manhandled or moved by animal or vehicle. Often a shield was fitted for the gunner's protection.

KPV 14.5 mm Vladimirov heavy machine-gun (USSR)

The KPV was used by the North Vietnamese and Viet Cong very successfully as an anti-aircraft arm. The gun was developed after World War 2, in the mid-1950s, by Vladimirov to fire the high-velocity round produced for the Degtyarev PTRD41 and PTRS anti-tank rifles after these weapons were phased out, as the ammunition had proved so successful. Its original conception was for it to be used as an anti-aircraft machine-gun. It was designed for simplicity of manufacture, with considerable use of stampings and some welding and riveting. Apart from the ejection port the gun was sealed against dust and dirt. The KPV was short-recoil operated with gas assistance provided by a muzzle booster. This was a departure from the usual Soviet gas operation, but had obviously been designed for aiding quick barrel changing. The air-cooled, quick-change barrel (weighing over 19 kg (41.8 lb) with jacket) was chromium plated and fitted with a muzzle booster and flash hider.

The AP-I or HEIT ammunition was fed into the gun from a 100-round continuous metallic closed-pocket belt, which could be broken down into handy 10-round groups. It could feed either way up, and the gun could take either right- or left-hand feeds. The gun was very heavy, weighing over 49 kg (108 lb) and measured over 2 m (2.2 yd) long. It had an effective range of 2,500 m (2,734 yd) in the ground support role and in the AA role a formidable effective range of over 1,500 m (1,640 yd). Towed-carriage mountings were provided for single, paired or quadrupled guns. These were known as ZPU1, ZPU2, and ZPU4. The ZPU2 version was encountered in considerable quantities in Vietnam, and claimed a substantial number of US aircraft of all types. ZPU4s were also used extensively in North Vietnam for protection of installations against US air strikes. They were often located on the bunds or 'dikes' around the paddy fields, as were other types of anti-air artillery, and suppressive strikes against them caused some destruction of the bunds. This led to the allegation that the Americans were deliberately attacking the 'dikes' to flood the countryside and ruin the rice crops (by drying the plants out).

FREE WORLD FORCES

M1919A4 .30 in medium and M2 HB .50 in heavy Browning machine-guns (USA)

The need for heavier machine-guns for support as well as for use on AFVs (armoured fighting vehicles) in Vietnam, gave these two World War 2 guns new leases of life. So useful did they prove, that the M2HB has resumed production in the USA and in Belgium for export. They were also used in the 1982 Falklands War. They were both used in the support role in Fire Bases in Vietnam, and the M1919A4 (being more portable) was used as a company and battalion support gun. Both guns were based on the M1917 .30 in medium machine-gun, although the water-cooling jacket was abandoned in favour of an air-cooled barrel. The M1919A4 had its barrel (which was heavier than that of the M1917) encased in a perforated steel jacket. The M2 .50 in was a development of a gun that was intended for aircraft use, increasing the mass of the barrel (hence the HB — heavy barrel — designation) and eliminating the artillery style oil buffer which had been installed to absorb the high recoil energy of the breech block.

Both guns were mounted on the light M2 tripod for ground fire. In the 1970s, some 250,000 of these tripods left over from World War 2 were discovered in British Army Ordnance storage and were converted for use as 'bore-sighting' equipment for rifles and machine-guns in Northern Ireland. Both guns were short recoil operated and belt fed. The M1919A4 uses a 250-round pocketed-cloth belt, and the M2HB a 100-round disintegrating metallic-link belt. Some M1919A4s were converted to the NATO 7.62 mm × 51 round for use by the US Navy. Both guns have, at 400–500 rounds per minute, a rather slow cyclic rate of fire. As a result of experience in Vietnam, and the growing shortage of the .30-06 M2 Springfield (7.62 mm × 63) ammunition, more M1919s are being converted to the 7.62 mm × 51 calibre cartridge. The Australian Department of Defence Engineering Development Department at Maribyrnong, Victoria, produced a conversion to take the NATO 7.62mm ammunition in the M13 disintegrating metallic-link belt and the

M2 .50 Browning heavy machine-gun emplaced on a hill top at Con Thien (USMC via MARS).

cyclic rate was increased to 650–750 rpm. Both guns had changeable barrels. Some models of the M2HB had their rate of fire increased to 700 rpm, but this heated the barrel up quickly and it had to be changed often.

The M2 weighed just over 38 kg (83.6 lb) and the M1919 14 kg (30.8 lb). The M2 tripod weighed another 6.35 kg (14 lb). The sights on both guns were a blade foresight and a leaf rearsight. The M1919 had an effective range of 900 m (984 yd) and the M2 1,400 m (1,531 yd). The M1919 could only fire on fully automatic, but the M2HB had a selective-fire capability. Both guns had a prominent cocking lever on the right sight of the body. The M2 had a two-hand grip with push-button trigger, whereas the M1919 used a single pistol grip with a semicircular lever trigger.

M60 7.62 mm general purpose machine-gun (USA)

This gun was introduced into US service in the late 1950s. It is notable for being the first GPMG in the US inventory, and for being the first US machine-gun with a quick-change barrel, although in the marks used in Vietnam this feature was less than satisfactory. It saw extensive service in the Vietnam War, and was adopted by the Australians as their GPMG. It was an automatic-only, gas-operated weapon feeding from a disintegrating metallic-link belt.

The Australians developed a box (holding 40 rounds of link) that could be attached to the weapon for easier carriage and firing of the weapon. This was a similar idea to the 50-round belt-feed box of the British L7 GPMG. The metal boxes made an awful rattle when carrying, and were useless when silence was needed on patrol or in covert operations. The Gurkhas came up with a novel solution to this problem in the Borneo Campaign. A 1958 pattern webbing water-bottle carrier had a large hole cut in the cover flap, and the carrier was attached to the body of the gun under the ammunition feed using D10 signals wire. The link was carefully coiled and placed in the water-bottle carrier, and the flap closed with the rounds led out through the hole and placed on the feed tray of the gun. This gave both silence and convenience of carriage. The practice has been widely adopted in the British Army and by the Australians. It was, of course, an unauthorized modification and officially frowned upon.

The M60's original feed system was based on that of the German MG42, and the piston and bolt assembly of the German FG42 was used. Vietnam experience led to modifications of the feed. The marks of the gun used in Vietnam had an odd arrangement of barrel, bipod and gas cylinder, which made barrel changing unnecessarily difficult and gave the gun's Number 2 crew member an equally unnecessary weight to carry. The bipod and gas cylinder were permanently attached to the barrel, and the carrying handle fitted to the receiver. When firing on sustained fire, the exterior temperature of the barrel could reach 500°F (literally glowing in the dark). To change the barrel, the whole assembly had to be removed, and this operation needed both crew members. Number 1 had to hold the gun secure by the butt and carrying handle, and Number 2 (wearing heat-resistant asbestos gloves) had to pull the barrel-bipod-gas cylinder assembly free after releasing the barrel locking lever. While Number 1 held the gun, Number 2 fitted the new barrel. Number 1 then had to readjust the zeroing setting to cater for the new barrel before resuming fire.

Experience gained in the Vietnam War led to the introduction of the M60E1. The rather flimsy carrying handle of the M60 was

Above *An M60 7.62mm machine-gun emplaced on the perimeter of the 173rd Airborne Brigade's positions prior to the assault on Hill 875 in November 1967* (US Army via MARS).

Below *A Marine Corporal firing an M60 from the hip — note expelled cases being ejected* (USMC via MARS).

replaced with a more robust one, and the gas cylinder and bipod mounted on the gun itself. The M60 had a straight-line recoil shape which made control easy when firing. It had the interesting features of a plastic heat guard on top of and underneath the body, forward of the trigger mechanism, and the bipod had heat shields attached so that when folded up the hands of the firer need not touch any hot metal. This was a great help when firing from the hip on the move or standing. A canvas belt carrier for a 100-round belt could be fitted to the left side of the gun, which kept the ammunition free of undergrowth. The gun weighed over 10 kg (22 lb) and was 1,105 mm (43.5 in) long. It had a fixed blade foresight and a U-notch leaf rearsight. The M60's effective range was 1,000 m (1,094 yd) on the bipod and 1,800 m (1,969 yd) on the M122 tripod.

The Australians introduced into the tactical use of the M60 two practices, based on experience. In jungle, the first reaction firefight takes place with only a few rounds being fired off while the soldiers take cover. Australian gunners used to fit a short belt of only about 15 or 20 rounds on the gun, which was enough for the first firing. A full belt was fitted after going to ground. They also designed and manufactured a 'ready reaction magazine' of 28 rounds, enough for the initial exchange of fire, which fitted on to the belt carrier attachment of the M60 and fed into the ammunition feed tray. After taking cover, a full belt was loaded. The ready reaction magazine stuck out of the side of the gun 'a bit like on the old Sten Gun' as it was described by an Australian veteran of the Vietnam War.

L4 7.62 mm Bren light machine-gun (UK)

Although a rather light LMG with a slow cyclic rate of fire (500 rpm), the Bren has continued to give good service since its first adoption in .303 in calibre in August 1938. When the British Army standardized on the NATO 7.62 mm × 51 ammunition in 1952, Mark II and Mark III Brens were converted by the Royal Small Arms Factory at Enfield Lock in Middlesex to take the new round. Barrels were made in the new calibre, and the breech block made for the Canadian 7.92 mm Bren was adopted. The 7.62 mm Bren was given the designation of L4, and various marks of this have since appeared. It has remained in British service with certain Territorial Army units, with the Royal Marines (who also use the L7 GPMG) and the Royal Navy, and is also used by many units when deployed in Northern Ireland. It was used extensively in the Borneo

Above *Now obsolete, the 'Ontos' was a lightly armoured air-portable tracked tank destroyer armed with six M40 106mm recoilless guns* (USMC via MARS).
Below *M110 8-in self-propelled howitzer with its recoil spade dug in firing at a distant Viet Cong target* (MARS).
Bottom *An observer spots for an M40 106mm recoilless gun mounted on a Jeep* (MARS).

Above *Personnel at the ARVN Armor School prepare newly acquired M-48s for training at Thu Duc, South Vietnam* (US Army via MARS).

Below *An M-48 just prior to setting off on an operation* (MARS). .

Above *General Lam, CO of the 2nd ARVN Division, and Brigadier-General Platt, CO of Tactical Force Delta (a Green Beret unit, not to be confused with the later 1st Special Forces Operational Detachment Delta formed by Charlie Beckwith), examine a captured Viet Cong DSh K38 machine-gun (USMC via MARS).*

Below *Men of the 4th Battalion, 173rd Airborne Brigade, move into position to assault Hill 875 near Dak To on 23 November 1967 (US Army via MARS).*

weapon to operate. Its IAs (immediate action drills) were simple and fast, and the gun could be manned for most of the time by one crew member if necessary. The bipod used could be extended, as each leg had a telescopic extension. This did, however, have the annoying tendency to catch in undergrowth and get pulled out. For most movement the bipod was folded back along the underside of the barrel. The L4 Bren was a gas-operated, selective-fire weapon with a very fast barrel change. It had an effective range of 600 m (656 yd), which was adequate for a section support weapon but a bit short for some defensive purposes. The foresight (attached to the changeable barrel) was a blade with protective 'ears', and the rearsight was a tangent leaf with an aperture hole calibrated in 50 m (55 yd) intervals from 200–1,650 m (219–1,805 yd). There was a V-notch battle sight on the bottom of the leaf near the hinge. The gun measured 1,133 mm (44.6 in) in length.

Because the Bren Gun was rather light on sustained fire, the Australian Army opted for the M60 GPMG with the added advantage of interoperability with the Americans in Vietnam, in spite of the disadvantages of this gun. The New Zealanders adopted the British L7 GPMG, which was a better-designed gun. Both armies, however, kept the L4 Bren as a section support weapon, and used it extensively in this role in Vietnam.

L2A1 7.62 mm heavy barrel FN FAL (Australia)

Made at the Small Arms Factory, Lithgow, New South Wales, the L2 was a slightly modified version of the Belgian *Fabrique Nationale* FAL HB (heavy barrel) and was similar to the Canadian C2 automatic rifle. It was used by the Australians and New Zealanders to give a measure of supporting fire to units other than the infantry. It was also useful on jungle patrols. It was used in these roles by both armies in Vietnam. Its basic features were those of the L1 SLR, with the addition of a heavier barrel and the restoration of the selective-fire setting. There was also a tangent-aperture leaf rearsight calibrated between 200 and 1,000 m (219 and 1,094 yd), with a V-notch battle sight. The foresight was a blade with protective 'ears'. It was gas operated and fed from a 30-round box magazine (interchangeable with that of the L4 Bren and the L1 SLR). It weighed 7 kg (15.4 lb) and measured 1,137 mm (44.8 in) in length. It had a higher cyclic rate than the Bren at 650 to 750 rounds per minute, and had a maximum effective range of 800 m (875 yd).

ANTI-ARMOUR WEAPONS

The principal characteristics of all armoured fighting vehicles (AFVs) are protection and mobility on the battlefield. In the case of infantry combat vehicles and some infantry support vehicles fire-power can be added to these attributes. It is a fact of military life that somebody will always come up with a counter to any advance, or 'edge', that the other side has developed. So it is with AFVs. From the time that Lieutenant H. W. Mortimore's tank signalled the arrival of the AFV on the modern battlefield at 05:30 on 15 September 1916 at the Battle of the Somme, the other side has been trying to knock them out. In fact this very tank received two direct shell hits not long after its arrival at the German trenches, which knocked it out and killed two of the crew. Thus, within half-an-hour of each other, the world was presented with a new weapon system and with its main counter — the artillery gun.

The anti-tank gun remained the principal answer to the tank, and its offshoot the armoured personnel carrier (APC), until the mid-1940s when free-flight rocket projectiles appeared both as man-portable weapons and as 'recoilless rifles'. This type of anti-tank weapon has remained in service with all armies ever since, and seems to have a lot more life left in it. It has been supplemented since the 1950s by the anti-tank guided weapon (ATGW). Thus three basic types of anti-tank weapon are in service side by side.

Of the artillery-type gun, the most effective now is another tank gun, and the role of the tank often seems to be defeating other tanks. The advent of the very successful Soviet T-34 tank in the summer of 1941 led the Germans to develop the concept of the Panzerzerstörer, the 'tank destroyer', or Jagdpanzer the 'tank hunter'. This function is now incorporated in all main battle-tank designs. In spite of this tank-against-tank battle, the tank never-theless presents a formidable problem for the infantry. This led to the introduction in 1944 of the Panzerschreck and Panzerfaust free-flight rocket-assisted grenade by the Germans. The British produced the PIAT gun (projectile, infantry, anti-tank) and the Americans the Bazooka shoulder-fired recoilless rifle. The Soviet arm was the RPG2, developed from the Panzerfaust. There were also a number of anti-tank rifles; the British had the Boys anti-tank rifle, the Americans the Browning and the Soviets the Simonov PTRS. These were not much use against the heavier armoured tanks of the later years of World War 2, but could still be effective against APCs.

Since the Second World War only the Soviets and the Warsaw Pact countries have persisted with the hand-thrown anti-tank grenade. Nevertheless, the principle incorporated in that device is used in the missiles and some of the gun rounds — the hollow or shaped charges designated HEAT (high explosive, anti-tank) and HESH (high explosive, squash head). The other principal anti-armour round is armour-piercing (AP) solid shot. This was the type of round fired by the anti-tank rifles. Their descendants, the heavy machine-guns such as the .50 in M2HB Browning, the 12.7 mm K38 DSh and the 14.5 mm KPV Vladimirov, though not much use against main battle tanks, can be devastating against APCs (especially the side armour) and light armoured vehicles (LAVs). LAVs used to be called 'soft-skinned' vehicles, a phrase that better describes their condition, and are things like Jeeps, Land Rovers and military lorries or trucks.

The Vietnamese did not use their T-55 MBTs much before the last year of the war in 1975, and those that they did use were mostly killed from the air by helicopter gunships or fixed-wing air strikes. One of the missiles used was the air-to-surface Maverick television-guided anti-armour missile. Another missile was also used in its ground role; the M151 TOW (tube-launched, optically-tracked, wire-guided) ATGW, usually mounted on Jeeps but sometimes fired from its tripod. The Soviet-built APCs that the NVA had were often similarly killed from the air, but when they were encountered by ground troops they were easily despatched by the anti-armour weapons possessed by the American and other troops. Building on the experience of World War 2 and the Korean War, it was found that the man-portable infantry anti-tank weapons such as the M20 'Super Bazooka', the L14 gun infantry 84 mm 'Carl Gustav', or the M72 (or L1) 66 mm LAW (light anti-armour weapon), were extremely destructive when fired at bunkers, sangars or buildings in which the enemy was under cover. They were also useful to blow a hole in the wall of a building when house clearing.

The Americans and their allies used armoured vehicles extensively during the war in Vietnam. These were mostly APCs, but often M48 MBTs were used on certain search-and-destroy missions. There was also a range of LAVs used. The main APC was the American M113, which was used by all the Free World forces, and this was often fitted with a turret and gun to act as a fire support vehicle (FSV). This large number of armoured vehicles presented the NVA and VC with a problem, and they employed a great variety of anti-armour weapons to counter it. These were mostly of Soviet origin, although the PRC versions were also used. Apart from hand-thrown anti-tank grenades, they used the RPG2 and RPG7V rocket launchers, captured American equipment (especially the M20), and a number of wheeled anti-tank guns and recoilless rifles. Most of the anti-armour effort during the Vietnam War was thus, naturally, on the Communist side.

In attacking an armoured vehicle such as a tank or APC, there are certain parts of it which are particularly vulnerable and other parts which can be defeated if the weapon used has enough penetrative power. The front part of the AFV is the least easy to defeat, for the thicker armour is also sloped into a wedge-shaped glacis and often reinforced by lengths of spare track bolted on. The side and rear armour is normally thinner than the front, and the most vulnerable parts arc thc underneath of the tank's body, the tracks and drive wheels, the turret ring and the top engine cover. The bottom of the AFV is generally more vulnerable than the top. An anti-armour team will therefore try for a side or rear shot. The main points of aim will be the tracks, drive sprockets, road wheels, side armour of the body and turret, and the turret ring. From a raised fire position, the team may be able to hit the engine cover. If the weapon they are manning fires projectiles with graze fuzes (meaning that a glancing strike will detonate the round) and sufficient penetrative power — such as a HEAT round — then a front end shot may be possible against the glacis and front of the turret. If the weapon is very accurate (such as the L14 'Carl Gustav'), with a thin warhead, then a turret ring shot may well be very effective. The L14 round has a long thin detonator head to facilitate this.

Anti-tank hand-grenades tend to strike the tank from above, as the thrown trajectory carries it high into the air and the grenade descends on to the vehicle nearly vertically. This gives the shaped charge the best angle to do its damage. However, the grenadier has to be very close to the tank, some 20 m (21.9 yd) away, which makes him vulnerable to the fire of the tank's guns and to any supporting infantry. It is a near-suicidal activity. The armour of APCs — even the front armour and glacis — is much thinner than that of tanks, and thus more easily defeated by the variety of available anti-armour weapons. Against these, light anti-armour weapons (LAWs) — such as the American M72 66 mm or the Australian version, the L1A2F1 66 mm — and rocket assisted rifle grenades — such as the Soviet RPG2 and RPG7V — can be devastatingly effective.

Heavier anti-armour weapons, such as the range of anti-tank

guns and recoilless rifles, have been supplemented by guided missiles. The principal ATGW (anti-tank guided weapon) in use in Vietnam during the war by ground troops was the TOW M151E2 heavy anti-armour weapon (HAW). This type of weapon can defeat any known main-battle tank, with a dramatic explosion. They tend to be guided electronically by means of a long wire connecting the missile with the gunner's control box on the weapon's firing platform. The USSR also has ATGWs, but none seems to have been used much, if at all, by the Communist forces in the Vietnam War

With ATGWs and free-flight rockets, there is a back-blast given off as the rocket motor is ignited. The gunners have to keep this back-blast area in mind when siting and firing their weapon, for not only will the dust and debris kicked up give away their position, but also fires can be started which will do the same and may even endanger the weapon's crew. Friendly troops caught in the back-blast area will receive nasty injuries, and so the weapon needs to be sited with this in mind too.

COMMUNIST FORCES

Type 51 90 mm rocket launcher (PRC)

This was a copy of the American M20 3.5 in 'Super Bazooka', with the same physical characteristics and performance. It broke into two parts for carriage. It was of fractionally larger calibre at 90 mm rather than the 3.5 in (88.9 mm) of the American weapon. When broken down into its two parts, which clipped together when carried, it measured 760 mm (29.9 in) in length and when assembled for firing it measured 1,530 mm (60.2 in). It weighed 5.45 kg (12 lb). The rocket was loaded into the rear end of the weapon by the Number 2, who also teased out a long wire which he wrapped around a connector on the outside of the barrel. When Number 1 squeezed the trigger, he in fact worked a magneto that sent an electrical current through the connector and down the wire to activate the rocket. Misfires could be a common problem if the wire was not properly connected and hangfires were not unknown. Misfire drill could be a hazardous business for the Number 2. The range of the weapon was 1,200 m (1,312 yd), but this was degraded by combat conditions and was really limited by the view and sight picture of the Number 1. The missile had a penetration of

267 mm. Many of this type of weapon used by the VC and NVA were in fact American M20s which they captured, or acquired by other means.

RPG2 and RPG7 (USSR), Types 56 and 69 (PRC), P27 (Czech) grenade launcher

These were shoulder-fired, man-portable weapons developed originally from the World War 2 German Panzerfaust (meaning mailed, or armoured, fist) — not to be confused with the modern German PZF44 Lanze, which is also known as the Panzerfaust and which has the same parentage as the Warsaw Pact weapons and looks remarkably like them. The RPG2 (Type 56) was eventually replaced by the RPG7V (Type 69) which had greater penetration, improved range, and certain other modifications. The Czechoslovakian P27 was essentially similar to the RPG2, but was larger, had better sights and fitted a bipod. It weighed 6.4 kg (14.1 lb) as opposed to 4.67 kg (10.3 lb) for the RPG2 (Type 56) when loaded, and was actually shorter (1,030 mm (40.6 in) compared to 1,194 mm (47 in)) in the launcher's length. The Soviet grenade of the RPG2 could penetrate 150–175 mm (5.9–7 in) of armour, the Chinese Type 50 grenade of the Type 56 launcher could penetrate 265 mm (10.4 in) and the Czech missile could penetrate 250 mm (9.8 in). The effective ranges were about the same, varying between 100 and 150 m (109 and 164 yd). Beyond this range LAVs could be effectively engaged still, but the grenade was less useful against armoured vehicles. The tube calibre was 40 mm (1.6 in) (P27 45 mm (1.8 in)) and the grenade was 80 mm (3.1 in) for the Type 56, 82 mm (3.2 in) for the RPG2, and 120 mm (4.7 in) for the P27.

The reload rate of the launcher was quite fast, and a good gunner could fire 4–6 rounds per minute with it. All these launchers were designed to be fired by one man, who also carried the reload grenades in a satchel on his back. Further reloads could be distributed around the supporting troops. All types could fit the Soviet NSP2 infra-red sight for low-light operation.

The RPG7V (Type 69) appeared in 1962, and was a product-improved version of the RPG2. It had an image-intensifier sight for low light as well as being able to fit the infra-red night sight. The grenades were percussion fired as with the RPG2. A cardboard cylinder containing the propellant was first screwed into the missile, which was then inserted into the muzzle of the launcher. The

North Vietnamese troops with RPG7 Type 69 anti-tank grenade launchers (MARS).

trigger was squeezed, which fired the missile. At a certain, very consistent, distance from the launcher the rocket motor ignited to accelerate the missile and this sustained the grenade out to about 500 m (547 yd). With the RPG7 grenades, four knife-like fins snapped outwards after the missile had cleared the muzzle of the launcher to stabilize it in flight. There were more, smaller fins at the rear end of the projectile which gave a slow turn in flight to the missile. This further improved its stability. In still air, the missiles had reasonable accuracy but if there was any cross wind they were somewhat erratic. When the motor had burned out, any wind tended to blow it bodily downwind and off course. Another disadvantage was the fuzing system, which was a piezo-electric type. This worked by producing a voltage to detonate the grenade when it was crushed against the target's inner skin. This could be shorted out by such simple means as placing wire mesh around the target. When the nose cone struck this, inevitably touching two strands of the wire, the fuze was shorted out rendering the missile inoperable. In common with many Soviet-designed anti-armour weapons, the grenades used a shaped-charge HEAT warhead. These grenade launchers are in widespread use, and were prominent in Communist forces' employment in Vietnam because of their great portability and availability. They were a great headache, and caused a lot of damage.

B10 and B11 (RG107) (USSR), Types 36, 52 and 65 (PRC), T21 (Czech) recoilless guns

These were recoilless guns of a type similar to the American M18A1 57 mm, M27 105 mm, M40 106 mm, and M67 90 mm and the British 120 mm battalion anti-tank gun (BAT, and later modifications were the CONBAT and WOMBAT). The Warsaw Pact weapons used a projectile which looked very like a mortar bomb. These were fin-stabilized HEAT bombs or shells, but there were a number of HE rounds available for direct and indirect fire at softer targets. The guns were breech loaded, with multi-vented breech blocks to allow the gases to escape to the atmosphere. They were all wheel mounted for manoeuvrability and could be pulled for short distances by two men. They also had tripod mounts, and the wheels could be disengaged to allow these to function. The Soviet B10 and B11 (PRC Types 52, 56 and 65) were heavier weapons and had to be fired from their mounts. The Type 36 and the

Type 36 57 mm recoilless gun together with DSh K38 heavy machine-guns (Christopher F. Foss via MARS).

Czechoslovakian T21 Tarasnice could also be shoulder fired. The maximum effective ranges were about 450 m (492 yd), and typically the rounds could defeat armour of around 250 mm (9.8 in) thickness.

The T21 weighed 20 kg (44 lb), the Type 36 just over 35 kg (77 lb), the B10 (Types 52, 56 and 65) about 87 kg (191 lb) and the B11 over 300 kg (660 lb). The length of the B11 was 3.5 m (3.8 yd), whereas the other types were all about 1.5 m (1.6 yd). They all had a rate of fire of around 6–7 rounds per minute. The PRC Type 52 was a copy of the American M20 RCL gun, and the Type 56 was an improvement of this, but whereas the Type 52 could fire either Chinese or American ammunition the Type 56 could only use Chinese natures. The larger of these RCL guns, when firing HE in the indirect-fire role, could reach ranges of about 6 km (3.75 miles). The Type 52 was quite popular with the NVA and VC because they combined firepower with light weight (maximum HE-indirect range of 6,675 m (7,230 yd), and HEAT-direct of 800 m (875 yd)) and could fire both PRC and American ammunition. They were often used in attacks on Fire Bases (such as at Plei Me) and other strong-points.

FREE WORLD FORCES

M20 3.5 in rocket launcher (USA)

This weapon, often called the 'Super Bazooka', replaced the M9A1 2.36 in Bazooka rocket launcher. Although used in Vietnam, it was on its way out of American service. It was however a very useful weapon, firing a 3.5 in HEAT rocket which was effective against AFVs, buildings or bunkers and sangars. The missile used a copper cone-shaped charge of a fifty/fifty mixture of RDX and TNT, with a percussion non-delay fuze. The rocket was magneto fired, and fin stabilized in flight. It had a maximum range of 1,100 m (1,203 yd) and a maximum range against armour of 110 m (120 yd) and could defeat some 130 mm (4.4 in) of armour. The weapon broke down into two parts which clipped together for carriage. In Vietnam it was mostly used as an anti-bunker weapon.

M72 66 mm HEAT rocket light anti-armour weapon (USA)

This one-man, throw-away type rocket launcher replaced the M20 for most purposes, and saw considerable service in Vietnam — mainly as a bunker buster. An Australian version is produced now called the L1A2F1 LAW. The M72 series consisted of two concentric tubes. The outer tube had a rubber- or PVC-encased pressel-switch trigger mechanism and pop-up rear and fore sights mounted on the top. The aluminium inner tube contained the missile. The open ends of the launcher were closed by flat front and rear covers. To arm the weapon, the covers were removed and discarded, and the tubes pulled apart until a sharp click was heard and felt. This was the inner tube locking into the outer tube in the launching position. The sights both popped up with this action. The launcher was placed on the firer's shoulder, steadied at the fore end with one hand while the other hand encircled the body of the weapon with the palm and thumb. The fingers were placed on the pressel-switch trigger. When the weapon was on target and the 10 m (11 yd) back-blast area clear the switch was firmly pressed. A safety handle first had to be pushed forward to the release (or 'arm') position. The rocket was fin stabilized in flight and was detonated by a piezo-electric crystal in the nose sending a small electric charge to the fuze in the base of the warhead. After firing, the launcher was discarded. A number of complete assemblies could be carried in a section (squad), each person could pack at least two if necessary. Each launcher assembly (with missile) weighed only 2.36 kg (5.2 lb). The maximum effective ranges were 300 m (328 yd) against stationary targets and 150 m (164 yd) against moving ones. The missile could defeat approximately 305 mm (12 in) of steel plate armour. It was very effective against sangars and bunkers.

M67 90 mm recoilless rifle (USA)

The M67 was an older type of weapon, but nevertheless served in Vietnam. It was comparatively lightweight (16 kg (35.2 lb)), portable, and served by a crew of two. It was intended for use against AFVs, but was also effective against sangars and bunkers. It was a breech-loaded, single-shot weapon shaped like a long tube with the sight assembly and firing mechanism offset to the side in opposite directions about half-way along the barrel. The breech was hinged on the right side, and had to be swung open by Number 2 to load the M371E1 HEAT round. It was then swung closed. When the rifle was fired, the rear end of the shell case broke up and was blown out of the back of the breech block. The M67 measured 1,346 mm (53 in) in length and could be fired from the shoulder or ground mounted. It had a maximum effective range of 400 m (437 yd) and was sighted to 800 m (875 yd). The shell could actually be fired as far as 2,000 m (2,187 yd). The weapon was air cooled, and when being used at the rapid rate of 10 rounds per minute the crew was supposed to observe a 15-minute cooling period after every five rounds.

L14 84 mm medium anti-armour weapon 'Carl Gustav' (Sweden)

Although a Swedish weapon (Swedish designation 84 mm 'Carl Gustav' M2 RCL gun), it was bought by the British and Australian armies as their medium anti-armour weapon (MAW) and given the designation L14. In this role it served in Vietnam with the Australians, although the Swedes were supporting the North Vietnamese. There was a variety of ammunition natures which could be fired by the gun; these included HEAT, HE, and illuminating. The gun was

A Carl Gustav 84mm medium anti-armour weapon; note also Model 45 9mm sub-machine gun (FFV-Ordnance Division via MARS).

very accurate, and the missile could defeat 400 mm (15.7 in) of armour. It had ranges of 450 m (492 yd) with HEAT, 1,000 m (1,094 yd) with HE, 1,300 m (1,422 yd) with smoke and 2,300 m (2,515 yd) with illuminating. Each HEAT round weighed 2.6 kg (5.7 lb), and each of the two gunners could carry four reloads.

The projectile had a long thin needle in the front which contained a piezo-electric fuze. The needle optimized penetration and stand off distance for the shaped-charge warhead. The shells of all natures were spin stabilized by a driving band at the rear of the projectile which was rotated by the rifling in the barrel. The driving band rotated independently of the body to ensure that the rate of spin did not degrade the HEAT effect of the round. Loading was done by Number 2, who opened the bell-like venturi at the rear of the gun to check that the gun was empty (or to remove the spent case from the previous firing), checked that the new round was the right way up and loaded it into the barrel. As the round was percussion fired, it was necessary for the percussion cap and the firing pin to match up and the Number 2 had to ensure this. The venturi was then closed. This action made the firing mechanism operative again. Number 2 then signalled Number 1 that the weapon was loaded. The gun could be fired from the shoulder in any of the standing, sitting, prone or supported positions that the infantryman used, but in prone positions the firer had to angle his body to the left away from the back-blast from the venturi.

The weapon was equipped with a bipod about half-way along

the barrel and the housing of this also acted as a shoulder stop. There were two pistol grips, one at the front to steady the weapon and one about half-way between the muzzle and the shoulder with the trigger mechanism. Sighting was telescopically assisted and was located on the left side of the gun. The length of the weapon was 1,130 mm (44.5 yd) and it weighed just over 14 kg (30.8 lb). It was thus highly portable. However, the shape of the gun (especially when the flexible bipod was fitted) was awkward and this could fatigue the crew members through having to use less than optimum carriage positions. It was a very effective weapon, and as a 'bunker buster' was devastating — this was demonstrated in Vietnam and was emphasized later in the Falklands War.

M40A1 106 mm (USA) and L6 120 mm WOMBAT (UK) HAW recoilless guns

Since the Vietnam War, both these guns have been replaced by ATGWs. The WOMBAT has been succeeded by the Euromissile 'Milan' and the M40 by TOW, although TOW also saw service in Vietnam. Mostly they were used mounted on vehicles, although the WOMBAT was often towed behind on its wheeled carriage and the M40 could be fired from a tripod mount (the front leg of which had a wheel for quick realignment). Both could fire HE as well as the normal anti-armour rounds, and provided the infantry battalion with something like its own artillery. The BAT series suffered from a large back-blast area which gave away its position after the first shell was fired, making it vulnerable to suppressive fire from other tanks than the one engaged. This gave rise to the description among infantry that it was a 'VC once only' weapon — any decorations were likely to be posthumous!

The L6 had a venturi breech similar to that on the L14 'Carl Gustav', which accounts for the enormous back-blast. The 120 mm shell was fired by electrical means. The current was provided by batteries enclosed in the firing arm. A .50 in (12.7 mm) spotting rifle was fixed to the barrel and calibrated to the trajectory of the 120 mm shells from the main gun. This rifle was the American M8 used on the M40. It fed from a 10-round magazine, and fired a tracer bullet which also had an explosive head. The tracer showed the track of the bullet, and the explosion of the head gave a white puff which marked the strike. When 'on target' the main gun was fired. The disadvantage with the spotting shots was that they too could give away the position of the gun. The L6 weighed 295 kg (649 lb), but could easily be laid on its wheeled carriage with the aid of two manhandling bars at the front of the muzzle (these folded back when the gun was in action). The gun was 3,860 mm (152 in) long, and stood 1,090 mm (42.9 in) high. The maximum range for a first-round hit was 1,000 m (1,094 yd). This is short by modern standards, but as a direct-fire artillery weapon in the context of the Vietnam War was adequate.

The M40 used the same spotting rifle (the M8) as the L6, with the same principle. The gun had an interrupted screw breech block, which was hinged on the left side. This was opened and closed by a characteristic breech-operating lever which stood above the rear of the weapon and was one of the means of identifying the gun. Although it was described as 106 mm, it was actually 105 mm. The designation was introduced to avoid confusion with the M27 105 mm RCL rifle, as soldiers tend to refer to the guns by their calibre rather than their classification. The M40 weighed nearly 210 kg (462 lb) when unloaded, and was 3,404 mm (134 in) long. It had a maximum range of nearly 8 km (5 miles), but the effective range was only 1,100 m (1,203 yd). The maximum range of the gun firing the anti-personnel tracer (APERS-T) round was 3,300 m (3,609 yd). It was frequently mounted on a Jeep or an M113, and used as a direct-fire infantry support weapon against Communist troops or bunkers.

M151E2 127 mm TOW heavy anti-armour weapon (USA)

The M151E2 HAW entered service in 1972 in time for the fighting following the NVA 'Easter Offensive' in Vietnam, when the Vietnamese crossed the DMZ in strength with tanks (T-55s) and other AFVs. Many of these vehicles were killed from the air, but a considerable number were engaged on the ground in some desperate fighting by ARVN and allied troops. The 'Easter Offensive' failed, and the military capability of North Vietnam was neutralized by the air offensive Operations Linebacker I and II later that year. TOW proved itself in Vietnam. The acronym TOW stands for 'tube-launched, optically-tracked, wire-guided missile'.

The system was made up of six units; tripod, traversing unit, launch tube, optical sight, missile guidance set and battery

TOW heavy anti-armour weapons mounted on Jeeps of the 1st Air Cavalry Division in Vietnam (AP via author).

A TOW being fired from a Jeep during Marine Corps tests in California (Hughes Aircraft Co via MARS).

assembly (housed in the missile guidance set). The missile was the BGM71A, which had an infra-red source in the tail for the gunner's missile guidance set to track. There were two motors; the launch motor and the flight motor. The M7 double-based propellant of the launch motor was completely burnt up before the missile left the launcher tube. The flight motor ignited about 12 m (13.1 yd) from the weapon to protect the crew. The guidance wires were paid out from two spools at the back of the missile, for the semi-automatic command-to-line-of-sight (SACLOS) guidance. The same missile was used in the airborne variant, which simplified logistics considerably. The BGM71A missile will defeat any known modern main-battle tank, and thus was extremely effective against the older T-55s of the NVA. It uses a HEAT shaped-charge warhead. The TOW system can be man-packed by its crew, or used from a vehicle. In Vietnam it was mostly used mounted on a Jeep or M113, or transported by vehicle and set up to cover set arcs of fire on its tripod. The weight of the complete system was 78.5 kg (172.7 yd), and each missile weighed an additional 24.5 kg (53.9 lb). The missile was fin stabilized in flight. It was contained in a tube for carrying and launching. The whole container was loaded into the launcher tube, and after firing the empty container was discarded.

MORTARS AND ARTILLERY GUNS

Since the Napoleonic Wars in the early years of the nineteenth century, modern battlefields have been increasingly dominated by artillery. Guns and mortars have become the major weapons, and other arms and services have been held by some (mostly artillerymen) to have been relegated to supporting or follow-up roles. In counter-revolutionary warfare (CRW), however, these weapons operate in support of the Infantry and cavalry. CRW is essentially an infantryman's war. Ground must be dominated and cleared of guerrillas, then held while normal government and police activity is restored. Expanding safe areas gradually restore government authority over the guerrillas' territory. To increase the numbers of available infantry for sweeps, searches, and patrolling armoured and artillery (and other) units are often 'dismounted'. Nevertheless, when contact is made with guerrillas in strength heavy supporting fire is necessary to break up their formations. This is true of mobile battles and defended locations under attack. Guns and battalion mortars may either operate from secure Fire Bases, or be mobile and fire from a movable Gun Line or Mortar Base. It depends on the nature of the operations under way, which option the force commander chooses. He may even select a combination of both. Airborne gunships and strike aircraft have increased the options for support since the advent of effective ground-to-air radio communications. In Vietnam, this was the role of the infantry's mortars and the artillery's guns, aided by the weapons mounted on tanks, armoured cars, and APCs — or should have been.

There is a rule-of-thumb division that mortars over 100 mm calibre are operated by artillery units, and below that by the infantry battalion. This evolved as a practical matter during World War 1, when trench mortars were located in Fire Bases in the infantry's trenches. The invention and development of the modern mortar is generally credited to a Dutch engineer — Menno, Baron van Coehoorn — in the late seventeenth century. The weapon has remained essentially the same, but improvements have of course been made. Accurate indirect-fire sighting systems have been added. The propellant has been incorporated in the base of the bomb, rather than in the launcher, and the weapon has been made highly portable. It nevertheless remains an indirect-fire weapon, and in its larger calibres the distinction between the mortar and the artillery gun known as the howitzer is very blurred indeed. Mostly this is a feature of the projectile — which is a self-propelled bomb — and the means of loading. Mortars are normally muzzle loaded and guns are breech loaded, however some large-calibre Soviet mortars are breech loaded to confuse the matter further. In Vietnam, most of the mortars in use by both sides were 'infantry mortars' in that they were below the 100 mm calibre. The normal Free World forces' mortar was of 81 mm, with smaller calibres also used below battalion level. The Soviet equivalent size was 82 mm, although the North Vietnamese manufactured an 81 mm mortar modelled on the American M19 60 mm or Soviet M36 82 mm mortar. All mortars manufactured since World War 1 use the Stokes and Brandt designs. Some are smooth bore and some rifled (which further confuses the distinction between them and artillery guns).

Essentially, the differences between artillery guns and mortars are as follows, with occasional exceptions. Mortars are indirect-fire weapons, whereas guns can fire both direct and indirect. Mortars are normally muzzle loading, whereas guns are breech loading and as such either vent the gases through the breech (recoilless guns) or use hydraulic pistons to absorb the shock and recoil. Guns are often rifled, whereas mortars are normally smooth bore. Mortar rounds are self-propelled by a ballistite cartridge in the base, whereas artillery gun shells are driven out of the barrel by a separate charge which may be contained in a shell case behind the projectile or be a separate 'bag charge'. Mortar rounds are fin stabilized, whereas shells tend to be stabilized in flight by the spin given by the rifling of the barrel.

In the Vietnam War the Americans tended to locate artillery Fire Bases in an interlocking pattern so that they could support operations. These Fire Bases had guns and mortars, and a unit operating against VC or NVA troops could call on artillery support from one or more Fire Bases. There was also mobile support from towed artillery, self-propelled (SP) guns, tanks and other AFVs, and mortars mounted in M113 APCs. Both mobile and Fire Base could be tasked to support a specific ground operation. Patrols could call on a nearby Fire Base for support, or could call for an air strike. In areas where there were operations going on, USAF forward air controllers (FACs) flew overhead (usually in slow fixed-wing aircraft, but also in helicopters) to liaise with the ground forces and direct strike aircraft to the target. There was usually a variety of aircraft 'on call' in the air, and the FAC could call up Puff or C-130 gunships, F-4 Phantoms, or others to aid the infantry and cavalry with guns, bombs and napalm. Placing a 105 mm artillery gun in a C-130 Hercules introduced a new dimension of airborne artillery. These gunships could shoot with accuracy even at a particular window in a given building. Such AC-130Ha performed spectacularly against NVA tanks and strongpoints during the 1972 invasion of the South.

The Vietnamese Communists used a variety of Soviet- and Chinese-supplied guns and mortars in their attacks on Free World forces' bases. American air bases were often under fire. During the evacuation of Kontum, USAF C-130s had to fly into the air strip while it was being shelled. Air attacks against the Communists provided the defenders of Kontum with spectacular 'son et lumière' shows during the nights.

COMMUNIST FORCES

The Communist forces in the Vietnam War used such a variety of mortars and guns (mostly from the USSR and PRC, but some even dating back to the time when they were being sponsored by the Japanese Imperial Army after the end of World War 2) that it is difficult to cover them all in the available space, but the principal ones are described below.

Light mortars

A calibre of 60 mm (2.4 in) has proved very successful for light mortars. The USSR used an even smaller calibre of 50 mm as did the Japanese Imperial Army, which also had a 25 mm mortar. The British and Commonwealth forces had the 2 in ML, which remained in service until the 1980s when it was replaced by a new design of similar calibre, the 51 mm ML. Some light mortars used by the Vietnamese Communists — mainly the VC — dated back to 1945 when the Japanese staked the Vietminh from their arms dumps. Some were from the French period, but most during the 'American phases' of the war were supplied by the PRC or USSR. Some were acquired from Free World sources, by capture, theft, or purchase, and a few were manufactured in North Vietnam. Typical light

A 60 mm mortar round discovered by South Vietnamese forces in an arms cache (IPS via MARS).

mortars used were the Type 31 (PRC), Type 63 (PRC), and M41 (USSR).

The Type 31 was a copy of the American M2 60 mm, and both were modelled on the French Stokes-Brandt M1935. These mortars had a square baseplate with a spade underneath for stability after bedding in. The front bipod could be screwed up and down for ranging. There was a handcrank at the end of the elevating screw housing. The Type 31 had a firing weight (mortar with bomb) of just over 20 kg (44 lb), and the M2 of 19 kg (41.8 lb). The maximum range was 1,530 m (1,673 yd) for the Type 31 and 1,820 m (1,990 yd) for the M2. Both were drop-fired weapons, in other words there was a fixed firing pin at the base of the barrel inside and when the bomb was dropped down the tube its own weight drove the ballistite cartridge on to the pin with enough force to fire the cartridge.

The Type 63 was really an updated version of the Type 31, with emphasis on portability for use in irregular and guerrilla warfare. It was much lighter in the firing position at 12.3 kg (27 lb) and had the same range as the Type 31. The basic features were the same except that there were angle plates at the rear corners of the baseplate for bedding in, rather than a rectangular spade. The Type 63 had one recoil cylinder, where the Type 31 had two. The weapon folded together for carriage, with the baseplate and bipod being placed under the barrel. Using the carrying handle on the top of the barrel, one man could easily carry it in rough country with the Number 2 mortarman carrying the ammunition. It had a slightly slower rate of fire at 15–20 rpm compared with 20–30 rpm for the Type 31 and M2. Its barrel length was also slightly shorter at 610 mm (24 in) as opposed to 675 mm (26.6 in) for the Type 31 and 726 mm (28.6 in) for the M2. All these mortars fired HE rounds, but the M2 also had an illuminating bomb, the M83.

The Soviet light mortars were of 50 mm calibre. The M41 50 mm did away with the bipod and shock absorber, and used a supporting yoke which was mounted on the baseplate for elevation, traverse and cross level. Gases from the firing were ducted away from a gas regulator by a pipe under the barrel. Its firing weight was 10 kg (22 lb) and it had a barrel length of nearly 600 mm (23.6 in). It fired HE rounds and had a range of 800 m (875 yd). Some American M19 60 mm light mortars were also in use by the Communist forces.

Medium mortars

These were mostly of 81 mm and 82 mm calibre, with Free World countries tending to use 81 mm and Communist states the 82 mm. However, the PRC and North Vietnam did produce 81 mm mortars mostly as copies of the American M1, with the PRC manufacturing 81 mm fragmentation projectiles based on the American M43A1 ammunition. Medium mortars proved very popular with all forces as they combined high portability with firepower. Apart from the NVN copy of the M1, weapons of these calibres in use were the PRC Types 20 and 53 and the USSR M36, M37, M37 New, M41 and M43. It is not clear in what quantities these were supplied as individual types. There was little variation between these types, although the PRC (and some of the older Soviet models) fitted wheels to the ends of the bipod legs. The weapon could then be towed from the muzzle. These wheeled versions had disadvantages in stability and maintaining cross level when firing, and the Soviets abandoned the idea with the M37 New. Although the Communists' weapons were usually 82 mm, they could fire NATO 81 mm rounds. This adaptability did not apply in reverse. The Communist weapons were automatic drop fired and had quite sophisticated aiming devices attached to the barrel about half-way up its length. Some used square or rectangular baseplates (M36 and M1 NVN copy), but most had circular ones. They all used a Brandt-type bipod with elevating screws and traversing gear at the top. They all weighed around 57 kg (114 lb) and had a barrel length of about 1,200 mm (1,312 yd). The rates of fire were between 15 and 25 rpm. The ranges were at a minimum about 100 m (109 yd) and at maximum approximately 3,000 m (3,281 yd). The bombs were impact detonated and weighed about 3 kg (6.6 lb) each. They were of HE and smoke natures. The Vietnamese developed a chemical delay fuze, which was activated on impact and delayed the explosion. This was used with HE and fragmentation rounds. The M1 NVN copy was popular with the VC because it could be broken down into three one-man loads.

Heavy mortars

Heavy mortars, of calibres above 100 mm, were not much used by the VC as they were not as portable as medium and light mortars, but they were used by the NVA. They were all moved on a two-wheeled carriage. The USSR had weapons of 107 mm (the M107/M38), two designs of 120 mm (M38 and M43) and one of 160 mm (M43). The PRC Type 55 120 mm was a version of the Soviet M43. The M38 107 mm was a scaled-down version of the M38 120 mm especially for use by Mountain Divisions. Both could be broken down into three loads for animal pack transport, or could be moved complete on their two-wheeled carriages, towed behind any suitable vehicle. The 107 mm M38 has a five-man crew, and the M107 a six-man crew. All these types could be drop fired (automatic) on to a protruding firing pin, or manually fired using a trigger device and lanyard. With the exception of the M43 160 mm they were all muzzle loaded. The 160 mm mortar was breech loaded and as a result could only be fired by lanyard and trigger. The barrel was swung upwards from the base, being pivoted on trunnions located not far from its centre point. The bomb was inserted and the breech closed. The barrel was then swung back down to the firing position. The shock from firing was absorbed by shock absorbers and a disc-shaped baseplate.

All these weapons had surprisingly short ranges when compared with NATO mortars: The M43 160 mm had a maximum range of 5,150 m (5,645 yd) and a minimum of 630 m (689 yd); the M43/Type 55 120 mm had a range of 5,700 m (6,234 yd) maximum and 460 m (503 yd) minimum; M38 120 mm had the same ranges as the M43 120 mm; and the M38/M107 107 mm mortars had a maximum range of 6,300 m (6,890 yd) and a minimum of 800 m (875 yd). The minimum ranges made for problems of sighting in the close country of Vietnam, and the maximum ranges left a lot to be desired — nevertheless the NVA did spectacular damage with these weapons.

Field guns

Many guns of this type supplied by the PRC and the USSR were used by the NVA, mostly during the main force offensives in 1972 and 1975, although they were used against the more accessible American installations and Fire Bases before these dates firing from sites in Cambodia and Laos (down the 'Ho Chi Minh Trail') or across the DMZ. They were of a variety of calibres from 76 mm to 130 mm: the Soviet M1942 ZIS-3 (PRC Type 54) division gun was 76 mm calibre; the D-44 (Type 56) was 85 mm; the M1955 and M1944 were 100 mm; the D74 (Type 60) and M37 A-19 were 122 mm; and the PRC Type 59 and 59-1 were 130 mm as was the Soviet M46 field gun. Typically field guns are expected to be fired on shallower trajectories than howitzers and so engage targets more directly, although indirect fire is also possible. Because of the shallower trajectories, however, shorter ranges are not as feasible as with howitzers and lower obstacle heights have to be accepted.

There is a family of gun-howitzers which can operate in a field gun or howitzer role. The Soviet M46 130 mm, of which the PRC Type 59 was a copy and the Type 59-1 a derivative, was a favourite weapon of the NVA and these were typical of the NVA use of field guns. The M46 was first seen in public in the 1954 May Day Parade in Moscow. It replaced the M1931/37 (A19) 122 mm field gun during the early 1950s in Soviet service. The recoil system, which consisted of an hydraulic buffer and hydro-pneumatic recuperator, was mounted over and under the 7.6 m (8.3 yd) long barrel. The gun was served by a crew of nine, it had a rate of fire of 5–6 rpm, and a range of 27,150 m (29,692 yd). Using bag charges the range with HE-fragmentation shells could be increased to 31,000 m (33,902 yd). These ranges were considerably greater than those of the American M101 and M102 105 mm howitzers, which were the main rivals of the M46, and therefore outgunned them. The M46 (or Type 59) was normally used by the NVA against American Fire

PRC Type 59 130mm gun-howitzers being limbered up to NVA trucks (MARS).

Support Bases. Because of the extra ranges, the NVA artillerymen were able to operate with virtual immunity from counter-battery fire. The M46 had a characteristic 'pepperpot' muzzle brake at the end of the barrel. It could fire various natures of case-type, variable-charge, separate-loading ammunition, which include fragmentation-HE and armour-piercing capped-tracer (APC-T) shells.

Howitzers

Among the howitzer types known to be available to the NVA are the M1938 (M30) (PRC Type 54) 122 mm and its replacement the D30 122 mm; the D74 (Type 60) 122 mm; the M1937 ML20 152 mm gun-howitzer and its replacement the D20 152 mm gun-howitzer (PRC Type 66); and the M1943 D1 (Type 54) 152 mm. Howitzers fire at a high angle with a lower charge than field guns, giving the shell a high, slow trajectory. They can thus lob shells on to a target, so that the projectile at the end of its trajectory falls and strikes the ground nearly vertically. This can aid penetration and optimize the blast and fragmentation effects. It also means that a target can be engaged from behind some quite substantial natural obstacles. It does, of course, require some competent forward observation officers (FOOs) and good communications from the forward observer to the gun line, although settings on the sights can be mathematically calibrated and targets can also be pre-registered.

97

The ranges that could be covered by these guns are: M1938 (Type 54) 12,400 m (13,561 yd); D30 15,400 m (16,842 yd) (21,000 m (22,966 yd) with a rocket assisted projectile (RAP)); D74 (Type 60) 24,000 m (26,247 yd); M1937 17,265 m (18,881 yd); D20 (Type 66) 17,410 m (19,040 yd); and M1943 (Type 54) 12,400 m (13,561 yd). These are generally comparable to similar guns in Free World service during the Vietnam War. However, the newer Soviet guns — the D20 152 mm and D30 122 mm — have ranges only comparable with the new British 105 mm light gun that did such prodigious service in the Falklands War. The light gun has a maximum range of come 17,000 m (18,591 yd), the D20 has the same range but the D30 has a range of only 15,000 m (16,404 yd) and needs RAPs to reach 21,000 m (22,966 yd).

The new NATO howitzers — the Anglo-German FH70 and the American M198, both 155 mm calibre — have ranges of around 24,000 m (26,247 yd) with normal ammunition and 30,000 m (32,808 yd) with RAPs. However none of these weapons was available during the Vietnam War, and the Free World howitzers were outranged on average by 1 km (0.625 miles) by the Soviet-PRC guns used by the NVA. The D74's range exceeded those of the heaviest FW guns (the M115 8 in and 5.5 in medium gun) by over 7 km (4.4 miles). Thus, careful siting by the NVA could put their howitzers out of range of counter-battery fire, making them only vulnerable to air strikes. NVA gun lines were therefore protected by various sorts of anti-aircraft weapons.

The M1937 152 mm had characteristic vertically-mounted spring-balancing cylinders on either side of the barrel forward of the shield (a similar feature to the British 5.5 in medium gun which was used by some RNZA batteries in Vietnam). It was served by a crew of nine, fired case-type variable-charge separate-loading ammunition and was towed behind tracked artillery tractors of the AT-S and AT-T types. The D20 (Type 66) 152 mm and the D74 (Type 60) 122 mm gun-howitzers were both served by ten-man crews. The D20 had a shorter, thicker barrel (5.2 m (5.7 yd)) and a larger double-baffle muzzle brake than those of the D74. All the guns were trail-towed with the muzzle to the rear with the exception of the D30 which was towed by the muzzle. In this case, the three trail arms were folded forward under the barrel for transit.

The D30 was a great improvement over the M1938 which it replaced. It had the recoil system sited on top of the barrel, as opposed to the over-and-under arrangement of the M1938. It could also be traversed quickly through 360° (6400 mils or milliradians). It had a seven-man crew, whereas the M1938 needed eight men to fire it. It was towed by the MTLB (which the NVA was not known to have possessed) or by ZIL-157 and Ural 375D 6 × 6 trucks. It had a slightly higher rate of fire at 7 to 8 rpm as opposed to the M1938's 5–6 rpm). It could fire most of the same natures of ammunition as the M1938, but also had a non-rotating fin-stabilized HEAT round for use against armour. All these shells were of the case-type, variable-charge, separate-loading nature.

Artillery rockets

The Soviet Army has used artillery rockets for many years, and has become famous for them since the Katyushas of 1941. It has passed on this enthusiasm to its allies and clients, and the Vietnamese Communists, therefore, used three types of artillery rocket; the BM14-16 and BM21 came from the USSR and the Type 63 107 mm from the PRC. The DKZ-B anti-building and anti-personnel free-flight rocket launcher was, in fact, a single tube from a BM21 with a tripod mount especially intended for use by guerrilla-type forces— this too was used by the NVA and VC. It broke down into two loads; the 2,460 mm (96.9 in) long, 22 kg (48.4 lb) tube and the 28 kg (61.6 lb) tripod mount. It had a range of 10,900 m (11,920 yd) and fired a 46 kg (101.2 lb), 122 mm rocket measuring 1,905 mm (75 in) in length. It was both fin stabilized and spin stabilized by the rifled tube. The mount had a panoramic sight and fitted quadrant. The missile could be set to impact detonation or delayed-action detonation.

The BM14-16 was mounted on a ZIL-151 or ZIL-131 6 × 6 truck and the BM21 on a Ural-375D 6 × 6, although both could be mounted on any suitable vehicle — even American ones. The Type 63 was mounted on a rubber-tyred split-pole carriage which could be towed by any suitable vehicle, or even yoked animal transport. It could also be mounted on a 4 × 4 or 6 × 6 truck, and on the PRC K-63 APC which the NVA used. A special model for use by mountain and airborne troops was developed which weighed 281 kg (618 lb) in the firing position (as opposed to 602 kg (1,324 lb) for the standard model), and this was ideal for guerrilla use. It could be broken down into man-packable loads. It had three banks of four 107 mm barrels mounted on the carriage. When in the firing position, the carriage's wheels were removed and the towing trails opened out into two legs to the rear. There were two further short legs in the front. The rockets were spin stabilized by the rifling in the barrels. The rockets could be fired from a single-round launcher as well as the 12-round assembly.

The Soviet BM14-16 was a 16-round 140 mm multiple-rocket system which first appeared in 1953. It was designed to be mounted on wheeled vehicles such as the ZIL-131 6 × 6 truck. It threw a 40 kg (88 lb) rocket to a range of about 6,000 m (6,562 yd), with a CEP (circular error probability — the average distance on impact that a projectile has deflected from its point of aim, some 50 per cent can be expected to land within the CEP) of 100 m (109 yd). Such CEPs made Soviet rocket systems almost into point attack weapons, rather than the area weapons that artillery systems normally are. The M14-OF rockets of the BM14 were spin stabilized by the rifling of the launcher barrels.

The 122 mm BM21 was a 40-round system mounted on a Ural-375D 6 × 6 truck, although any suitable lorry could be used. The rockets were fin stabilized, and two types could be fired from the four banks of ten launcher tubes. There was a 1.9 m (2.1 yd) short rocket with a range of 11,000 m (12,030 yd), and a 3.23 m (3.53 yd) long rocket with a range of 20,380 m (22,288 yd).

The DKZ-B single-rocket system used the short rocket. The short rocket could also be fitted with an additional motor to reach a range of 17,000 m (18,591 yd). The warhead types used included smoke, chemical, and HE-fragmentation. In Vietnam, the NVA used the HE-fragmentation type to attack FW positions. These systems appeared briefly during the 1968 Tet Offensive, later during the 1972 Easter Offensive, and again in 1975.

FREE WORLD FORCES

Light mortars

During the Vietnam War, American infantry units found that the M1 and M29 81 mm medium mortars were too heavy and awkward to be used outside the Fire Bases for support. As a result, they had to rely on the old M19 60 mm light mortar which was going out of service. This gave it a new lease of life. It was, really, the only light mortar used by the FW forces, although some of the smaller contingents used the M2 60 mm from which the M19 was developed.

The M19 was a smooth-bore, muzzle-loading weapon which

could be either drop or manually fired. It could fire HE, smoke and illuminating rounds, and there were four possible incremental (or 'booster') charges that could be added to drive the bombs to greater ranges. There were two possible baseplates; the M1 which was small and allowed the weapon to be hand held and fired without the bipod, and the M5 which was a rectangular plate with ribs underneath and must be used with the M2 bipod. With the M1 baseplate, only one booster charge could be used. Using the M5 baseplate, a minimum range for the HE bomb was 45 m (49.3 yd) and a maximum was 1,814 m (1,983 yd) using booster Charge 4. The M19 needed a crew of two. With the bipod and M5 baseplate it weighed just over 21 kg (46.2 lb) and with the M1 baseplate only some 9 kg (19.8 lb). It had an overall length of 819 mm (32.2 in). It could maintain a rate of fire of 8 rpm for an indefinite time, or a maximum of 30 rpm for short periods. The smoke bomb was white phosphorus, which could also be used in an anti-personnel role. The bombs were impact detonated.

The New Zealand Army also employed the British 2 in OML light mortar, which by the time of the Vietnam War only had smoke rounds on issue, although a supply of HE rounds had been purchased from India for the Borneo Campaign and may well have been available for Vietnam. The HE bomb was reintroduced by Royal Ordnance Factories during the middle 1960s and these were available for patrol and platoon support. The ML 2 in was manually fired by trigger with a short lanyard and weighed just over 4 kg (8.8 lb). It was nearly 700 mm (27.5 in) long and had a two-man crew, although it could be fired and loaded single-handed. The baseplate was a small rectangular spade, measuring 165 by 165 mm (6.5 by 6.5 in). HE rounds could be fired to a maximum range of 490 m (536 yd).

Medium mortars

There were three medium mortars in use by FW forces in Vietnam. These were the ageing American M1 81 mm, its replacement the M29 81 mm and the British L16 OML 81 mm. The L16 was also made by the Australians and designated the F2. This type of mortar is normally deployed at battalion level and manned by soldiers from the Support Company. Mortar fire controllers (MFCs) and their teams are sent to lower-level sub-units to direct the fire of the tubes, but any officer, NCO or patrol commander should be able to

South Vietnamese Marines being instructed in the use of the M29 81 mm mortar (US Navy via MARS).

direct fire of both mortars and artillery guns. The Americans tended to deploy the battalion mortars in Fire Support Bases, but mobile support from the medium mortars was also available from APC-mounted 81 mm weapons. Although 81 mm mortars are sup-posedly man-packable, the individual loads are rather too heavy for comfort in rough and close country. If a battalion is operating on foot, and needs to take its mortars with it and give support to its forward elements at the same time, the usual method is to split the mortar section up into pairs of 'tubes'. These pairs leap-frog forward, with two tubes always ready to fire. In Vietnam, with the high availability of helicopters it was more effective simply to fly the 'mortar baseplate' forward to a new mobile Fire Base half a section at a time.

The M1 was declared obsolete in March 1970 and replaced by the M29. Both these mortars, and the L16, were automatic (drop-fired) weapons with high angles of fire. A product-improved version of the M29 — the M29A1 — was introduced also in 1970. All were served by three- or five-man crews. The M1 weighed 60.1 kg (132.2 lb), the M29 48.5 kg (106.7 lb) and the L16 36.6 kg (80.52 lb) in the firing position. The L16 and the M29 had circular baseplates, whereas the M1 had a rectangular one. All used the Stokes-Brandt style of adjustable bipod for controlling elevation and traverse, and to give stability when firing. They fired various natures of ammunition including HE, white phosphorus (WP), and illuminating rounds. Booster charges were available to increase the ranges. The L16 has nine available charges (including the Primary Charge) in small, intermediate and large sizes. The HE round L15A3 could be fired to a minimum range of 180 m (197 yd) and a maximum of 520 m (569 yd) on the Primary Charge, and to a minimum of 2,100 m (2,297 yd) on Charge 8 Small and maximum of 5,660 m (6,190 yd) on Charge 8 Large. The stated maximum range for the M29A1 using the M374A2 HE round was 4,595 m (5,025 yd), and for the M1 (using the M43A1 HE round) it was 3,016 m (3,298 yd). Most of the bombs used point-detonating fuzes (PDFs), but the American M362 HE and M375 WP bombs could be fitted with a proximity fuse (VT) to give an airburst. The fuze could be quickly reset to point detonate.

Heavy mortars

The only heavy mortar in FW service during the Vietnam War was the American M30 4.2 in which was used from Fire Bases or from the M106 variant of the M113 APC especially modified to operate the M30. The mortar was originally designed to fire only smoke or chemical rounds. However, when an HE and an illuminating round were introduced, the weapon's versatility was increased. There were later several HE rounds it could fire, and with the M329A2 bomb a maximum range of 6,800 m (7,437 yd) could be reached with a blast-and-fragmentation area of 40 × 20 m (43.7 × 21.9 yd). The bombs were spin stabilized by the rifled barrel, although the propellant charges could be adjusted as on other mortars.

The M30 was a muzzle-loaded, drop-fired (automatic) weapon. It could be disassembled into five loads and in this form it could be manhandled for short distances. It had a circular baseplate, which was connected to a standard by a bridge assembly. The standard consisted of the elevating, traversing, and recoil mechanisms and was fitted at the top end to the barrel and at the bottom to the bridge. It served instead of the bipod of most other mortars. The telescopic sight mechanism was the M53, which had coarse elevations of eighteen graduations each of 100 mils (1° is about

17 mils). Fine elevations were made by a micrometer with one hundred 1 mil graduations. The whole mortar in the firing position was very heavy, weighing 305 kg (671 lb). The barrel was some 1.5 m (1.6 yd) long.

Field guns and light howitzers

Western armies have favoured light howitzers with a field gun capability for some years. During World War 2, British and Commonwealth units used the famous 25-pounder gun-howitzer and the Americans the M2A1 105 mm light howitzer. The M2A1 was redesignated after World War 2 as the howitzer light towed 105 mm M101 and M101A1, and under this classification was used in Vietnam. British and some Commonwealth armies (notably Australia and New Zealand) replaced the 25-pounder with the Italian OTO-Melara Model 56 105 mm pack howitzer in the late 1950s. In Vietnam the Australians also used the American M101.

The Americans produced a new light howitzer in the early 1960s to replace the M101. This was the M102 105 mm which first saw service in Vietnam in February 1964. Some design problems were

Above right *Engineers dig an ammunition bunker for a battery of M102s near Khe Sanh in April 1968* (US Army via MARS).

Right *105 mm howitzer mounted in an AC-130 Pave Aegis gunship, May 1972* (USAF via MARS).

Below *M102 105 mm howitzers of the 319th Artillery Battalion firing in support of the 173rd Airborne Division at Dak To in August 1967* (US Army via MARS).

A captured Soviet AK47 assault rifle being used by a US Ranger on patrol along the Dong Nai River in 1970 (US Army via MARS).

butt) or AKMS (folding butt) that were issued to the Soviet Army from 1959 onwards found their way to the Communist forces in Vietnam.

SKS 7.62 mm Simonov (USSR) and Type 56SKS (PRC) self-loading rifles

The SKS (and the Type 56SKS) was a conventional gas-operated, self-loading rifle of a similar generation to the American M14. Its remarkable feature was the permanently-attached folding bayonet, the tip of which lay in a recess in the forestock when not required. The Chinese actually called the weapon the Type 56SA carbine. This copy of the SKS featured a longer barrel and had a needle bayonet. The rifle fed from an attached 10-round box magazine, which had to be loaded through the breech opening using either single rounds or a 10-round magazine charger. Although the magazine was non-detachable, a unique feature of the weapon was the release catch which allowed the magazine to swing

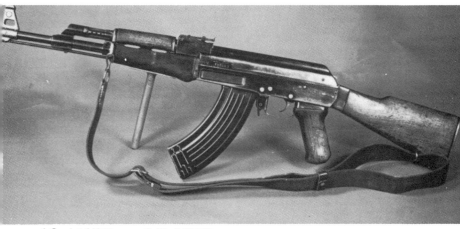

A Soviet AK47 assault rifle (MARS).

whose concept of use was to put down a heavy weight of fire while closing with the enemy so as to 'keep his head down' and then to shoot the rifle like a sub-machine-gun in the close quarter battle. Although the weapon was gas operated, there was no gas regulator unlike on most Western rifles. It fed from a detachable 30-round box magazine and had an effective range of 400 m (437 yd). It measured 868 mm (34.2 in) in length, and weighed over 5 kg (11 lb) with a loaded magazine. The weapon came in two forms; one had a fixed wooden butt stock and the other had a double-strut folding metal butt stock which was operated by a press button release above the pistol grip. The folding-butt version measured 699 mm (27.5 in) when the butt was folded forward.

The Chinese Type 56 did not have the folding-butt variant. Later models were fitted with a permanently-attached, triangular bayonet that folded back underneath the barrel when not needed. It was estimated that a single VC or NVA sniper equipped with this reliable weapon could hold a well-sited position against an entire company. The Chinese folding-butt variant of the AK47 was known as the Type 56-1, but did not feature the fixed bayonet of the later Type 56s. By 1968 most NVA and VC main force units were equipped with Type 56-1s.

Although the Soviet Union gradually took over from the PRC as the principal supplier of the Vietnamese, very few (if any) of the slightly modified variant of the AK47 known as the AKM (wooden

discovered in combat, and the weapon underwent major modifications to solve them. It became the standard gun of Airborne and Air Mobile Divisions, and certain other selected units, and the M101 remained as the main artillery light gun. The 105 mm cannon was eventually mounted in the later marks of C-130 gunships (the AC-130H Pave Aegis) and did sterling work during the 1972 offensive against NVA armoured vehicles, notably tanks, especially at Dak To and An Loc. Neither the M101 nor M102 fitted a muzzle brake at the end of the barrel, whereas the Model 56 PH did. The M101 and Model 56 PH used split trails, with spades at each end that dug in on firing to help stability. The M102 used an aluminium two-wheeled box carriage, and had a circular baseplate under the forward part of the carriage which was lowered to the ground in the firing position (a feature similar to that of the British 25-pounder gun-howitzer). This facilitated rotating the gun through 360° (6,400 mils) which was further aided by a ribbed roller at the rear of the trail. Both the M101 and M102 used hydro-pneumatic recoil systems in an over-and-under layout, whereas the Model 56 PH used a hydraulic buffer and helical recuperator under the barrel slide.

The Italian gun weighed 1,290 kg (2,838 lb) in the firing position and had a maximum range with a normal HE shell of 10,575 m (11,565 yd). With RAPs this range was extended to 13,000 m (14,217 yd). It was served by a crew of seven, and could be towed behind a 4 × 4 vehicle such as a Land Rover. It could sustain a rate of fire of 4 rpm for 30 minutes and 3 rpm for an hour. In an anti-tank role, it could fire at a rate of 8 rpm. It fired the same range of ammunition as the M101, including the M67 HEAT round.

The M101 weighed 2,030 kg (4,466 lb) in the firing position, and the later M101A1 weighed 2,363 kg (5,199 lb). The M102 was much lighter, weighing only 1,496 kg (3,291 lb) in both the firing and travelling positions. Both guns were served by eight-man crews, and were designed to be towed by a 6 × 6 truck. The rates of fire were similar to those of the Model 56 PH. The M102 had an overall rate of 10 rpm. The M101 could manage 8 rpm for the first 30 seconds, 4 rpm during the first 4 minutes, and 3 rpm during the first 10 minutes of firing. It had a maximum range of 11,270 m (12,325 yd). The M102 had a maximum range with the HE (M1) round of 11,500 m (12,577 yd) and with the M548 HERA (high explosive, rocket assisted) round 15,100 m (16,514 yd) could be achieved. The relatively light weights of the M102 and Model 56 PH meant that they could be easily heli-lifted by a variety of military helicopters including the workhorse of the Vietnam War, the Bell UH-1 Iroquois ('Huey'). Such guns were usually teamed with mortars, and protected by machine-guns in sangars, in Fire Support Bases, although they could be positioned by helicopter to give mobile gun lines to support particular operations of major units and formations.

Medium guns and howitzers

There were three types of medium guns on towed carriages used by the FW forces in Vietnam; these were the American M114A1

COMMUNIST FORCES

Tanks

Although tanks were used by the Communists in dribs and drabs, it was in the 1972 offensive that they really used them in numbers. Usually when they used them in 1972, they seemed to be trying to apply the Soviet armoured warfare doctrines with tanks and other armour spearheading an infantry attack. During April 1972, the 9th Viet Cong and 5th NVA Divisions advanced down the axis of Route 13 from Cambodia through the town of Loc Ninh to An Loc where they were held by a reinforced 5th ARVN Infantry Division. The ARVN formation had on call massive air support from both VNAF and USAF squadrons, and from helicopter gunships of 1st US Cavalry Division (the last US Army Division remaining in Vietnam), but they had little artillery support.

The VC and NVA Divisions spearheaded their advance by T-54/55 main battle tanks. Many of these were destroyed by airstrikes, or by gunships. The AC-130 Pave Aegis (with a 105 mm cannon) aircraft killed many, as did the TOW armed Cobras of the 1st US Cavalry Division. Six T-54/55 MBTs, for example, were driven down a main north-south street in An Loc in a co-ordinated tank and infantry attack on April 13 towards the ARVN Command Post. The lead tank was immobilized by ARVN troops using an M72 LAW. At the same time the ARVN Commander — Lieutenant General Nguyen Van Minh — cleared three US Army Cobras to engage the remaining tanks, four of which were either immobilized or destroyed. The problem for the Communists was that the Soviet and PRC tanks were not proof against NATO-type anti-armour weapons and tactics, and also that Soviet tank doctrine does not necessarily work against a prepared and well-equipped enemy in close country and urban areas. The Soviet Army is not good at fighting in built up areas (FIBUA) — Stalingrad notwithstanding!

The VC and NVA had PT-76 (PRC Type 62) light tanks, T-34/85 medium tanks, and T-54/55 (PRC Type 59) main-battle tanks. The PT-76 types were used during the later stages of the war in armoured cavalry battalions of one tank company (seven to ten PT-76/Type 62s) to two APC companies (using BTR-60PA or K-63s). During the 1968 Tet Offensive, the Communists were using PT-76s in dribs and drabs. However, they did achieve some notable successes. One was the overrunning of the Special Forces base at Lang Vei (near Khe Sanh) on 7 February 1968; the PT-76's

Above *PT-76 in very non-Vietnamese surroundings!* (Finnish Army via MARS).

Above left *Soviet T-54 medium tank; this vehicle is actually in service with the Finnish Army* (Finnish Army via MARS).

Left *T-55 medium tank at speed* (Finnish Army via MARS).

Below left *South Vietnamese troops inspect a T-54 knocked out by a TOW heavy anti-armour weapon near Kontum* (Hughes International via author).

first appearance in the war. It mounted a 76 mm D56T gun and the PRC Type 62 had an 85 mm gun. Both types had a coaxially-mounted 7.62 mm machine-gun and a DShKM 12.7 mm machine-gun for anti-aircraft defence (although it can be used for ground fire). The PT-76 had a combat weight of 14 tonnes (13.8 tons) and the Type 62 had a combat weight of 18 tonnes (17.7 tons). The armour was between 10 and 14 mm (.39 and .55 in) thick. The maximum road speed was 50 kph (31.3 mph), and the ground pressure was 0.5 kg/cm^2 (8 psi).

The World War 2 T-34/85 was brought out of storage in the 1960s and some were fitted with the wheels and engine of the T-54 MBT. It had an M1944 85 mm gun which had a range of just over 13 km (8.1 miles). It could fire anti-armour rounds and an HE-fragmentation projectile. The tank had a road speed of 55 kph (34.4 mph), and a ground pressure of 0.83 kg/cm^2 (13.3 psi). The T-34/85 weighed 32 tonnes (31.5 tons) and was manned by a crew of five. The thickest armour was 90 mm (3.5 in) at the turret mantlet and the thinnest was 18 mm (.71 in) on the top of the hull and turret.

The T-54/55 was equipped with a D10T 100 mm gun which had

A Soviet T-34/85 medium tank as used by the NVA (IWM via MARS).

an indirect-fire range of 14,600 m (15,967 yd) and fired various anti-armour rounds as well as two HE natures. The road speed was about 50 kph (31.3 mph), and the ground pressure 0.81 kg/cm^2 (13 psi). It weighed 36 tonnes (35.4 tons), and had a four-man crew. The thickest armour was the turret front at 203 mm (8 in), and the thinnest was the 20 mm (.78 in) of the hull floor. The hull side armour was 70 mm (2.8 in) and the glacis was 100 mm (4 in) at a 60° angle.

Armoured personnel carriers and reconnaissance vehicles

The Soviet Union supplied the Vietnamese Communists with three of their current types of APC — the BTR-152, BTR-50, and BTR-60 — but not the BMP-1, which was just being issued to Soviet Motor Rifle Divisions mainly in the GSFG (Group of Soviet Forces, Germany) at the time of the 1972 invasion of the South. It is likely that the mining of Haiphong Harbour during Operation Linebacker and the costly 1972 campaign deterred them from sending this new tracked APC in case some were captured. At that time it was still a relatively unknown quantity in the West, and it does not do to give potential enemies too easy access to one's equipment. In any case the 1973 October War in the Middle East — and the equipment build-up that went before it — drew off any that were available

114

for export to friendly countries. The USSR also supplied the current armoured reconnaissance vehicle — the BRDM-2 — which was first seen in public in the Soviet Union in 1966. The PRC supplied its copy of the BTR-152, called the Type 56 APC, and its own production K-63 tracked APC. It also provided the Type 55 APC, which was a PRC copy of the older Soviet BTR-40.

The BRDM-2 was an amphibious scout car made of all-welded steel armour which was 14 mm (.55 in) thick. It normally had a crew of four. The driver sat at the left front, and the vehicle commander on the right. Both were provided with bullet-proof windshields which were further protected by armoured shutters that were hinged at the top. The vehicle was a 4 × 4 with an additional two wheels on either side in the middle. These were normally kept raised, and only lowered by the driver for crossing ditches and to give better cross-country performance. The vehicle was driven in water by a single water jet at the rear of the hull. The BRDM-2 was entered through two roof hatches situated just behind the driver-vehicle commander's vision blocks. A turret — the same as was mounted on the BTR-60PB — could be fitted in the centre of the vehicle. There was a single firing port on each side of the hull. The water-cooled V-8 GAZ-41 engine was located at the rear. The armament was a turret-mounted 14.5 mm machine-gun and a coaxial 7.62 mm machine-gun. The BRDM-2 could also be equipped with the AT3 Sagger ATGW or the SA9 Gaskin SAM. The Saggers were fitted in a six-missile mount in place of the turret. The SA9 mount only entered Soviet Army service in 1972 and was not available for the Vietnam War.

The BTR-152 was quite an old APC. It first appeared in 1949, and was the first Soviet APC to be made after World War 2, although it is still in service today. It could be used as an artillery tractor as well as an APC, and one of its variants (BTR-152A) was an anti-aircraft vehicle equipped with twin 14.5 mm KPV heavy machine-guns in a 360°-traverse manually-operated turret. It had an appearance not unlike the American World War 2 M2 and M3 half-tracks, although the BTR-152 was all wheeled. It was a 6 × 6 vehicle, and was not amphibious. It was made of all-welded steel and the six-cylinder ZIL-123 engine was placed in the front. The driver and vehicle commander sat immediately behind the engine compartment, and the troops sat along the sides of the troop compartment facing inwards. The troop compartment had no top cover, and troops could exit over the sides as well as out of the rear doors. There were three firing ports down each side of the vehicle and two more in the

Soviet BTR-60s during an amphibious exercise (US Navy via MARS).

rear (on either side of the doors). The hull side armour was only 9 mm (.35 in) thick, and the front armour was 13.5 mm (.53 in). A spare wheel was mounted on the outside of the left-hand rear door. Armoured shutters (which were controlled by the driver) protected the radiator of the engine from damage by small-arms fire. The normal vehicle armament was a 7.62 mm SGMB machine-gun or a 12.7 mm DSh KM heavy machine-gun on the front mounting and SGMBs on each of the two side mountings. The BTR-152K variant had full overhead armour protection with two roof hatches. The vehicle had a crew of two and could carry seventeen troops.

The BTR-50P was based on the PT-76 light tank chassis and was a track-laying APC with hull side armour of 14 mm (.55 in) and front armour of 11 mm (.43 in) at 60°. The V-6 engine was at the rear, the open-topped troop compartment for twenty men in the centre and the covered crew compartment was at the front. The crew consisted of the driver and the vehicle commander. The passengers entered and left by climbing over the sides. The normal armament was a 7.62 mm SGMB machine-gun which was pintle mounted. It was a fully amphibious vehicle which was propelled in water by two water jets at the rear of the hull.

The BTR-60P was an 8 × 8 wheeled APC which was fully amphibious and was developed as a replacement for the BTR-152 (PRC Type 56) at the end of the 1950s. It was made of all-welded steel armour, which at its thickest part (the front hull) was 10 mm (.39 in) at 80° on the upper part and 45° on its lower part. It was driven by two six-cylinder GAZ-49B petrol engines mounted in the rear of the hull on land, and by a single water jet (also at the rear of the hull) in water. The driver and commander sat in the front. The driver was on the left and the vehicle commander on the right. The troop compartment for sixteen men was open topped, and the soldiers sat on bench seats across the width of the hull facing forward. There were two half doors and three firing ports one each side of the vehicle. The main armament was a 7.62 mm SGMB or PKB machine-gun mounted on a pintle on the commander's right and operated by him. Some BTR-60Ps had the heavier 12.7 mm DSh KM machine-gun in this position. There were mounts on each side of the hull for further 7.62 mm machine-guns. The BTR-60PB variant had a turret fitted behind the driver-commander positions. This was the same turret that was mounted on the BRDM-2. It was equipped with a 14.5 mm KPV and a 7.62 mm PKT machine-gun, and all functions were manually operated. The BTR-60 had a maximum road speed of 80 kph (50 mph) and in water a speed of 10 kph (6.3 mph) could be reached.

The K-63 tracked APC was a PRC design developed in the late 1960s. It was based on the PRC Type 62 light tank, which was a modified copy of the USSR PT-76, and was a slightly scaled down version having four road wheels instead of six, for example. The glacis of the front hull was squared off, and the hull rose higher above the tracks. It was operated by a crew of four and carried ten passengers who sat facing each other along the sides of the hull. The crew consisted of the driver, vehicle commander, gunner and loader. The gunner and loader were situated to the rear of the vehicle in the middle, with the loader forward of the gunner and behind the driver. He had his own single-piece, rear-opening roof hatch. The gunner manned a 12.7 mm Type 54 heavy machine-gun (USSR DSh KM). The passengers entered and loft through a single door in the rear of the hull, giving the K-63 a rear view not unlike the British FV432 APC. The Australian Army tested some captured K-63s and reported that it had excellent cross-country performance. It had a maximum road speed of 60 kph (37.5 mph). It was fully amphibious, and was driven in water by the tracks, being able to reach a speed of 5.7 kph (3.6 mph). The engine was a six-cylinder diesel. There were two known variants. One mounted a 122 mm Type 54 (USSR M1938) howitzer in the rear instead of the troop compartment, to become a self-propelled gun, and the other mounted a multi-barrelled rocket launcher system (MRS). This APC and its parent light tanks were used by both the Vietnamese Communists and by the PRC People's Liberation Army (PLA) when it invaded border areas of North Vietnam in 1979, as well as having been used during the American phase of the war.

FREE WORLD FORCES

Tanks and self-propelled guns

The most widely used FW tank in Vietnam was the American M48, although some M60s, M551s, and British Centurions of the Commonwealth Forces were present. Various self-propelled guns (SPGs) such as the M107, M110 and especially the M109 were deployed.

The M551 Sheridan light tank-reconnaissance vehicle had a crew of four and a combat weight of nearly 16 tonnes (15.7 tons). It had an interesting main armament, which was the M81 combined gun and missile launcher. It fired a number of conventional rounds with combustible cartridges, as well as launching the Shillelagh MGM51A infra-red guided missile which had a HEAT shaped-charge warhead and was effective against all contemporary armour. In 1968, 64 M551s were sent to Vietnam where, during the subsequent year, a number of defects were found. Secondary

Above right *An M-60 makes its way through a mountain village* (MARS).

Right *M-551 General Sheridan armoured reconnaissance/airborne assault light tank* (Detroit Diesel Allison via MARS).

Below right *A mud-besmattered Sheridan light tank on a training area in Kentucky, USA* (US Army via MARS).

Below *Centurion tanks in Vietnam with the Australian Army; overhead is an RAAF UH-1H Iroquois helicopter* (Defence PR, Canberra, via MARS).

Above *An M107 175mm self-propelled gun near Tuy Hoa in October 1966* (US Army via MARS).

Above left *US Marines M-48s being ferried ashore aboard LCTs at Da Nang in March 1965* (USMC via MARS).

Left *View from an LCT landing M-48s at Da Nang* (US Navy via MARS).

Below left *Marines and an M-48 in a clearing during operations north of Cam Lo in February 1967. In the background is a CH-46 helicopter evacuating wounded* (USMC via MARS).

armaments were an anti-aircraft .50 in (12.7 mm) machine-gun and a coaxially-mounted 7.62 mm machine-gun. It was made of an all-welded aluminium armour hull and an all-welded steel turret. The maximum road speed was 70 kph (43.8 mph), and the tank had a ground pressure of 0.49 kg/cm^2 (7.8 psi). It was powered by a six-cylinder turbo-charged Detroit Diesel Model 6V53T diesel engine.

The M48 was rushed into service during the Korean War of the early 1950s, and had to be subsequently rebuilt for issue to units afterwards. Early marks had a petrol engine, and only the M48A3 and later variants were fitted with a diesel (the same engine, incidentally, that was installed in the M60 series). The boat-shaped hull was made of cast steel. The hull front armour was between 100 and 120 mm (3.9 and 4.7 in) thick and the sides were 76 mm (3 in). The turret front had 110 mm (4.3 in) of armour. The tank was manned by a crew of four. The main armament was a 90 mm M41 gun with a coaxially-mounted 7.62 mm M73 machine-gun. Mounted

in the commander's cupola was a .50 in (12.7 mm) M2 HB Browning heavy machine-gun which could be aimed and fired from inside the turret. The main gun was normally fitted with a characteristic T-shaped blast deflector. The ground pressure was 0.78 kg/cm^2 (12.5 psi). The combat weight was around 48 tonnes (47.2 tons), and the maximum road speed was about 48 kph (30 mph).

The M109 155 mm SPG was first issued to the US Army and US Marine Corps in June 1963. It had an all-welded aluminium turret and hull, and a loaded weight of nearly 24 tonnes (23.6 tons). It was manned by a crew of six. The main armament was an M126 155 mm howitzer and a .50 in (12.7 mm) Browning M2 HB machine-gun was fitted as secondary armament in front of the commander's cupola, mainly for anti-aircraft use. The M109 was driven by an eight-cylinder, turbo-charged diesel engine. It was a track-laying vehicle with seven road wheels and two drive sprockets. It had a maximum road speed of 56 kph (35 mph), and a ground pressure of 0.77 kg/cm^2 (12.3 psi).

The M126 cannon could throw various natures of ammunition (including six types of HE) out to 20,000 m (21,872 yd), and a HERA (high explosive, rocket assisted) round to 24,000 m (26,247 yd). It provided FW forces in Vietnam with a valuable means of mobile heavy-fire support.

Armoured personnel carriers and reconnaissance vehicles

The principal APC used by the FW MAF, the Americans and the ARVN during the Vietnam War was the American M113 series. Equipped with various armaments, this vehicle was also used in reconnaissance and fire support roles. The USMC also used their LVTP5A1 amphibious APC. The Cadillac Gage V-100 wheeled reconnaissance vehicle was also used, as were some British Ferret scout cars in the FV701 Mark 2/2 variant.

The M113 was an all-welded aluminium tracked APC with a combat weight of nearly 12 tonnes (11.8 tons). It was powered in the original mark by a Chrysler 75M V8 petrol engine, but the M113A1 and all later variants were fitted with a Detroit Diesel six-cylinder Model 6V53 diesel engine. It had a ground pressure of 0.55 kg/cm^2 (8.8 psi). Its maximum road speed was 68 kph (42.5 mph). It had a crew of two and could carry eleven passengers in the APC role. The armour thickness varied between 12 and 38 mm (.47 and 1.5 in). Entry (and exit) to the troop compartment was over a single ramp-type rear door which was hinged at its base. The normal armament was a single 0.50 in Browning M2 HB which was mounted at the commander's centrally located cupola. In its variants, there was the M106 (and M106A1) 107 mm mortar carrier mounting the 4.2 in heavy mortar, the M125 (and M125A1) 81 mm mortar carrier, and the M132 (and M132A1) flamethrower, all of which were used in support roles in the war.

The Australian Army added various weapons to the M113 to

M113A1 in action in Vietnam with its .50 Browning machine-gun (FMC via MARS).

M113s of the 25th Infantry Division during an offensive in April 1968 (US Army via MARS).

make a number of fire support vehicles. The American Cadillac Gage T50 turret armed with a 0.30 in and a 0.50 in machine-gun, and a T50 turret with twin 7.62 mm machine-guns were two such, and both were employed in the light reconnaissance vehicle role. They were designated M113A1 APC/LVR. Another Australian variant was the M113A1 FSV (Saladin), which had the turret and armament of the British Saladin armoured car fitted. This consisted of the all-welded steel turret with a 76 mm L5A1 gun that fired HE, HESH, smoke and illuminating rounds, a coaxially-mounted 7.62 mm machine-gun (or 0.30 in MMG), and a pintle-mounted 0.30 in MMG on top of the turret to the right front of the commander's hatch. This last was originally for anti-aircraft defence.

The Ferret FV701 Mark 2/2 was a variant of the Mark 2 especially modified for service in the Far East. It was a wheeled 4 × 4 scout car made of all-welded steel, with 12 to 16 mm (.47 to .63 in) of armour at 50° and 35° at the front hull. It was powered by a rear-mounted six-cylinder Rolls-Royce B60 Mark 6A petrol engine. The combat weight of the vehicle was nearly 4.5 tonnes (4.4 tons), and had a maximum road speed of 93 kph (58.1 mph). It had a crew of two. The driver was centrally placed in the front. The commander-gunner sat behind him in the manually-operated

An M113 charging through a river somewhere in Vietnam during the early 1970s (FMC via MARS).

turret. The Mark 2/2 had a collar fitted between the top of the hull and the turret, which raised the turret and gave the commander-gunner a better field of fire and protected observation. The armament was a single 0.30 in MMG. The Ferret, like the V-100, was widely used for patrol work and for convoy escort.

The Cadillac Gage V-100 Commando (which the US Army designates the M706) was an all-welded steel, 4 × 4-wheeled APC. It had a crew of three and could also carry nine soldiers. It had a gross weight of over 7 tonnes (6.9 tons), and was powered by a V8 Chrysler 361 petrol engine which gave it a maximum road speed of 100 kph (62.5 mph). There was a variety of armaments that were fitted to the V-100 in Vietnam. There were three turret variants: a turret mounting twin 0.30 in machine-guns; a turret with a single 0.30 in MMG and a single 0.50 in Browning M2 HB HMG; and a turret fitting a General Electric 7.62 mm M134/GAU-2B/A Minigun as used in helicopter gunships. The V-100 was also fitted with the TOW heavy ATGW system. Further weapons could be mounted at the rear of the vehicle and operated by the soldiers in the troop compartment. One typical method was to mount an extra 0.50 in M2 HB HMG. It was a fully amphibious vehicle, being driven in water by its wheels.

ANTI-AIRCRAFT WEAPONS

Air defence is a great problem for modern armies, as strike aircraft can devastate military formations. In Vietnam, American B-52s in Iron Hand operations (the codename for tactical missions over South Vietnam and Cambodia in support of ground troops) broke up and even obliterated many VC and NVA formations as they were assembling for attacks. One such B-52 strike at An Loc in April 1972 destroyed an NVA unit as it was about to launch its attack with armour support. The Communists' supply line of the Ho Chi Minh Trail was constantly attacked from the air. North Vietnam itself was frequently the subject of air operations during Operation Rolling Thunder (March 1965 to October 1968) and Operation Linebacker I (10 May to 23 October 1972) and Linebacker II (17 to 29 December 1972). Communist forces were constantly subject to American, VNAF, and RAAF operations in the South. NVA troops, installations and air bases in the north were frequently attacked by the USAF, US Navy, and USMC Air Wing aircraft.

To combat this massive air threat from the ground, the Vietnamese Communists had a variety of anti-aircraft guns and missiles. An escalating development of anti-air weapons and radars versus electronic counter-measures, air tactics and organization, and suppressive strikes, took place. The USSR supplied the North

SA3 Goa surface-to-air missiles during a parade in Hanoi (MARS).

A pair of SA7 Grail portable anti-aircraft missiles (Crown Copyright MoD via MARS).

Vietnamese with SA2 Guideline, SA3 Goa and SA6 Gainful air-defence guided missiles, and later with the shoulder-launched SA7 Grail man-portable missile. All of these caused many casualties among US aircraft and their crews. The SA7 was particularly troublesome in the South, claiming many helicopters and fixed wing aircraft. The USSR also supplied a range of air-defence guns (anti-aircraft artillery, or AAA) including the M44 85 mm, M38/39 37 mm, ZU23 23 mm, ZSU23-4 and the ZPU4 14.5 mm AA machine-gun. The PRC provided the Type 63 twin 37 mm self-propelled AA gun. The vehicle-mounted SA9 Gaskin (carried on a BRDM-2) was also supplied by the Soviet Union.

Communist troops were taught to fire at aircraft with whatever weapons they had to hand. The result was a barrage of small arms and heavier fire, which not only affected the pilots' run-in to the target but also caused some aircraft and crew casualties. As a result of this, NATO armies reintroduced this air defence tactic which had gone out of fashion since the 1950s.

Air defence was not a problem for American, ARVN and FW MAF troops in South Vietnam. Even so, batteries of Hawk missiles were

Above *A Hawk missile battery on Hill 327 as a part of the Da Nang airfield defences in 1965* (USMC via MARS).

Left *A Redeye close-range anti-aircraft missile being demonstrated by a soldier of the 82nd Airborne Division* (US Army via MARS).

deployed with the USMC 3rd MAF (Marine Amphibious Force) at Da Nang as part of their standard equipment. Also, Redeye man-portable shoulder-fired air-defence missiles were deployed as part of standard equipment scales. These were not needed as the NVAF was only really met in combat in the skies over North Vietnam, where their MiG-17s proved to be quite a problem.

CONCLUSION

The thirty-year-long war in Vietnam saw the use of nearly all the weapons in the armouries of both Western and Eastern blocs. As a result it has not been possible to give a comprehensive account in this book, so only the principal and most interesting weapons employed by ground forces have been included. There were many other weapons used during the war as a great deal of improvization occurred, both using unconventional weapons and using normal weapons in an unusual way. For example, the M18 Claymore anti-personnel mine became a principal weapon in close-country ambushes. The Australians and New Zealanders were all regular soldiers, with considerable recent combat experience in South-East Asia among the senior NCOs and battalion officers of the rank of Captain and above, and were therefore probably the most innovative. The Australians took to lining the sides of their lorries with steel plate and fitting Claymores around the vehicle with the initiating devices in the cab with the driver. If ambushed, the driver would fire all the Claymores and drive on. An Australian SAS officer, Duncan Gordon, invented a modified automatic shot-gun (based on the Remington Automatic, favoured for jungle patrols in Malaya and Borneo) which could fire belt-fed ammunition. Shot-guns were very good weapons for scouts and certain others on patrols in close country. Bows and arrows were also used for silent killing on patrols and covert operations.

The Viet Cong and NVA, and the Vietminh before them, developed a nasty range of booby traps especially for use on forest paths. There were the familiar 'panji-panji' stakes of sharpened bamboo, which were later refined to be steel spikes, often with a rifle cartridge included. There were various heavy, spiked balls which were suspended over paths and activated by tripwires to swing down into the oncoming patrol. There were also various tripwire-activated booby traps using anti-personnel fragmentation grenades, or even bows and arrows. These weapons were the most de-moralizing side of the jungle warfare.

War is never a romantic occupation, and CRW is particularly unpleasant. The effects of warfare and the number of casualties can be limited by professionalism and discipline among the troops fighting it, but ultimately the soldier's main purpose is to get at the enemy and either injure him or kill him. Higher commanders are able to refine this to taking and holding ground, or clearing it of any enemy presence. The infantryman's war is more immediate and terrifying, and CRW is predominantly a foot soldier's conflict. It is also filled with long periods of inactivity and boredom. Good weapons make any war easier to fight and easier to win. Good tactics are constructed around the power and characteristics of these weapons. In the case of the war in Vietnam, the strategy employed was often inappropriate to the nature of the conflict, and the work of the skilled soldiers of the Americans and their allies was undermined by blunders from above.

GLOSSARY

A
AA anti-aircraft.
AAA anti-aircraft artillery.
ACP auto (or automatic) Colt pistol.
AFV armoured fighting vehicle.
AK Avtomat Kalashnikova – Kalashnikov's assault rifle.
AP anti-personnel.
APC armoured personnel carrier
APC-T armour-piercing capped tracer.
APERS-T anti-personnel tracer.
Armd armoured.
Armr armour.
ARVN Army of the Republic of Vietnam (ie. South Vietnam).
AT anti-tank.
ATk anti-tank.
ATGW anti-tank guided weapon.
AT-S artillery tractor, medium *(Russian initials)*.
AT-T artillery tractor, heavy *(Russian initials)*.

B
BAT battalion anti-tank (gun).

C
CEP circular error probability.
CQB close quarter battle.
CRW counter-revolutionary warfare.
CS Gas a non-lethal, riot control agent.

D
DIC Division d'Infanterie Coloniale.
Div division.
DMZ de-militarized zone (the border between North and South Vietnam).
DSh KM Degtyarev-Shpagin K38 heavy machine-gun (modified).

E
ECM electronic counter measures.
ECCM electronic counter counter measures.

F
FAC forward air controller.
FAL Fusil Automatique Léger.

H
HAW heavy anti-armour weapon.
HB heavy barrelled.
HE high explosive.
HEAT high explosive, anti-tank.
HERA high explosive, rocket assisted.
HESH high explosive, squash head.
HK Heckler und Koch (West German arms manufacturer).
HMG heavy machine-gun.
HP high powered/haut puissance.

I
IA immediate action.
ICP Indo-China Communist Party.
inf infantry.

K
KPV tank heavy machine-gun designed by Kalashnikov.

L
LAV light armoured vehicle.
LAW light anti-armour weapon.
LMG light machine-gun.
LRP long range penetration.
LRRP long range reconnaissance patrolling.

M
MAAG Military Assistance Advisory Group, Vietnam.
MAC Military Airlift Command, USAF.
FIBUA fighting in built-up areas.
FN Fabrique Nationale (Belgian arms manufacturer).
FOO forward observation officer (artillery).
FSV fire support vehicle.
FW Free World.
FW MAF Free World Military Assistance Forces.

G
GCI ground control intercept radar.
GPMG general purpose machine-gun.
GR Gurkha Rifles.
GSFG Group of Soviet Forces, Germany.

MACV Military Assistance Command, Vietnam.
MAF Marine Amphibious Force, USMC.
MAW medium anti-armour weapon.
MBT main battle tank.
MEF Marine Expeditionary Force, USMC.
MFC mortar fire controller.
MG machine-gun.
mil milliradian — the metric angular measurement used by NATO armed forces. One mil is 'the angle which subtends a base of one metre at one kilometre distance'. There are 6,400 mils in a circle.
MMG medium machine-gun.
MRS multi-barrelled rocket launcher system.
MTLB a Soviet tracked high mobility load carrying vehicle.

N
NATO North Atlantic Treaty Organisation.
NCO non-commissioned officer.
NGS naval gunfire support.
NVA North Vietnamese Army.
NVN North Vietnam.

P
PDF point detonating fuze.
PIAT projector, infantry, anti-tank.
PKB a modification of the Soviet *pulemet Kal'ashnikova* (Kalashnikov machine-gun) (PK).
PKT a PK modified for fitting in an AFV.
PLA People's Liberation Army.
PRC People's Republic of China.

R
RAAF Royal Australian Air Force.
RAIR Royal Australian Infantry Regiment.
RAP rocket-assisted projectile.
RCL recoilless.
RDX a World War 2 acronym for the explosive compound Cyclotrimethylenetrinitramine, also known as Cyclonite.
REI Régiment Étrangère d'Infanterie.

REP Régiment Étrangère de Parachutistes.
RIC Régiment d'Infanterie Coloniale.
RL rocket launcher.
RNZA Royal New Zealand Artillery.
RNZIR Royal New Zealand Infantry Regiment.
rpm rounds per minute; revolutions per minute.
RVN Republic of Vietnam (ie. South Vietnam).

S

SAC Supreme Allied Commander; Strategic Air Command, USAF.
SACLOS semi-automatic command to line-of-sight.
SAM surface-to-air missile.

SAS Special Air Service Regiment.
SEAC South East Asia Command.
SF Special Forces; sustained fire.
SGM a modification of the Soviet Goryunov machine-gun.
SGMB a further modification of the SGM.
SLR self-loading rifle.
SMG sub-machine-gun.
SMLE short magazine Lee Enfield.
SP self-propelled.
SPG self-propelled gun.

T

TOW tube-launched, optically-tracked, wire-guided ATGW.

U

USAF United States Air Force.
USASF United States Army Special Forces.
USMC United States Marine Corps.
USN United States Navy.
USSR Union of Soviet Socialist Republics.
UZRG a Soviet grenade fuze.

V

VC Victoria Cross; Viet Cong.
VNAF Vietnamese Air Force.
VT variable time.

W

WOMBAT War Office Modified Battalion Anti-Tank gun.
WP white phosphorus.

INDEX